American Political Parties
in the 21st Century

American Political Parties in the 21st Century

DAVE BLEVINS

McFarland & Company, Inc., Publishers
Jefferson, North Carolina, and London

LIBRARY OF CONGRESS CATALOGUING-IN-PUBLICATION DATA

Blevins, David.
    American political parties in the 21st century / Dave Blevins.
       p.   cm.
    Includes bibliographical references and index.

    ISBN 0-7864-2480-X (softcover : 50# alkaline paper) ∞

    1. Political parties—United States—Directories. I. Title.
JK2265.B54   2006
324.273—dc22   2006008718

British Library cataloguing data are available

Cover photograph ©2006 PhotoSpin.

Manufactured in the United States of America

McFarland & Company, Inc., Publishers
  Box 611, Jefferson, North Carolina 28640
    www.mcfarlandpub.com

Contents

viii • Contents

Preface

Politics. Religion. Sports. These three topics are sure to ignite intense conversation and debate wherever they are discussed — over the office water cooler, at local bars, or anywhere else two or more people congregate. Arguing politics is popular for three reasons— anyone can join the argument, everyone has an opinion, and there is no clear-cut right or wrong.

The importance of politics to the average citizen in today's America appears to be on the rise, judging by the attention paid to it by the mass media, the intensity of the public debate in several forums, and the growing number of political parties active in the country. Politics and political movements have always been an integral part of our history, were the driving force for the Pilgrims leaving England for the "New World," and continues to be a spark that drives immigrants (both legal and illegal) to our shores on a daily basis.

Despite a recent seemingly fervent interest in political movements by the voters, there is also a startling paradox in voting trends, which has seen a steady decline over the past decades in the percentage of eligible voters participating in the political process. While there have been many theories presented to explain this paradox, the trend continues today and most experts predict this lack of political participation to continue into the future. Initially viewed in this light, the proliferation of minor parties might seem surprising. However, most third parties claim to eschew national politics and work either to improve their local communities, one district at a time, or to focus on specific issues, such as immigration, taxes, and the like.

Unlike any period in our recent history, there is a growing resentment in America among voters against the two primary established and entrenched political parties, the Democrats and Republicans. Almost all new parties that have formed in the past 25 years are a result of the two parties' perceived lack of ability to address common problems of the average citizen. While many parties focus on specific subjects of interest (such as the Green Party and the Veterans Party of America, among others), the growing anger and mistrust allows these parties to attract new members and to grow. Many feel that the Democrats and Republicans are basically the same party with their differences being cosmetic, at best. The perception that both parties have deserted their core values has led people either to drop out of the political process or to form their own political parties to address apparently ignored issues and values.

While today's political environment is a result of our history and other socio-economic factors, this book focuses only on political parties active since 2000, of which there are more than 180, big and small. Listings in this book include the two major national parties, regional (such as the Southern Independent Party), and state/local entities (such as the Charter Party of Cincinnati). Each entry includes party name, address, telephone and fax numbers, launch date, email and web site addresses, a review of the party's history and activities, an abbreviated inclusion of the party's platform, and a listing of any affiliates. For more detailed information about the party or a full description of their platform, please refer to each party's web site.

The information detailed in this book was primarily gathered from direct contact with each political party or through the use of materials provided from their respective web sites. Additional information was also gathered through several political-related books and web sites. Please see the Bibliography for a complete listing of reference sources.

Introduction

In today's America, the political climate and agenda are mainly controlled by two parties, the Democrats and the Republicans, both of which have been active, in one form or another, for more than 150 years. These two parties have been able to dictate and guide the political direction of America over the last two centuries and have been the primary architects of this country's political structure and foreign policy. The paradox of their longevity is that their size, power, and influence have now been turned against them. The continuous decline in voting trends and the dissatisfaction of large blocs of voters have caused many citizens to turn their backs on both parties, claiming that they are controlled by special interest groups, are always searching for more money to consolidate their power, and increasingly ignore the American voter and their concerns.

While it is beyond the scope of this book to provide an in-depth analysis of the major parties and their goals, it can be stated in simple terms that the Democrats believe that the government is responsible for solving all social ills while the Republicans support seeking solutions from individual initiative and business. However, many voters today feel there are no fundamental differences between the two parties and that they both focus too much energy on special interest money and enhancing the lives of an elite few while ignoring the plight of average Americans. The sheer size and reach of these two parties force them to cater to special interest groups and to approach voters from a "lowest common denominator" point of view. These factors have led many citizens to believe that both parties have abandoned their core principles in order to remain in power, gather more money, and enact legal obstacles to any challenge to their political hegemony. This dissatisfaction with the status quo leads voters to take one of two paths: turn their back on the political process or join with like-minded citizens and form a third party.

Rise of the Third Party

While third party political groups (commonly called minor parties) have always existed in American history (even the Republican Party, at its inception, was a third party to the Democrats and Whigs), the rise of voter dissatisfaction with the political status quo has led to a rapid increase in the number of active third parties in today's America. Their political experience and recognition of why past parties have failed, along with available funds and technology, have made it easier to form third parties, although it is still extremely difficult to have an impact on national politics (such as electing members to Congress or electing a president) since the Democrats and Republicans have been very successful in establishing severe legal obstacles to ballot access for minor parties.

Because of the tremendous barriers to national ballot access built into our political system, most third parties focus on affecting local, state or regional political decisions or on specific topics of interest (such as immigration, taxes, education), although the goal of almost all entities is to grow. There is almost an inevitable contradiction in this arrangement. Third parties want to grow in membership and to have representatives in multiple states so that they can have a larger political influence over issues that matter to them. The logical result of this is that as parties grow in size, they tend to lose focus on their core beliefs, thus generating resentment and dissatisfaction among some of their members, who then leave the political process altogether or form offshoot parties in an attempt to regain their initial focus. And the cycle continues.

The net result is that a party either remains focused on only local politics (school boards, city governments), continuously reinvents itself as internal factions develop, or fades from the political landscape. Whichever path is followed, these third parties, by and large, will never achieve national prominence or have the chance to affect national policies or elections. However, they can play prominent, and in some cases dominant, roles in their communities and have the ability to shape their own political environment.

Future of Political Parties

It seems apparent that America's national politics will continue to be dominated by a two-party system, with a third party occasionally achieving national prominence because of a charismatic figure's catching the media's attention or because their support of some specific issue that will briefly put them in the national spotlight. However, the Democrats and Republicans are too entrenched to fear any real threat to their national political stranglehold in the foreseeable future.

It is, however, undeniable that there is no slow-down of voter dissatisfaction and revolt against this long-time established two-party system. While this book features more than 180 minor party organizations, this figure is sure to rise as more voters abandon national politics and focus on their local communities or niche concerns. Once local breakthroughs are made, the viability of third parties becomes more accepted, and smarter use is made of the internet's ability to organize like-minded people, there will be an outbreak of these dedicated organizations, the number of which will dwarf those in existence today. The future of politics as it affects our day-to-day lives in our local communities will soon be dominated, not by the Big Two, but by a proliferation of third parties.

AMERICAN POLITICAL PARTIES

Alaskan Independence Party

P.O. Box 58462, Fairbanks, AK 99711; *Telephone:* 907-488-4310; *Fax:* 907-488-1955; *Email:* contact party through its web site; *Web site:* http://www.akip.org

Founded in the 1970s and officially recognized as a political party in 1984 by the State of Alaska, the Alaskan Independence Party advocates an "Alaska First, Alaska Always" policy that is focused around the land and resource development. The party strives to restore the American Republic to its founding principles of a constitutional government that acknowledges God and defends the family. With 20,000 registered members, the AIP is the only political party in Alaska that is comprised of Alaskans, staffed by Alaskans, and financed by Alaskans.

The AIP's activities began in earnest in the mid–1980s and by 1986 the party's candidates for Governor and Lt. Governor (Joe Vogler/Rowe) received 5.5% of the votes cast for Governor, which earned the AIP Recognized Political Party status. By 1998, their candidate for Governor (Sullivan) ran for office without a Lt. Governor running mate and received only 1.92% of the votes cast. However, there was still a sufficient number of voters registered under the party name to retain Recognized Political Party status.

The party's Preamble states that all political power is inherent in the people; that all government originates with the people and is instituted to protect the rights of the individual; that all persons have a natural right to life, liberty, the pursuit of happiness, and the enjoyment of the rewards of their own industry; and that all persons are equal and entitled to equal protection under the law.

The AIP supports States' Rights; abolishing all property taxes; the complete repatriation of public lands held by the federal government to the state and people of Alaska; preserving the Alaska Permanent Fund; direct popular election of the attorney general, all judges, and magistrates; the right of the individual to keep and bear arms; the rights of parents to privately or home school their children and to provide them equal access to a proportional share of all public money provided for educational purposes; and the privatization of government services.

All-African People's Revolutionary Party

P.O. Box 863, New York, NY 10116; *Email*: contact party through its web site; *Web site*: http://members.aol.com/aapprp/index2.html

The All-African People's Revolutionary Party promotes the concept of African unity, embraces the fundamental needs and characteristics of African civilization and ideology, and works for economic and technological advances. The party supports Pan-Africanism (defined as a total liberation and unification of Africa under Scientific Socialism); Black Power (the belief that real black freedom will only come when Africa is politically united); and Scientific Socialism (the idea that modern technology can be reconciled with human values, in which an advanced technical society is realized without the social upheaval and deep schisms that occur in capitalist industrial societies).

The All-African People's Revolutionary Party (A-APRP) was founded by Dr. Kwame Nkrumah, who introduced the party's concepts and philosophies in his book, *Handbook of Revolutionary Warfare*, which was released in 1968. As he envisioned, the A-APRP aims to be a coordinating organization for all revolutionary political parties in the African world, with its purpose being to create and manage the political-economic conditions necessary for the emergence of an All-African People's Revolutionary Army that will lead the military struggle against Colonialism, Zionism, Imperialism, and all other forms of capitalist oppression and exploitation. Through this struggle, the A-APRP promotes Pan-Africanism, which will eventually evolve into a United Socialist African government that will encompass the entire African continent. The ideology of the A-APRP is Nkrumahism-Toureism, which takes its name from the founder, and his primary colleague in arms, President Ahmed Sekou Toure.

The All-African Women's Revolutionary Union is the women's wing of the A-APRP. Its main focus is the education and organization of African women so that they can make significant contributions to the African Revolution and National Liberation Struggle.

Affiliates. *California*: P.O. Box 2302, Berkeley, CA 94702. *Colorado*: P.O. Box 3165, Denver, CO 80201. *Georgia*: P.O. Box 42126, Atlanta, GA 30311; *Telephone*: 707-808-6062. *Illinois*: P.O. Box 87549, Chicago, IL 60680; *Telephone*: 773-955-3906. *Louisiana*: P.O. Box 8035, New Orleans, LA 70182. *Maryland*: P.O. Box 1304, Baltimore, MD 21203; *Telephone*: 410-385-3351. *Massachusetts*: P.O. Box 1286, Boston, MA 02119; *Telephone*: 617-445-4204. *Michigan*: P.O. Box 06824, Detroit, MI 48206; *Telephone*: 313-869-8343. *Missouri*: P.O. Box 4681, St. Louis, MO 63108. *Mississippi*: P.O. Box 3760, Tougaloo, MS 39174. *New Jersey*: P.O. Box 1287, Newark, NJ 07101. *New York*: P.O. Box 300, New York, NY 10027; *Telephone*: 718-671-0142. *North Carolina*: P.O. Box 824, Raleigh, NC 27602; *Telephone*: 919-231-6887. *Ohio*: P.O. Box 14736, Cincinnati, OH 45250, P.O. Box 200524, Cleveland, OH 44120. *Pennsylvania*: P.O. Box 13389, Philadelphia, PA 19101; *Telephone*: 215-471-6508. *Tennessee*: P.O. Box 3597, Memphis, TN 38173; *Telephone*: 901-725-5732. *Texas*: P.O. Box 224113, Dallas, TX 75222; *Telephone*: 817-792-3064. *Virginia*: P.O. Box 12505, Richmond, VA 23241; *Telephone*: 804-745-3962. *Washington, D.C.*: P.O. Box 43793, Washington, D.C. 20010; *Telephone*: 202-483-4333.

Aloha Aina Party

The Aloha Aina Party is a resurgence of a political party that was once called the Home Rule Party and has recently re-formed to better serve native Hawaiians and to give them more of a voice in statewide politics. In 1900, many Hawaiians, frustrated at the loss of their sovereignty, ignored the Republican and Democratic parties and formed the Home Rule Party shortly after Hawaii became a U.S. territory. In its first election that year, the "Hawaiians for Hawaiians" party gained control of the territorial House and Senate, and sent pro-monarchy advocate Robert Wilcox as the first Hawaii delegate to Congress. The Home Rulers (as they were called) often spoke Hawaiian instead of English and initially tried to pass legislation to free native prisoners from jail and to license kahunas as physicians. Within several years, however, the Home Rule Party lost Prince Jonah Kuhio Kalanianaole Piikoi to the Republican Party and after two more elections, the party faded away in 1912. There is a movement currently underway in Alaska to re-activate this party.

America First Party

1630A 30th Street #111, Boulder, CO 80301; *Telephone:* 866-767-8721; *Fax:* 303-265-9230; *Email:* info@AmericaFirstParty.org; *Web site:* http://www.americafirstparty.org

The America First Party seeks to restore the Old Constitutional Republic and the ideals of the Founders of America. The party supports limited government; protection of natural and civil rights, including the right to life; the Second Amendment; states' rights; an America First foreign and trade policy; the end of foreign aid; the return of our soldiers from other countries to protect our own homeland; the roll back of the power and size of government to the original intentions of the nation's founders; and the promotion of Judeo-Christian values upon which the nation was founded.

The AFP intends to organize in all fifty states following a grassroots development strategy that will focus first on winning state and local elections, followed by House and Senate elections, concluding with fielding candidates for the Presidency.

Using the slogan "Fighting For Faith, Freedom, and the Constitution to put America First," the America First Party was founded on April 15, 2002 by a group of supporters of well-known commentator Pat Buchanan (a former speech writer for President Richard Nixon). This group, also known as the "Buchanan Brigade," broke away from the more-established Reform Party to form this new social conservative and fair trade political party, with strong ties to the Religious Right movement. Closely following the views of Buchanan, the AFP is dedicated to "protect our people and our sovereignty ... promote economic growth and independence ... encourage the traditional values of faith, family, and responsibility ... ensure equality before the law in protecting those rights granted by the Creator ... and to clean up our corrupted political system."

Shortly after the AFP was created, ten state chapters of the Reform Party defected and joined the AFP, further eroding the support base of the Reform Party. The AFP lost impetus when its national chair, vice chair, and treasurer all resigned in mid–2003 after allegedly clashing with a group of supporters of the ultra-right militia movement leader Bo Gritz, who had purportedly grabbed control of key party elements. However, many in the AFP dispute this theory and insist that the leaders left due to serious financial problems and personality divisions within the party. The party's prominence and influence waned quickly as many of the AFP state parties left the national party soon after the top leaders had resigned. The party's 2003 National Convention was canceled and the party decided not to field a Presidential candidate for the 2004 election. A group of Buchanan supporters made a move and re-gained control of the party and refocused their efforts on building the party's strength through its state affiliates.

Learning from past mistakes made by other political entities, the AFP developed a simple party structure. Its National Committee has complete authority over all aspects of the national party; its National Convention is granted primary authority over the platform and the nominations for President and Vice-President; and its Executive Committee coordinates the daily operations of the party in compliance with the resolutions of the National Committee.

In an effort to directly assail the deeply-entrenched two-party system that currently dominates the American political landscape, the AFP aims to offer a populist, conservative alternative that appeals to citizens (both active and non-active voters) who are looking for a voice that represents their views to "put America first" and lead the country back to its founding principles.

The party's foreign policy platform is basically isolationist in nature and focuses on America. The founding principles of the AFP are that the government must "put America First" and not be swayed into placing international interests above America's interests. The party insists that the government not cede authority to international organizations, such as the United Nations, the World Trade Organization, the World Bank, and the World Court. The AFP wants the

United States to withdraw from the United Nations and insists that the U.N. be forced to relocate outside of the United States.

Domestically, the AFP wants less government and more sovereignty for American citizens. The party does not support federal income or property taxes and feels the government should encourage personal savings and investment. The party defends the traditional family unit based on one man and one woman and believes that the federal government should in no way be allowed to interfere with how parents raise their children. The AFP supports overturning Roe vs. Wade; prayer in school; State's Rights; dismantling the Department of Housing and Urban Development and the Department of Education; eliminating funding for the National Endowment for the Arts, the National Endowment for the Humanities, and the Corporation for Public Broadcasting; the right of citizens to possess and bear arms; using the military to help patrol America's borders; curtailing legal immigration; and the designation of English as the official language of the United States.

In the business arena, the party wants the government to withdraw from international trade agreements, such as the North American Free Trade Agreement, and wants the government to help American businesses stay in America. The AFP support a "Buy American" policy; implementation of a self-sufficient energy policy; an end to taxpayer bailouts of corporations and foreign governments; passing a federal balanced budget amendment; and the payment of the Federal Debt.

The party's primary focus is on cleaning up the federal government, both in scope and on how it operates. The AFP feels that corruption and special interests organizations have made the federal government inefficient and not answerable to the American people. The party supports numerous governmental changes, including a limit on gifts and outside sources of income; prohibiting federal officials from becoming lobbyists for at least five years after leaving office; requiring that all legislative bills address only one issue and do not allow riders; requiring that all donations to political organizations must come from actual persons who are citizens and registered to vote or from other political committees; and retaining the Electoral College.

Affiliates. *California*: P.O. Box 370, Lompoc, CA 93438; *Email*: info@afpca.us; *Web site*: http://afpca.us. *Colorado*: 40 West Littleton

Boulevard #210-337, Littleton, CO 80120; *Email*: colorado@america
firstparty.org; *Web site*: http://colorado.americafirstparty.org/.
Florida: P.O. Box 382, Christmas, FL 32709; *Telephone*: 407-249-1689.
Idaho: 1212 Savannah Street, Caldwell, ID 83605; *Telephone*: 208-
459-9225. *Illinois*: P.O. Box 3381-9093, St. Charles, IL 60174. *Indiana*:
Indiana Patriot Party; *Email*: contact party through its web site; *Web
site*: http://www.patriotparty.us/state/in. *Massachusetts*: P.O. Box
61126, New Bedford, MA 02746; *Telephone*: 508-997-3606; *Email*:
MassAFP@americafirstparty.org; *Web site*: http://massachusetts.
americafirstparty.org/. *Mississippi*: 405 River Road, Greenwood, MS
38930; *Telephone*: 662-453-8412; *Email*: chairman@msreformparty.
org; *Web site*: http://mississippi.americafirstparty.org/; http://www.
msreformparty.org. *Missouri*: 807 Englehart Lane, Marble Hill, MO
63764; *Telephone*: 573-238-2266; *Email*: contact party through its web
site; *Web site*: http://www.rpmo.org. *New York*: 24–52 44th Street #A2,
Astoria, NY 14468; *Telephone*: 718-545-0669; *Email*: info@afpny.org;
Web site: http://www.afpny.org. *Ohio*: 200 Tillman Avenue, Greene-
ville, OH 45331; *Telephone*: 877-448-6417, 937-548-9200; *Email*:
afpoinfo@yahoo.com; *Web site*: http://www.afpohio.com. *Pennsylvania*: P.O. Box 62, West Decatur, PA 16878; *Telephone*: 814-342-8320.
Wisconsin: RR3, Muscoda, WI 53573; *Telephone*: 608-532-6281.

America Founding Fathers Party

P.O. Box 108, University Park, IA 52595; *Telephone*: 770-471-
3931; *Email*: chair@americafoundingfathersparty.org; *Web site*: http:
//www.americafoundingfathersparty.org

The America Founding Fathers Party believes that the current two-
party system is a corruption of the intentions of the Founding Fathers
of a limited government and has given the American people the tyranny
of a quasi-democratic, socialist, intrusive, unlimited government with
very few, if any, freedoms left for the people. The AFFP believes that third
parties fail in American politics because of the belief that a President
must be elected before state legislators and that these emerging parties
believe that they can beat the Democrats and Republicans at their own
game with a better vision and a superior plan to lead the country.

Learning from the failures of other third-party organizations,
the AFFP approaches political survival with the belief that the cur-

rent two-party system itself is the problem, and that the solution lies in creating a new political system outside the Democratic-Republican sphere of influence. The goal of the AFFP is to return America to constitutional governance through independent, constitutionally-committed citizen legislators.

The national organization of the AFFP aims to echo the ideals and goals of the Founding Fathers while the party's affiliated state organizations totally control the national entity, exactly as the Founding Fathers envisioned for the federal government. The AFFP does not provide a Presidential candidate; encourages a return to independent citizen legislators at the local and state levels; and does not nominate, endorse, or finance any political candidate (although independent candidates are encouraged to seek the support of local AFFP members).

Affiliates. *California*: America First Party of California, P.O. Box 370, Lompoc, CA 93438; *Email*: info@afpca.us; *Web site*: http://afpca.us. *Colorado*: 8200 South Quebec Street #243, Suite A3, Centennial, CO 80112; *Email*: contact party through its web site; *Web site*: http://www.americafoundingfatherpartyofcolorado.com/. *Connecticut*: 862 Colorado Avenue, Bridgeport, CT 06604; *Telephone*: 203-367-6048; *Email*: info@AmericaFoundingFathersPartyofCT.org; *Web site*: http://www.americafoundingfatherspartyofct.org. *Michigan*: *Email*: contact party through its web site; *Web site*: http://www.affpmi.us.

American Centrist Party

2141 North University Drive #212, Coral Springs, FL 33071; *Email*: munger@americancentristparty.com; *Web site*: http://www.americancentristparty.com

Not limiting its membership to only those who take positions defined as being in the political center; the American Centrist Party tries to attract those interested in re-defining the American political system as it was envisioned by this country's founders. The ACP states it is committed to a policy of inclusion, so long as those who hold political views which lean to either end of the spectrum are tolerant of others who may not agree with those beliefs. The purpose of the ACP is to unite all Americans in an effort to make the United States a better place.

The American Centrist Party believes that too many so-called third party organizations focus on single-issue politics, thus limiting their appeal to a wider audience. The ACP attempts to address all major American political issues in the hopes of making America a better place while attracting a larger membership base.

The ACP supports separation of church and state; the declining influence of special interest groups in national politics; strong protections for individual credit information; canceling the Federal Communications Commission's indecency fine; a flat tax for all citizens and businesses; institution of a national health care system and limits on malpractice suits; less federal government interference in state operations; the end to the idea of career politicians; elimination of individual federal income taxes; a Taxpayers' Bill of Rights; returning all military troops to the United States and closing all foreign bases; the creation of a Border Security Force within the Department of Homeland Security; and the formation of local Civil Defense Teams.

American Fascist Party

P.O. Box 78, Garfield, GA 30425; *Email*: contact party through its web site; *Web site*: http://americanfascistparty.net

The American Fascist Party is dedicated to the cause of fascism and is active in creating a fascist political party in the United States. In spite of what many might believe, the AFP stresses that its beliefs do not echo the Nazi philosophies of Adolf Hitler and that it is not a racist political party. The party supports the separation of church and state; states' rights; a smaller role for the federal government in the lives of its citizens; and a limited foreign policy role, although the AFP does not adhere to a strict isolationist policy.

American Heritage Party

P.O. Box 241, Leavenworth, WA 98826; *Telephone:* 888-396-6247; *Email:* hq@ahparty.org; *Web site:* http://www.americanheritageparty.org

The American Heritage Party, formerly the Washington State affiliate of the U.S. Taxpayers Party/Constitution Party, broke away from that group in 2000 because of religious grounds (believing that while the Constitution Party is a Religious Right organization, it is not explicitly a Christian party). The AHP describes itself as "a political party that adopts the Bible as its political textbook and is unashamed to be explicitly Christian ... [and] whose principles are drawn from Scripture." The AHP aims to become a national conservative party, with the ultimate goal of fielding candidates around the nation at various political levels. The party fielded candidates for Congress, Governor, and local offices in Washington in 1998, but ran just one local candidate in 2000 and 2002.

The party's main stated goals include strengthening the Lordship of Jesus Christ over politics; promoting God's Word, through the Holy Bible, as the absolute authority upon which their principles rest; ensuring that party members, leaders, and nominees for public office meet Biblical and constitutional qualifications; promoting the Gospel of Jesus Christ as a nationwide and international message; redefining the political debate from "liberal vs. conservative" to "Christian faith vs. unbelief"; promoting Christ-centered solutions to the problems in America; restoring a comprehensive Biblical world view among Christians; and mobilizing Christians at the local level to develop a strong base as a foundation from which to launch state and national candidates.

The American Heritage Party rejects man-centered politics and the politics-as-usual mentality in building its strength. The party believes that "no political work founded on pragmatism and inclusiveness, bought and paid for by special interests, and whose primary goal is political power for today, can hope to effect long term national reform. Christian political action is more than the religious servant of the secular two-party establishment, more than just another special interest group competing in a pragmatic struggle for political power, and more than just a voice of protest against the latest liberal innovation."

The AHP views itself as a political and philosophical emancipation movement, working to liberate American families from the grip of socialism while promoting the Christian world view and looking to the Gospel for the answers to today's ills. The party believes that the American people must be freed from the cynicism and indifference toward politics and government and that the AHP's success will depend on its ability to rally a disenfranchised electorate around a common cause, thus capturing the hearts and imaginations of the people.

The AHP's basic tenet is that the current two-party system has played an integral role in the rise of socialism and the decline of freedom in America. By reducing the debate of ideas to the self-serving struggle for political power, the two-party system has handed America's future over to bureaucrats and special interests. The party believes that many Americans have been intimidated by the current, deeply entrenched establishment; demoralized by political pragmatism and the "lesser of two evils" philosophy; and have consequently given up and withdrawn from political involvement. The AHP calls for the end to the two-party system as the only way for Americans to regain control of their government and its political institutions.

The AHP supports the God-ordained boundaries of the family, the church, and the state; the restoration of the civil government to its proper role as minister of law, justice, national defense and as a defender of life, including that of the unborn child; the repeal of every law, tax, and government program which denies, supplants, or obstructs the design and intended operation of God's civil, religious and social order; the replacement of the secular public school system with an educational system that respects individual freedom of conscience and reinforces the Biblical role and responsibility of the family as the educator of youth; the reduction of the prison system into a system of just restitution for the victims of crimes and capital punishment for murderers; and the recognition of God's providential plan for nationhood.

The party also supports the sanctity of life and the prohibition of abortion; the right of citizens to bear arms; capital and corporal punishment and a judicial system that protects the rights of victims over the rights of criminals; end to property taxes; abolishing the U.S. Department of Education; eliminating the Food and Drug Administration; repealing the Social Security Act; abolishing the Federal Reserve System; eliminating the income tax and the Internal Revenue Service; eliminating the Federal Election Commission; designating English as the official language of the United States; and ending U.S. funding for the United Nations.

Affiliates. *Idaho*: idaho@ahparty.org. *Virginia*: virginia@ah party.org. *Washington*: 17725 West 17th Avenue, Lynnwood, WA 98037; *Telephone*: 888-396-6247; *Fax*: 425-670-8421; *Email*: ahp@ americanheritageparty.org, washington@ahparty.org.

American Independent Party

The American Independent Party was established in 1967–1968 by Alabama governor George Wallace to be the platform for his 1968 run for the presidency. Ultimately, he and running mate Curtis E. LeMay were on every presidential state ballot and received 13.5% of the popular vote and 46 electoral votes. During the 1968 presidential campaign, the party's main positions were opposition to the Civil Rights Act of 1964 and to federal government welfare programs.

In 1970 representatives from 38 states established the American Party as the successor to the American Independent Party and in 1972, nominated former Congressman John G. Schmitz of California for president. In 1976 the American Party split again into the American Party, which included more northern conservatives and Schmitz supporters, and the American Independent Party, which focused its political efforts on the deep South. Both of the parties have continually nominated candidates for the presidency and other offices, but neither has had much national success.

The American Independent Party is still active in the state of California, where it has become the state affiliate for the national United States Constitution Party.

AIP presidential candidates over the years have included George Wallace (1968), John G. Schmitz (1972), Lester Maddox (1976) from the American Independent Party, Thomas Jefferson Anderson (1976) from the American Party, John Rarick (1980) from the American Independent Party, Delmar Dennis (1984 and 1988) from the American Party, Diane Beall Templin (1996 and 2004) from the American Party, and Don Moore (2000) from the American Party.

Governor George C. Wallace (D-AL) founded the AIP and ran as its first Presidential nominee in 1968. Running on a right-wing, anti–Washington, anti-racial integration, anti-communist platform, Wallace carried nearly 10 million votes (14%) and won five Southern states. Although he returned to the Democratic Party by 1970, the AIP continued operations and moved further to the political right.

The 1972 AIP nominee, John Birch Society leader and Congressman John G. Schmitz (R-CA), carried nearly 1.1 million votes (1.4%). The 1976 AIP Presidential nominee was former Governor Lester Maddox (D-GA), a vocal segregationist who received far less support and votes than did Schmitz. The AIP last fielded its own national Presidential candidate in 1980, when the party nominated white supremacist ex–Congressman John Rarick (D-LA), who subsequently garnered only 41,000 votes nationwide. The AIP still fields local candidates in a few states, mainly California, but now acts primarily as a state affiliate party of the national Constitution Party. Since 1980, the AIP has co-nominated the Constitution Party's Presidential nominee.

American Independent Party of California (state affiliate of the Constitution Party)

8158 Palm Street, Lemon Grove, CA 91945; *Telephone:* 619-460-4484; *Email:* join@aipca.org; *Web site:* http://www.aipca.org/

On July 8, 1967, formal organization of California's American Independent Party was completed at a convention held in Bakersfield. A constitution and declaration of principles were adopted and officers were elected. The party endorsed limited constitutional government, the rights of the states to govern their own local affairs, educational systems without federal bureaucratic or court interference, and a foreign policy based on America's best interests, not world opinion.

In 1967, Governor George C. Wallace of Alabama ran for President on a new party ticket, the American Independent Party. Second to Alabama, California was the next most important state in the election according to the Wallace campaign and his supporters were encouraged with the formation of the American Independent Party of California, which basically supported their candidate's political positions. In addition to California being the most populous state in America, it also had the earliest ballot qualification deadline for the 1968 presidential election, January 2, 1968. The procedures for ballot qualification in California were difficult and required a new political party to either secure 66,000 voter registrations showing affiliation with the new party (a very difficult task in such a short time) or to present a petition with over 660,000 valid voter signatures (a less difficult, but not easy task to accomplish). Garnering the necessary signatures was an arduous process and it soon became clear to the campaign that the signature drive was proceeding too slowly for Wallace to qualify for the state ballot in 1968. To give his campaign a boost, Wallace visited California in October 1967 for a week of rallies; his campaign opened more than 45 Registration Centers in the most populous areas of the state; and a massive radio, television, and newspaper advertising campaign was launched.

He visited the state again in late November. His campaign efforts proved to be successful and more than 100,000 additional verified signatures were collected, more than enough to qualify for the state's presidential ballot. His California victory encouraged his campaign and in 1968 Wallace was able to qualify for the presidential ballot in every state of the nation.

A period of turmoil followed for the California party as Wallace's profile became more prominent. Wallace campaign leaders did not want the AIP of California to operate as a separate entity from the Wallace campaign but instead to be a state affiliate of his political ambitions. The California leaders had no intention of being a subservient party and had their own ideas on how to operate, which inevitably led to conflict between the AIP and the Wallace campaign.

On August 3, 1968, delegates to the state convention of the American Independent Party adopted the party's first platform, which held tremendous significance for AIP activists who had joined the new party because they wanted major changes in public policies. Many party leaders had specific legislative proposals they wanted addressed and the platform gave them an opportunity to participate in the decision-making process. Its platform in place, the party needed a rallying point to garner support. Governor Wallace, their presidential candidate, would have been a natural choice but he had turned away from the state party organization. With no high-profile option, party activists rallied around the 1968 platform, which would become the cornerstone of future national and state party activities.

The 1968 election brought Governor Wallace seven percent of the California vote and over 482,000 votes out of his national total of almost 10 million. Problems simmered underneath the political surface between the AIP and the Wallace Campaign until 1971, when both entities buried the hatchet and joined forces for another Wallace presidential run. However, before the AIP could play any significant role in his campaign, Wallace was shot by a would-be assassin, wounded, and was forced to end his presidential bid. From that moment on, Wallace was no longer a political factor and played no further leadership role in the AIP.

However, the AIP's earlier efforts to maintain independence paid off and the party began to grow in influence and in members. The AIP of California has been continually ballot-qualified since January 1968 and over the years has affiliated itself with several national political parties. Since 1991, the AIP (which now has more than 300,000 registered members) has been the California state affiliate of the U.S. Taxpayers Party (later renamed the Constitution Party). The AIP's main tenets include respect for life; fiscal responsibility; a reduced role of government in people's lives; reduction of the tax burden; crime control; protection of American businesses, workers, and farmers from unfair foreign competition; and an America-first non-interventionist foreign policy.

Due to its relatively long existence, the AIP has developed a full national and international position platform addressing today's problems and trouble areas. The party supports an end to all undeclared wars; ending debt financing of both Federal and State governments; abolishing the federal income tax; terminating all international trade agreements such as the North American Free Trade Agreement, the World Trade Organization, and the proposed Free Trade Area of the Americas; reducing immigration and stopping all government subsidies to illegal aliens; keeping God in the pledge of allegiance; encouraging the development of private schools and home schooling; the right of citizens to bear arms; term limits; the abolition of the Federal Reserve system, the Internal Revenue Service, and the federal Department of Education; the U.S. ending its membership in the United Nations; and a slowdown of legal immigration.

American Nationalist Union

P.O. Box 426, Allison Park, PA 15101; *Fax*: 724-443-4240; *Email*: mail@anu.org; *Web site*: http://www.anu.org

Founded in 1995, the American Nationalist Union is the largest nationalist political organization in the United States and publishes

The Nationalist Times, a monthly newspaper. The ANU is not affiliated with any political party, but supports individual candidates and third parties which share its political views.

The ANU calls for a united block of voters to support candidates who stand for nationalist principles and feels it is time for America to end its fracturing of political voices into hundreds of splinter groups, thus reducing their effectiveness.

American Nazi Party

P.O. Box 85942, Westland, MI 48185; *Email*: staff@americannazi party.com; *Web site*: http://www.americannaziparty.com

Formed in 1959, the American Nazi Party considers itself a political-educational association that is committed to bringing American National Socialism, first created by the late George Lincoln Rockwell, into the 21st Century. Although American National Socialism encompasses various issues of concern to Aryan Americans (including a healthy environment, children's welfare, and freedom of belief without fear of government persecution), the two primary tenants focus on the Struggle for Aryan Racial Survival and Social Justice for White Working Class people throughout America. Recognizing that its past activities, some historically extreme, have lost the party support, the ANP is adopting new strategies that include no uniforms or ranks, and no public, anger-provoking rallies or marches. The party works through small cells and individual activism to spread their message and to garner new members. To help spread its message, the Party publishes the monthly newsletter, *The White Worker*.

George Lincoln Rockwell (1918–1967), the founder and leader of the American Nazi Party, was one of the most controversial figures in the United States. Though known as one of the most public advocates of racist and anti–Semitic politics, Rockwell was also media savvy and used the attention he garnered to play a larger role in the public arena than his small number of followers would normally have justified. Whatever else his legacy, it is generally recognized that Rockwell laid the foundation for what he called the "White Power" movement in the United States. It is also accepted that most of the organizations within current right-wing, white supremacist U.S. politics, except the Ku Klux Klan, are philosophical descendants of Rockwell and the American Nazi Party, including the Skinheads, the National Socialist Vanguard, the Order, the Aryan Nation, the White Aryan Resistance, and the New Order. Rockwell is recognized as one of the first U.S. white supremacists to understand the value of connecting his political movement to a religious philosophy that provided a theological justification for racist and anti–Semitic violence.

American Pagan Party of Massachusetts

180 Church Street, Lowell, MA 01862; *Email*: paganparty@hot mail.com; *Web site*: http://www.geocities.com/mass paganparty/

The American Pagan Party of Massachusetts operates to defend the constitution of the state of Massachusetts and is currently working to ensure that the state proposal banning same-sex marriage does not pass. The APPMA considers itself defenders of GLBT rights (Gay, Lesbian, Bi-sexual, Transgender).

American Party of the United States

P.O. Box 612, Tooele, UT 84074; *Telephone:* 800-456-8683; Fax: 801-596-3662; *Email*: liberty@theamericanparty.org; *Web site*: http://www.the americanparty.org

The American Party of the United States, more commonly referred to as simply The American Party, was organized in March 1969 within the ranks of the state parties that had supported Alabama Governor George Wallace for President in 1968 and became a separate splinter group in 1972 when it broke away from the more established American Independent Party. Since its inception, the party has nominated candidates in every election for president and vice president but has come to realize that it can be more effective, and can garner more power and influence, by focusing its efforts on getting state candidates elected to Congress.

The party's presidential aspirations have not fared well. From its high mark during the 1976 election, when the party's candidate, Tom Anderson, finished sixth with 161,000 votes, the party's presidential candidate of 1996 (attorney Diane Templin) garnered only 1,900 votes. The party's 2000 presidential nominee, former California State Senator Don Rogers, did even worse and did not qualify for ballot status in any state.

The American Party is religious; pro-life; pro-gun; anti-tax; advocates an end to farm price supports and subsidies; supports privatization of the U.S. Postal Service; supports the right of citizens to own and bear arms; opposes federal involvement in education; supports abolition of the Environmental Protection Agency; supports repeal of the North American Free Trade Agreement; supports the complete decontrol of energy production; supports the death penalty; opposes minimum wage laws; opposes land use zoning regulations; opposes convening a Constitutional Convention; and opposes U.S. membership in the United Nations, the Central American Free Trade Agreement, the Free Trade Area of the Americas, NAFTA, the New World Order, communism, socialism, and the Trilateral Commission.

The party's highest honor is the Walter Brennan Award given to that "American who has rendered extraordinary service above and beyond the call of duty to God and America!" Members of the American Party believe that the original United States Constitution and Bill of Rights were prepared and adopted by men acting under inspiration from Almighty God; that there are solemn compacts between the people of the states of this nation which all officers of government are under oath to obey; and that the eternal moral laws expressed therein must be adhered to or individual liberty will perish. The party publishes the *Eagle*, the official national monthly publication of the American Party in the United States.

American Patriot Party

P.O. Box 451, Kinsman, OH 44428; *Email*: chair@patriotparty. us; *Web site*: http://www.patriotparty.us

Formed in March 2003, the American Patriot Party supports returning the federal and state government back to the system originally envisioned by the Founding Fathers as laid out in the Constitution, including: returning all powers back to the states from the federal government that are not specified by the Constitution and educating the American people about the U.S. Constitution, the Declaration of Independence, and the Bill of Rights.

The APP supports a crackdown on illegal immigration; making English fluency a requirement of U.S. citizenship; abolishing the Internal Revenue Service; repealing the federal income tax; the right of citizens to bear arms; imposing steeper taxes and tariffs on imported goods; abolition of the centralized Federal Reserve System and the Department of Education; the U.S. developing a self-sufficient energy policy; term limits for elected officials; withdrawing the U.S. from the Untied Nations and the World Trade Organization; imposing a foreign policy of non-interventionism; and ending federal involvement in education.

The National Patriot Party is the national level of the American Patriot Party.

Affiliates. *Alabama*: *Email*: contact party through its web site; *Web site*: http://www.patriotparty.us/state/al/index.htm. *Alaska*: *Email*: contact party through its web site; *Web site*: http://www.patriot party.us/state/ak/index.htm. *Arizona*: *Email*: az.chair@patriotparty. us; *Web site*: http://www.patriotparty.us/state/az/index.htm. *Arkansas*: *Email*: contact party through its web site; *Web site*: http://www. patriotparty.us/state/ar/index.htm. *California*: *Email*: ca.chair@patri otparty.us; *Web site*: http://www.patriotparty.us/state/ca/index.htm. *Colorado*: *Email*: co.chair@patriotparty.us; *Web site*: http://www. patriotparty.us/state/co/index.htm. *Connecticut*: *Email*: ct.chair@ patriotparty.us; *Web site*: http://www.patriotparty.us/state/ct/index. htm. *Delaware*: *Email*: contact party through its web site; *Web site*: http://www.patriotparty.us/state/de/index.htm. *Florida*: *Email*: fl. chair@patriotparty.us; *Web site*: http://www.patriotparty.us/state/ fl/index.htm. *Georgia*: *Email*: contact party through its web site; *Web site*: http://www.patriotparty.us/state/ga/index.htm. *Hawaii*: *Email*: hi.chair@patriotparty.us; *Web site*: http://www.patriotparty.us/state/ hi/index.htm. *Idaho*: *Email*: contact party through its web site; *Web site*: http://www.patriotparty.us/state/id/index.htm. *Illinois*: *Email*: il.chair@patriotparty.us; *Web site*: http://www.patriotparty.us/state/ il/index.htm. *Indiana*: *Email*: contact party through its web site; *Web site*: http://www.patriotparty.us/state/in/index.htm. *Iowa*: *Email*: contact party through its web site; *Web site*: http://www.patriot party.us/state/ia/index.htm. *Kansas*: *Email*: contact party through its web site; *Web site*: http://www.patriotparty.us/state/ks/index.htm. *Kentucky*: *Email*: ky.chair@patriotparty.us; *Web site*: http://www. patriotparty.us/state/ky/index.htm. *Louisiana*: *Email*: contact party through its web site; *Web site*: http://www.patriotparty.us/state/la/

index.htm. *Maine*: *Email*: me.chair@patriotparty.us; *Web site*: http://www.patriotparty.us/state/me/index.htm. *Maryland*: *Email*: contact party through its web site; *Web site*: http://www.patriotparty.us/state/md/index.htm. *Massachusetts*: *Email*: contact party through its web site; *Web site*: http://www.patriotparty.us//ma/index.htm. *Michigan*: *Email*: contact party through its web site; *Web site*: http://www.patriotparty.us/state/mi/index.htm. *Minnesota*: *Email*: mn.chair@patriotparty.us; *Web site*: http://www.patriotparty.us/state/mn/index.htm. *Mississippi*: *Email*: ms.chair@patriotparty.us; *Web site*: http://www.patriotparty.us/state/ms/index.htm. *Missouri*: *Email*: contact party through its web site; *Web site* http://www.patriotparty.us/state/mo/index.htm. *Montana*: *Email*: mt.chair@patriotparty.us; *Web site*: http://www.patriotparty.us/state/mt/index.htm. *Nebraska*: *Email*: contact party through its web site; *Web site*: http://www.patriotparty.us/state/ne/index.htm. *Nevada*: *Email*: nv.chair@patriotparty.us; *Web site*: http://www.patriotparty.us/state/nv/index.htm. *New Hampshire*: *Email*: contact party through its web site; *Web site*: http://www.patriotparty.us/state/nh/index.htm. *New Jersey*: *Email*: contact party through its web site; *Web site*: http://www.patriotparty.us/state/nj/index.htm. *New Mexico*: *Email*: nm.chair@patriotparty.us; *Web site*: http://www.patriotparty.us/state/nm/index.htm. *New York*: *Email*: ny.chair@patriotparty.us; *Web site*: http://www.patriotparty.us/state/ny/index.htm. *North Carolina*: *Email*: nc.chair@patriotparty.us; *Web site*: http://www.patriotparty.us/state/nc/index.htm. *North Dakota*: *Email*: contact party through its web site; *Web site*: http://www.patriotparty.us/state/nd/index.htm. *Ohio*: *Email*: oh.chair@patriotparty.us; *Web site*: http://www.patriotparty.us/state/oh/index.htm. *Oklahoma*: *Email*: contact party through its web site; *Web site*: http://www.patriotparty.us/state/ok/index.htm. *Oregon*: *Email*: or.chair@patriotparty.us; *Web site*: http://www.patriotparty.us/state/or/index.htm. *Pennsylvania*: *Email*: pa.chair@patriotparty.us; *Web site*: http://www.patriotparty.us/state/pa/index.htm. *Rhode Island*: *Email*: contact party through its web site; *Web site*: http://www.patriotparty.us/state/ri/index.htm. *South Carolina*: *Email*: contact party through its web site; *Web site*: http://www.patriotparty.us/state/sc/index.htm. *South Dakota*: *Email*: sd.chair@patriotparty.us; *Web site*: http://www.patriotparty.us/state/sd/index.htm. *Tennessee*: *Email*:

tn.chair@patriotparty.us; *Web site*: http://www.patriotparty.us/state/ tn/index.htm. *Texas*: *Email*: tx.chair@patriotparty.us; *Web site*: http: //www.patriotparty.us/state/tx/index.htm. *Utah*: *Email*: contact party through its web site; *Web site*: http://www.patriotparty.us/state/ut/ index.htm. *Vermont*: *Email*: contact party through its web site; *Web site*: http://www.patriotparty.us/state/vt/index.htm. *Virginia*: *Email*: va.chair@patriotparty.us; *Web site*: http://www.patriotparty.us/state/ va/index.htm. *Washington*: *Email*: wa.chair@patriotparty.us; *Web site*: http://www.patriotparty.us/state/wa/index.htm. *West Virginia*: *Email*: wv.chair@patriotparty.us; *Web site*: http://www.patriotparty.us/state/ wv/index.htm. *Wisconsin*: *Email*: wi.chair@patriotparty.us; *Web site* http://www.patriotparty.us/state/wi/index.htm. *Wyoming*: *Email*: contact party through its web site; *Web site*: http://www.patriotparty. us/state/wy/index.htm.

American Reform Party

10 Aida Court, Lodi, NJ 07644; *Telephone:* 973-777-3838; *Email:* downingr@optonline.net; *Web site:* http://www.americanreform.org

In August 1996, after trying to activate a national party for almost a year, the American Reform Party was established, guided by the National Reform Party Committee, which voted unanimously to declare independence from Ross Perot and his National Organizing Committee, which had been formed in Nashville, Tennessee. Party leaders decided that it was essential for the new party to grow beyond the influence of a single individual if it was to succeed as a credible third party choice for the American people.

A splinter group of the Reform Party, the American Reform Party (formerly known as the National Reform Party Committee), was founded in September 1997. The ARP broke away from Ross Perot's Reform Party, claiming that the Perot organization was unfocused and anti-democratic when the memberships' views clashed with Perot's views. The ARP fielded candidates for state and federal offices in Reform Party primaries against candidates backed by Perot's Reform Party in 1998. The ouster of Perot's allies from control of the Reform Party at the July 1999 national convention looked like a move towards ending the split. However, the restoration of control to the Perot forces in early 2000 and subsequent takeover of state party affiliates by the Buchanan forces destroyed any move by the ARP to rejoin the Reform Party.

Instead, the ARP ultimately shifted towards the political left and opted to endorse (but not co-nominate) Green Party Presidential nominee Ralph Nader in the 2000 elections. Since then, the ARP has become virtually invisible on the political scene and has fielded only four state and local candidates nationwide in 2002 (in addition to co-endorsing several other third party candidates).

The American Reform Party supports paying down the national debt and eliminating federal deficits; a balanced budget; reducing the number and size of federal agencies; bringing congressional and federal pensions in line with those in the private sector; instituting a national sales or a graduated flat tax; term limits for elected officials; replacing the Electoral College with popular votes; remaining a member of the United Nations; restoring normal diplomatic trade relations with Cuba; establishing a firm cap of 200,000 immigrants per year; and a strong national Environmental Protection Agency and national conservation efforts.

Affiliates. *Alabama*: *Email*: contact party through its web site; *Web site*: http://www.americanreform.org/ARP-State-Affiliates/alabama.html. *Alaska*: *Email*: contact party through its web site; *Web site*: http://www.americanreform.org/ARP-State-Affiliates/alaska.html. *Arizona*: *Email*: contact party through its web site; *Web site*: http://www.americanreform.org/ ARP-State-Affiliates/arizona.html. *Arkansas*: *Email*: contact party through its web site; *Web site*: http://www.americanreform.org/ ARP-State-Affiliates/arkansas.html. *California*: *Email*: contact party through its web site; *Web site*: http://www.americanreform.org/ ARP-State-Affiliates/california.html. *Colorado*: *Email*: contact party through its web site; *Web site*: http://www.americanreform.org/ ARP-State-Affiliates/colorado.html. *Connecticut*: *Email*: contact party through its web site; *Web site*: http://www.americanreform.org/; *Web site*: http://www.americanreform.org/ARP-State-Affiliates/connecticut.html. *Delaware*: *Email*: contact party through its web site; *Web site*: http://www.americanreform.org/ ARP-State-Affiliates/delaware.html. *District of Columbia*: *Email*: contact party through its web site; *Web site*: http://www.americanreform.org/ARP-State-Affiliates/district-of-columbia.html.

Florida: Email: contact party through its web site; *Web site:* http://www.americanreform.org/ ARP-State-Affiliates/florida.html. *Georgia: Email:* contact party through its web site; *Web site:* http://www.americanreform.org/ ARP-State-Affiliates/georgia.html. *Hawaii: Email:* contact party through its web site; *Web site:* http://www.americanreform.org/ ARP-State-Affiliates/hawaii.html. *Idaho: Email:* contact party through its web site; *Web site:* http://www.americanreform.org/ ARP-State-Affiliates/idaho.html. *Illinois:* 1062 North Old Mill Road, Palatine, IL 60067; *Telephone:* 847-359-2999; *Fax:* 847-359-2996; *Email:* contact party through its web site; *Web site:* http://www.americanreform.org/ ARP-State-Affiliates/illinois.html. *Indiana: Email:* contact party through its web site; *Web site:* http://www.americanreform.org/ ARP-State-Affiliates/ indiana.html. *Iowa: Email:* contact party through its web site; *Web site:* http://www.americanreform.org/ ARP-State-Affiliates/iowa. html. *Kansas: Email:* contact party through its web site; *Web site:* http://www.americanreform.org/ ARP-State-Affiliates/kansas.html. *Kentucky: Email:* contact party through its web site; *Web site:* http://www.americanreform.org/ ARP-StateAffiliates/kentucky.html. *Louisiana: Email:* contact party through its web site; *Web site:* http://www.americanreform.org/ ARP-StateAffiliates/louisiana.html. *Maine: Email:* contact party through its web site; *Web site:* http:// www.americanreform.org/ARP-State-Affiliates/maine.html. *Maryland: Email:* contact party through its web site; *Web site:* http://www.americanreform.org/ ARP-State-Affiliates/maryland. html. *Massachusetts: Email:* contact party through its web site; *Web site:* http://www.americanreform.org/ARP-State-Affiliates/massachusetts.html. *Michigan: Email:* contact party through its web site; *Web site:* http://www.americanreform.org/ ARP-State-Affiliates/michigan.html. *Minnesota: Email:* contact party through its web site; *Web site:* http://www.americanreform.org/ ARP-State-Affiliates/minnesota.html. *Mississippi: Email:* contact party through its web site; *Web site:* http://www.americanreform.americanreform.org/ARP-State-Affiliates/mississippi.html. *Missouri: Email:* contact party through its web site; *Web site:* http://www.americanreform.org/ ARP-State-Affiliates/missouri.html. *Montana:* 2210 West 22nd Street, Billings, MT 59102; *Telephone:* 406-248-9277; *Fax:* 406-248-3974; *Email:* contact party through its web site; *Web site*: http://www.american reform.org/ARP-State-Affiliates/montana.html. *Nebraska*: *Email*: contact party through its web site; *Web site*: http://www.american-reform.org/ARP-State-Affiliates/nebraska.html. *Nevada*: *Email*: contact party through its web site; *Web site*: http://www.americanreform. org/ ARP-State-Affiliates/nevada.html. *New Hampshire*: *Email*: contact party through its web site; *Web site*: http://www.americanreform. org/ARP-State-Affiliates/new-hampshire.html. *New Jersey*: 10 Aida Court, Lodi, NJ 07644; *Telephone*: 973-777-3838; *Email*: downingr@ optonline.net; *Web site*: http://www.americanreform.org. *New Mexico*: *Email*: contact party through its web site; *Web site*: http://www.americanreform.org/ARP-State-Affiliates/new-mexico. html. *New York*: P.O. Box 2352, Aquebogue, NY 11931; *Telephone*: 631-369-0048; *Email*: contact party through its web site; *Web site*: http://www.americanreform.org/ATP-State-Affiliates/newyork.html. *North Carolina*: *Email*: contact party through its web site; *Web site*: http://www.americanreform.org/ARP-State-Affiliates/north-carolina. html. *North Dakota*: *Email*: contact party through its web site; *Web site*: http://www.american-reform.org/ARP-State-Affiliates/north-dakota.html. *Ohio*: *Email*: contact party through its web site; *Web site*: http://www.americanreform.org/ARP-State-Affiliates/ohio.html. *Oklahoma*: *Email*: contact party through its web site; *Web site*: http://www.americanreform.org/ARP-State-Affiliates/oklahoma.html. *Oregon*: *Email*: contact party through its web site; *Web site*: http://www.americanreform.org/ARP-State-Affiliates/oregon.html. *Pennsylvania*: *Email*: contact party through its web site; *Web site*: http://www.americanreform.org/ARP-State-Affiliates/pennsylvania. html. *Rhode Island*: *Email*: contact party through its web site; *Web site*: http://www.americanreform.org/ARP-State-Affiliates/rhode-island.html. *South Carolina*: *Email*: contact party through its web site; *Web site*: http://www.americanreform.org/ARP-State-Affiliates/ south-carolina.html. *South Dakota*: *Email*: contact party through its web site; *Web site*: http://www.americanreform.org/ARP-State-Affiliates/south-dakota.html. *Tennessee*: *Email*: contact party through its web site; *Web site*: http://www.americanreform.org/ARP-State-Affiliates/tennessee.html. *Texas*: *Email*: contact party through its web site; *Web site*: http://www.americanreform.org/ARP-State-Affiliates/

texas.html. *Utah*: 1799 Heritage Center, Salt Lake City, UT 84112; *Web site*: http://www.amreicanreform.org/ARP-State-Affiliates/utah.html. *Vermont*: *Email*: contact party through its web site; *Web site*: http://www.americanreform.org/ARP-State-Affiliates/vermont.html. *Virginia*: 2503 Columbia Pike, Box 153, Arlington, VA 22204; *Fax*: 703-892-2272; *Email*: contact party through its web site; *Web site*: http://www.americanreform.org/ARP-State-Affiliates/virginia.html. *Washington*: *Email*: contact party through its web site; *Web site*: http://www.americanreform.org/ARP-State-Affiliates/washington. html. *West Virginia*: *Email*: contact party through its web site; *Web site*: http://www.americanreform.org/ARP-State-Affiliates/west-virginia.html. *Wisconsin*: http://www.americanreform.org/ARP-State-Affiliates/wisconsin.html. *Wyoming*: 607 N2W, Riverton, WY 82501; *Telephone & Fax*: 307-856-3581; *Email*: contact party through its web site; *Web site*: http://www.americanreform.org/ARP-State-Affiliates/ wyoming.html.

American Renewal Party

Email: info@americanrenewalparty.org; *Web site*: http://www. americanrenewalparty.org

The American Renewal Party is a new organization dedicated to presenting a viable third party alternative to the American people. The Party believes that "the political agendas pushed by the powerful elite, the multinational corporations and the corrupt, morally bankrupt professional politicians who are their 'paid servants' will no longer be tolerated by decent, hard working Americans that have been paying the bills for their failures! We are going to take back our government from those who would limit the peoples voice over their own destiny!"

American Synthesis Party

P.O. Box 40099, Augusta, GA 30909; *Telephone*: 706-736-7796, 706-722-4055; *Email*: info@mypoliticalparty.com; *Web site*: http://www.mypoliticalparty.com

The American Synthesis Party was formed in January 2000 and supports a strong national defense; space exploration; a national sales tax; free international trade; population control to preserve national and economic resources; strong environmental protection; nuclear power; educational overhaul and strong national standards; English as the official language; restricted immigration; capital punishment; religious freedom but no government support; legalize abortion in the cases of rape, incest, endangerment to the mother, and detection of fetal abnormality; and prayer in school (basically, a moment of silence).

The concept of ideological synthesis is central to the philosophy of the party with the basic idea being that the most functional ideology that would best serve the public interest is a composite of elements that are commonly more closely associated with both the ideological left and the ideological right. The ASP believes that it is important for Americans to reach a consensus over divisive issues and ideologies, because not doing so causes a chasm between the citizens and its government and with each other. The party believes that until such a synthesis is adopted by the people, as an alternative to liberalism or conservatism, political leaders will govern without a mandate and the United States will stumble along without direction. The ASP feels that it is up to the people to reach a consensus and to agree on important issues and ideas, and to relay that consensus to its political leaders.

This syntheses of ideas adopted and agreed to by the American people would change the currently-dominated two-party system because there would be a mixture of ideas, both conservative and liberal, instead of the current process of basically casting votes for liberalism by choosing Democrats or conservatism by selecting Republican candidates. The ASP's position is that today's political climate is an "all or nothing" choice for the voter, whereas the country's political goals would be better served by having a synthesis of ideas across the political spectrum; essentially choosing the ideas that make the most sense for America instead of blindly supporting liberal or conservative ideologies.

Through recent analysis of political trends, the ASP has identified several indications that the polarization of the two major parties has increased in recent years. There is a growing rift between the views held by members of each party and voting strictly along party lines has become more frequent. As this polarization has increased and the two parties have become dominated by unrepresentative groups on the political left and the political right, many people have abandoned the parties to join independent organizations or to become non-voters. Recently this trend has accelerated and membership numbers of the major parties have declined, as a proportion of the total population. While still dominant, this loss of membership clout has gradually weakened both the Republican and Democratic parties and has spurred voter exodus to independent third parties or to bail out of the political process altogether. This process can clearly be seen in the fact that the vast majority of U.S. citizens do not vote, whether out of apathy or party alienation.

This non-voting trend is one of the guiding forces behind the creation and operation of the American Synthesis Party. While the ideological polarization of the two major political parties has increased over recent years, most Americans continue to hold a mixture of both liberal and conservative views on political issues. Thus, most Americans do not strongly identify themselves with either the political left or the political right and perceive the ideologically-polarized electoral and policy-making processes to be increasingly unrepresentative and out of touch with their views. The ASP believes that a natural consequence of these events is the synthesis of political ideas to bridge the gap between citizens and their elected leaders, which can only be achieved through a third party.

Autonomy Party

6282 North 12th Street #105, Oakdale, MN 55128; *Email*: autonomy_party@wowmail.com; *Web site*: http://www.freewebs.com/autonomyparty

The main goal of the Autonomy Party is complete freedom for the individual and a complete dismantling of corporations. The party supports the idea that all drug war prisoners should be freed and compensated for their losses; the abolition of the Federal Communications Commission, the Federal Bureau of Investigation, and the Central Intelligence Agency; the abolition of federal currency and a reliance on bartering; students should be paid to attend college; limitation of urban sprawl; a maximum annual salary cap for every worker established at $500,000 a year; lowering the minimum age to

30 for presidential candidates; maintaining the operation of the United States Postal Service; eliminating the flag and anthem of the United States; no tax breaks for religious institutions; complete separation of church and state; the repeal of all anti-nudity laws; encouraging the use of the bicycle as a more prominent mode of transportation; the budget of the military should never exceed the monies going toward education and human charity; Congress be dissolved and replaced by a unicameral legislative system which is appointed by the chief executive; a ban on the sale, manufacture, distribution and consumption of intoxicating substances; gay and lesbian rights; the building of more public libraries; the banning of all guns; the building of a network of public transportation systems that would span the entire country; universal health care; the elimination of all gambling and all gambling-related devices; the end to all abortions; and the government financially compensating individuals who have been wrongfully convicted and imprisoned.

Bear Flag Party (California Secessionist Party)

Email: contact party through its web site; *Web site*: http://www. bear-flag-party.8k.com

The Bear Flag Party is a southern California-based organization that promotes greater freedom, if not independence, for California from the rest of the United States, and recreating the Bear Flag Republic of 1846. The party not only advocates separation of California from the rest of America, but it also supports the idea of dividing the state of California into two separate entities, Northern California and Southern California.

Being Human Party (of Utah)

1678 Hickory Lane, Provo, UT 84604; *Telephone*: 801-367-1761; *Email*: info@beinghumanparty.com; *Web site*: http://www.beinghumanparty.com

The mission of the Being Human Party is to "promote world peace through non-violent, global political, spiritual, and ethical initiatives that foster respect for and protect the relevancy and sovereignty of each human being. The party's beliefs also state that "all creation is one and indivisible and that the human family inhabiting earth alongside the many other species of life is also one and indivisible and interdependent with those species."

The Being Human Party supports developing alternative energy sources; reducing military spending by withdrawing troops from foreign soil; eliminating the World Trade Organization and the North American Free Trade Agreement; prohibiting the Central Intelligence Agency from meddling in the affairs of other nations; strengthening ties to the United Nations; dismantling the Bureau of Indian Affairs; rescinding the Patriot Act; eliminating all subsidies and buyouts; and allowing citizens to carry concealed weapons, but banning assault weapons.

Birthday Party

Pocatello, ID; *Email*: contact party through its web site; *Web site*: http://birthdayparty.cjb.net

The Birthday Party was formed on February 12, 1999, which was, coincidentally, President Abraham Lincoln's birthday; hence the party's name. The party is heavily involved in American and high school politics and no current members of the party are over 35 years old. The party believes that "each individual has the right to control his or her own body, action, speech, and property. Government's only role is to help individuals defend themselves from force and fraud."

British Reformed Sectarian Party

3108 Moss Drive, Cocoa, FL 32922; *Telephone*: 321-638-8960
Local political party.

California Secessionist Party (see Bear Flag Party)

Capitalist Party of Georgia

2871 Buchanan Highway #A, Dallas, Georgia 30157; *Email*: cpofga@cpofga.org; *Web site*: http://www.cpofga.org

The Capitalist Party of Georgia, established in December 2002, supports the idea that "economic freedom paves the way for political freedom" and proposes a smaller, less intrusive government. Its basic tenets endorse limited government, individual liberty, free market capitalism, and a strict constitutional interpretation. The mission of the Capitalist Party is to develop an organization and movement of volunteers to support citizens who will run as a candidate of the Capitalist Party of Georgia or on a platform consistent with its ideals.

Cascadian National Party

P.O. Box 3272, International Station, Seattle, WA 98114; *Email*: cnp4cascadia@angelfire.com; *Web site*: http://www.angelfire.com/wa3/cascadia/index.html

The Cascadian National Party calls for greater freedom and autonomy from the United States of the Cascadian region, more commonly known as the Pacific Northwest. Members of the party believe that the United States has become far too powerful and increasingly oppressive throughout the world and even within its own borders.

The party's basic goals are to institute a peaceful separation from the federal government and to create the Republic of Cascadia; force a total withdrawal of all U.S. federal forces, agencies, and institutions on Cascadian soil to be replaced by a Cascadian government; establish a democratic partnership government between the states of Oregon and Washington; conserve and safeguard the environment; merge the state legislatures of Oregon and Washington into a one-chamber state assembly; eliminate victimless crimes as punishable offenses; eliminate the Electoral College; withdraw from the North Atlantic Treaty Organization; establish Cascadian embassies and consulates around the world; establish an International Institute of Peace, a think tank and meeting center to research and resolve international disputes; establish Cascadia as a nuclear-free zone; develop alternate energy sources; avidly enforce anti-pollution laws and the forced cleanup of all toxic sites; create a Department of Native Affairs that will address the needs and issues of all tribes; increase the federal minimum wage to $14.00 per hour and increase the wage based on the cost of living; institute a 35-hour work week; abolish vice laws regarding prostitution and gambling; abolish the death penalty; implement a universal Cascadian-wide health care system at the state level; support the abortion rights of women; cut funding for scholastic sports programs and use the saved money to update textbooks and improve school facilities; implement sex education training at an early age within the school system; oppose the use of advertising and commercials in all public schools; introduce the Metric system into public schools; reduce the size of classrooms to a 15 to 1 teacher ratio; raise automobile efficiency standards to 48 miles per gallon by 2010; implement English as the region's official language, although the party does support the idea of students learning at least two foreign languages; expand the area of Cascadia to include Canada's British Columbia and the northern counties of California; and ensure the strict separation of church and state.

Charter Party (of Cincinnati, Ohio)

517 Finlay Street, Cincinnati, OH 45214; *Telephone*: 513-621-3455

The Charter Party (party organizers prefer the term Charter Committee) was founded in 1924 and claims to be the "oldest active independent political party" in the United States. The party came into existence during a time when Cincinnati government was under the control of a corrupt Republican administration. At the rime, Cincinnati was often called the most corruptly-governed major city in the United States and was still under the influence of the Boss Cox era, established by George Cox in the 1880s.

Republican reformers began the Cincinnatus Association and in 1923 lawyer Murray Seasongood became the leader of the reformers' successful anti-tax campaign. The Cincinnatus Association led to the formation of the Birdless Ballot League, which advocated nonpartisan elections. The term "birdless" referred to the use of the Republican eagle and Democratic rooster as party symbols on the ballot. In 1924, the Birdless Ballot League joined with other reformer groups to create the City Charter Committee, which established a 32-member city council, six of whom were elected at-large. Only candidates nominated in a city-wide primary by the Republican and Democratic parties were eligible to run and in 1924 there were 31 Republicans and one Democrat on the council.

The new municipal charter enacted in 1925 established a city manager-council form of government (abolishing the mayor-council system) and a civil service bureaucracy to replace political patronage. The new charter created a nine-member council and mandated nonpartisan municipal elections and proportional representation.

Although the Charter movement started with Republican reformers, the party quickly became allied with the Democrats against the entrenched Republican party. Democratic candidates ran as Charterites and by the 1950s Republicans labeled them socialists.

In 1959 Democrats splintered from the Charterite coalition, which caused a splitting of the progressive vote with the Democrats throughout the 1960s. During this time, the Charterites barely survived the return of Republican rule and only had one elected official in 1961.

In 1969, the Charterites again joined with the Democrats in a formal coalition that took control of city government in 1971. The two parties divided the two-year mayoral term into two one-year periods that alternated between them. The Democratic-Charterite coalition was able to function for almost 17 years and lasted until 1986. In recent years, the Charter Party has sought to expand beyond Cincinnati and has endorsed candidates in neighboring jurisdictions, such as Covington, Kentucky.

Over its history, the Charter Party has supported liberal and progressive causes, including reducing pollution, establishing cost-of-living wage increases for municipal employees, maintaining a public inventory of municipal property, and the right-to-know law, in which employers are required to inform employees of the risks of handling hazardous materials. The Charter Party currently includes Democrats, Republicans, and Independents and advocates an activist government to address public problems.

Christian Falangist Party of America

P.O. Box 1106, Newton, NC 28658; *Email*: admin@falange.us; *Web site*: http://www.falangist.org

Founded in Philadelphia, Pennsylvania, in September 1985, the Christian Falangist Party of America is "dedicated to fighting the 'Forces of Darkness' which seek to destroy our Western Christian Civilization. The CFPA is not a hate organization and does not condone acts of violence or hatred towards those of differing or opposing viewpoints and lifestyles nor does it condone racism or anti–Semitism in any form." The CFPA has no connection with the Spanish Falange nor any other neo–Fascist/anti–Democratic groups who use the name

Falangist. The party is also not affiliated with the American Falangist Party in California. The CFPA supports the Constitution, the Bill of Rights, and nationalistic loyalty to the United States of America.

The Christian Falangist Party of America was founded on the third anniversary of the assassination of Bashir Gemayel, the then-president elect of Lebanon and the head of that country's Phalange Party, also known as the Kataeb. Often referred to as the Christian Phalangist Party of Lebanon or the Christian Phalange Party of Lebanon, its members have always called themselves Christian Phalangists.

Seeing a need in America for an organization like the Kataeb, organizers formed the CFPA as an alternative political party, hoping to fill the gap between the Conservatives and the Fascists. The founders wanted to form a right wing party that saw both communism, socialism, and radical Islam as a threat to world freedom and western Christian civilization. Its position on radical Islam went largely ignored until the attack on the World Trade Center twin towers in September 2001. Since that time, the party has experienced steady growth and has plans to open a national office.

The party's main goals are to "fight for the preservation of western and Judeo-Christian civilization, the defeat of the New World Order, and the destruction of the Forces of Darkness." The party supports the return of the military draft; the right of citizens to own and bear arms; outlawing public displays of homosexual behavior; a cap on legal immigration; return the value of the American dollar back to the silver standard and abolishing the Federal Reserve System; volunteer prayer in school; abolishing abortion; and the separation in jail of dangerous criminals from non-violent prisoners.

Christian Freedom Party

c/o Vision 2020 Design Team, 723 Woodlawn Avenue #203, Saint Paul, MN 55116; *Telephone*: 612-221-4432; *Email*: thomasharens@christianfreedomparty.com;*Web site*: http://www.christianfreedomparty.com

Established in mid 2004, the Christian Freedom Party believes that the philosophies and teachings of Christianity are progressive by works and morally absolute by values and that members can't be true to Christian principles and vote for a Democrat or a Republican. Church organizations cannot propose a platform of Christian

Social Justice and then justify lobbying and voting based solely on single issues, such as pro-life or anti-gay marriage.

The principal mission of the Christian Freedom Party is "to begin reaching out to and educating the silent majority of progressive, moderate and other true Christians whose faith has been politically misrepresented by the Christian Right Wing, vilified by the liberal democratic establishment for being pawns of single-issue groups, and unfairly labeled by the public as being all of one political persuasion." The CFP aims to give true Christians an alternative choice to the two major parties.

The Christian Freedom Party also works to expose the Christian Right Wing in their "unholy alliance with republicanism, which is the corrupt use of individual and corporate wealth." The CFP makes a distinction between the Christian Right Wing and the Republican Party as a whole and does not support the Democratic Party, which in the CFP's view also accepts just as much corrupt monies as the Republicans.

The party supports limited federal government control of citizens lives, eliminating smokestack emissions and increasing alternative energy sources; eliminating abortion, universal health care for all; strong environmental protections; legalization for undocumented immigrants already working in the United States; and full funding of efforts to cure the world-wide AIDS epidemic.

Christian Party

803 East Magnolia, Arcadia, FL 34266; *Telephone*: 863-494-9696
Local political party.

Citizen Party of Florida

519 Richmond Street, Dunedin, FL 34698; *Telephone*: 727-735-0080
Local political party

Committee for a Unified Independent Party

225 Broadway #2010, New York, NY 10007; *Telephone*: 800-288-3201, 212-609-2800; *Fax*: 212-609-2801; *Email*: national@cuip.org; *Web site*: http://www.cuip.org

The Committee for a Unified Independent Party is a nonprofit political center that develops strategies and provides leadership training for America's growing independent movement in an effort to make the political culture more democratic by encouraging activist citizen participation. Founded in 1994 and re-launched in January 2003, the CUIP has mounted numerous legal, legislative, and political challenges to bipartisan and special interest control of the electoral process. The CUIP disseminates its message through its publication, *The Neo-Independent*.

Common Good Party (Human Progress Network)

610 Ethan Allen Avenue, Takoma Park, MD 20912; *Telephone*: 301-891-2996; *Email*: pazpax@hpn.org; *Web site*: http://www.commongoodparty.org

The Common Good Party works in conjunction with the "Government for the People" social movement to "implement the actions needed to bring about the Common Good State, initially in America and eventually world-wide, as the next higher level of human society." The party works with a coalition of non-partisan organizations and social activists, united to reform the government of the United States.

A non-profit educational organization, the Human Progress Network is the organizer of the coalition of which the Common Good Party belongs. Through research and analysis of the problems that face the world today, the network concluded that solutions must be global in nature. This conclusion led the think tank to initiate the Government for the People movement and the Common Good Party.

The Common Good Party does not plan to be on election ballots, like other third parties, but aims to endorse candidates willing to support the goals of the Government for the People movement. The function of the Government for the People movement is to bring about needed changes to the Constitution for reforming the legislative branch of government. The movement also seeks a transforming presidency to ensure that the executive branch of the government works together with a reformed Congress. All of these efforts would be aimed at making the federal government more responsive to the needs of its citizens.

Common Sense of America Party

Email: contact party through its web site; *Web site*: http://www.commonsensenow.org

The Common Sense of America Party believes that the nation's and the world's problems can only be resolved if citizens play an active role, which cannot occur in today's environment of big money domination in worldwide politics. In America, the party supports an increase in social security benefits for the elderly; free universal health care; and free college tuition for all students who attend institutions of higher learning.

The party's main appeal is geared to those disillusioned and disappointed voters who feel they are always presented with a "lesser of two evils" political choice for the offices of President and Vice President of the United States that are offered through the dominance of the Democratic and Republican Parties. In an attempt to reach a wide base of support, the party tries to appeal to all ranges of the political spectrum, including fiscal conservatives/social liberals and fiscal liberals/social conservatives.

Affiliates. *Alabama*: Alabama@CommonSenseNow.org. *Alaska*: Alaska@CommonSenseNow.org. *Arizona*: Arizona@CommonSense Now.org. *Arkansas*: Arkansas@CommonSenseNow.org. *California*: California@CommonSenseNow.org. *Colorado*: Colorado@Common SenseNow.org. *Connecticut*: Connecticut@CommonSenseNow.org. *Delaware*: Delaware@CommonSenseNow.org. *Florida*: Florida@ CommonSenseNow.org. *Georgia*: Georgia@CommonSenseNow.org. *Hawaii*: Hawaii@CommonSenseNow.org. *Idaho*: Idaho@Commo Sense.org. *Illinois*: Illinois@CommonSenseNow.org. *Indiana*: Indiana@CommonSenseNow.org. *Iowa*: Iowa@CommonSenseNow. org. *Kansas*: Kansas@CommonSenseNow.org. *Kentucky*: Kentucky@ CommonSenseNow.org. *Louisiana*: Louisiana@CommonSenseNow. org. *Maine*: Maine@CommonSenseNow.org. *Maryland*: Maryland@ CommonSenseNow.org. *Massachusetts*: Massachusetts@Common SenseNow.org. *Michigan*: Michigan@CommonSenseNow.org. *Minnesota*: Minnesota@CommonSenseNow.org. *Mississippi*: Mississippi @CommonSenseNow.org. *Missouri*: Missouri@CommonSenseNow. org. *Montana*: Montana@CommonSenseNow.org. *Nebraska*: Nebraska@CommonSenseNow.org. *Nevada*: Nevada@Common-

SenseNow.org. *New Hampshire*: NewHampshire@CommoSenseNow .org. *New Jersey*: NewJersey@CommonSenseNow.org. *New Mexico*: NewMexico@CommonSenseNow.org.*New York*: NewYork@CommonSenseNow.org. *North Carolina*: NorthCarolina@CommonSenseNow.org. *North Dakota*: NorthDakota@CommonSenseNow. org.*Ohio*:Ohio@CommonSenseNow.org. *Oklahoma*: Oklhoma@CommonSenseNow.org. *Oregon*: Oregon@CommonSenseNow.org. *Pennsylvania*: Pennsylvania@CommonSenseNow.org. *Rhode Island*: RhodeIsland@CommonSenseNow.org. *South Carolina*: SouthCarolina@CommonSenseNow.org. *South Dakota*: SouthDakota@ CommonSenseNow.org. *Tennessee*: Tennessee@CommonSenseNow. org. *Texas*: Texas@CommonSenseNow.org. *Utah*: Utah@CommonSenseNow.org. *Vermont*: Vermont@CommonSenseNow.org. *Virginia*: Virginia@CommonSenseNow.org. *Washington*: Washington@Common SenseNow.org. *West Virginia*: WestVirginia@CommonSenseNow.org. *Wisconsin*: Wisconsin@CommoSenseNow.org. *Wyoming*: Wyoming@ CommoSenseNow.org.

Commonwealth Party of America

Email: contact party through its web site: *Web site*: http://www. commonwealthparty.net

The Commonwealth Party supports limited government; regional and local governmental autonomy; lower taxes; freedom of religious choice; an end to the policies of the welfare state; the right of citizens to own and bear arms; elimination of affirmative action programs and racial quotas; English being designated the official national language; an end to abortion; decriminalization of drug use and possession; expanding the borders and territory of the United States through purchases of foreign or foreign controlled lands; categorizing selected beaches and parks for topless or nude swimming and sunbathing; and adopting the metric system as the standard of measurement for all regulation and commerce.

Communist Organization for the Fourth International (see League for the Revolutionary Party [LRP] — Communist Organization for the Fourth International [COFI])

Communist Party USA

235 West 23rd Street, New York, NY 10011; *Telephone*: 212-989-4994; *Fax*: 212-229-1713; *Email*: cpusa@cpusa.org; *Web site*: http://www.cpusa.org

Formed in 1919, the Communist Party USA's main political goals are "to defeat the agenda of the ultra-right; creating reforms to put people before profits; end racism, gender discrimination, and homophobia; and guarantee justice, economic security and basic needs for all."

The Communist Party USA is "an organization of revolutionaries working to bring about social change in a conscious, progressive direction." The party offers candidates; publishes a weekly newspaper and a monthly magazine; organizes major demonstrations for social change; and supports workers' struggles for decent wages and working conditions.

The party's philosophy is based on Marxism-Leninism and on the needs of the working class as a whole. It considers itself a consistent advocate for the unity of the multiracial, multinational, male-female, young and old working class. The party's unity efforts encompass all religions; areas of the country; national origins; legal and undocumented immigrants; the unemployed; and the homeless.

The party believes that the capitalist system is set up to produce profits, not goods or services that people need, and to serve the interests of a tiny minority of the super-rich. Today's monopolistic capitalist ruling class dominates all major areas of society, including government and policy-making institutions. Under this entrenched system, issues are not decided by how much the people benefit but on how they affect the financial bottom line of major corporations.

The Communist Party USA supports universal health care; guaranteed retirement pensions; improved social security benefits; strong environmental protections; full funding of education at all levels; amnesty of all immigrants; a massive transfer of federal money from the defense budget into social programs; and an increase in the level of income at which one is exempt from federal income tax.

Despite relatively recent events and predictions, the party firmly believes that Communism isn't dead or irrelevant in today's world. As proof, the party points to the fact that in the late 1980s and early

1990s many countries that were socialist fell due to capitalist economic pressure, popular unrest, mistakes in rule, and governmental shortcomings. To fill the void, capitalism has been restored in many of these countries, resulting in a significant drop in the living standards and well being of the people. Problems resulting from the rise of capitalism in these countries includes declining health and life expectancy, increasing unemployment, poverty, infant mortality, suicide, sexism, racism, and right-wing nationalism. Proof positive, says the CPUSA, that communism is still a viable and necessary political system. The party believes that as long as capitalism exists, with all its perceived ills, there will always be a need and desire by the people for the Communist Party.

The CPUSA was founded in 1919 with most of its membership originally coming from the left wing of the Socialist Party. In the 1920s, the party opposed the Palmer Raids, which led to the government arresting and deporting many perceived radicals and Communists. The CPUSA supported the newly-developing Soviet Union against the military intervention of the United States and other capitalist countries. The party built strike solidarity in Gastonia, North Carolina, with mine workers in West Virginia, and began efforts to unionize basic industry through the Trade Union Unity League and the Trade Union Educational League.

In the 1930s, the party organized various factions to fight for unemployment insurance, which was a radical idea at the time. The CPUSA endorsed a national retirement program, which eventually became Social Security. The party led efforts to organize basic industries in auto, steel, and rubber and in California members initiated efforts to unionize Japanese and Filipino immigrant farm workers.

In the 1940s, the party fought fascism and more than 15,000 of it members joined the armed forces to serve during World War II. During this time, many countries, including the United States, were wary of the rising wave of change around the world, including national liberation struggles and of colonies demanding freedom from their old colonial oppressors. The American response to this international rising tide of discontent took the form of McCarthyism, loyalty oaths, expelling Communist members from unions, and Congressional investigating committees that violated the rights of citizens, the CPUSA fought back and supported the Progressive Party in the 1948 elections.

During the 1950s, the party continued supporting the fight against worldwide repression and saw a massive defection of liberals who wanted to prove they weren't "soft on communism." Other efforts included circulating the the Stockholm Peace Appeal, which garnered the signatures of hundreds of thousands of Americans; opposing the Korean War, and helping to bring about the beginning of the American Civil Rights Movement.

In the 1960s the party helped begin the movement against the war in Vietnam and its members volunteered for Mississippi Summer, a project that brought northern volunteers south to help with voter registration. After several decades of absence, in 1968 the CPUSA ran candidates for President and Vice-President. Moving into the 1970s, the party led the movement to Free Angela Davis, helped workers and families cope with double-digit inflation, continued to protest the Vietnam War, and continued to run candidates for national and local offices.

In the 1980s, the party opposed Reaganomics; protested American military activities in Nicaragua, El Salvador, Panama, Grenada, and Lebanon; worked against apartheid in South Africa; and helped re-establish the Young Communist League. In the 1990s, the party joined in the opposition to the Gulf War and the North Atlantic Treaty Organization's bombing of the former Yugoslavia and continued its work within the labor movement. Currently the CPUSA opposes terrorism while protesting the military activities spearheaded by the Bush administration.

The CPUSA condemns capitalism as "very undemocratic and unpatriotic because it gives no say in the economic decisions made by corporations, which can affect the lives and livelihoods of hundreds or thousands of workers and kill whole communities. It ignores borders whenever there is money to be made. The almost overwhelming force of money in politics is the opposite of free speech." The party espouses the idea that communism and revolutionary activities will save the people from the evils of capitalism. The CPUSA believes "that it is possible to make peaceful systemic changes by using the electoral process, the Constitution, and the Bill of Rights." The level of peace would depend on the capitalists, the fascists, and the politicians who would fear any changes to their power base and the status quo.

The basic unit of the CPUSA is the club, which can range in size from a few members up to several dozen. The party attempts to locate each club in a specific neighborhood, shop, or industry and tries to conduct meetings at least twice per month. The club collects dues, discusses member activities, elects their leadership, and recruits new members.

Every four years, the party holds a national convention, which sets basic policy and elects national leaders, including the National Committee, which sets policy between conventions. The National Committee is a political body of about 140 members from around the country, one of its duties being the election of national officers.

The CPUSA views socialism "as a precursor to communism. Socialism is a stage of development where society transforms itself into an economic system based on production for use rather than production for profit and where social need plays a much larger role in political and economic decisions. Before a communist society can be constructed, the remains of society based on exploitation, racial and social divisions, and where there are still inequalities in pay, distribution of goods, and other social divisions will need to be overcome. All Communists are for socialism, seeing it as a transition stage to communism, a higher stage of economic, political, and social development and freedom. However, all socialists aren't for communism, which some view as too radical. Socialism is social ownership of the main means of production and the control of the economy that is run in the interests of the working people ... the transition from Socialism to Communism reduces the state apparatus to minimal administrative functions and will provide people with the full benefits of the labor they engage in ... the production of the necessities of life will be plentiful and society will no longer suffer shortages of food, housing, jobs, health care and education."

Affiliates. *Arizona*: P.O. Box 26912, Tucson, AZ 85726; *Telephone*: 520-623-5280. *California*: 405 14th Street #810, Oakland, CA 94612; *Telephone*: 510-251-1120; *Fax*: 510-251-1050; 1251 South St.

Andrews Place, Los Angeles, CA 90019; *Telephone*: 323-733-3415; *Email*: socal@cpusa.org. *Connecticut*: P.O. Box 1437, New Haven, CT 06506; *Telephone*: 203-624-4254; *Email*: ct-cpusa@pobox.com. *District of Columbia*: *Email*: dc-cpusa@geocities.com; *Web site*: http//www.geocities.com/CapitolHill/Senate/8216. *Florida*: P.O. Box 222444, Hollywood, FL 33022. *Georgia*: *Email*: cpga@cpusa.org. *Illinois*: 3339 South Halsted, Chicago, IL 60608; *Telephone*: 773-446-9930; *Fax*: 773-446-9926; *Email*: cpillinois@cpusa.org. *Indiana*: P.O. Box 64575, Gary, In 46401; *Telephone*: 219-938-1538; *Email*: redsteel46403@netscape.net. *Maine*: 102 Twitchell Road, South Paris, ME 04281; *Telephone*: 207-743-2183. *Maryland*: P.O. Box 39187, Baltimore, MD 21212. *Massachusetts*: 550 Massachusetts Avenue, 2nd Floor, Cambridge, MA 02139; *Telephone*: 617-354-2876; *Email*: jacruz@cpusa.org; *Web site*: http://www.crosswinds.net/~macp/. *Michigan*: P.O. Box 47097, Oak Park, MI 48237; *Telephone*: 313-438-3080. *Minnesota (and North and South Dakota)*: 300 East 4th Street #611, St. Paul, MN 55101; *Email*: csminn@csminn@cpusa.org; *Web site*: http://csminn.cpusa.org. *Missouri*: P.O. Box 11523, St. Louis, MO 63105. *New Jersey*: P.O. Box 6356, Jersey City, NJ 07306; *Email*: district@nj.cpusa.org; *Web site*: http://nj.cpusa.org/. *New Mexico*: 2203 North Twisted Juniper Road, Rio Rancho, NM 87124; *Telephone*: 505-892-3480. *New York*: 235 West 23rd Street, 7th Floor, New York, NY 10011; *Telephone*: 212-924-0550; *Email*: cpny@cpusa.org. *North (and South) Carolina*, *Email*: contact party through its web site; *Web site*: http://www.geocities.com/CapitolHill/Senate/9744. *Ohio*: P.O. Box 93951, Cleveland, OH 44101; *Telephone*: 216-939-1547; *Email*: oh@cpusa.org. *Oregon*: P.O. Box 3201, Portland, OR 97208; *Telephone*: 503-402-1868. *Pennsylvania (Eastern Pennsylvania and Delaware)*: 4515 Baltimore, Philadelphia, PA 19143; *Telephone*: 215-222-8895; *Fax*: 215-222-8895; *Email*: cpepa@snip.net; *Web site*: http://epa.cpusa.org/, http://de.cpusa.org/; *Western Pennsylvania*: 5024 Penn Avenue, Pittsburgh, PA 15224. *Rhode Island*: Center for Workers Education, P.O. Box 25015, Providence, RI 02905. *Tennessee*: *Email*: cpusamtn@excite.com. *Texas*: P.O. Box 226147, Dallas, TX 75222; *Email*: contact party through its web site; *Web site*: http://tx.cpusa.org/. *Utah*: 978 Cheyenne Street, Salt Lake City, UT 84104; *Telephone*: 801-973-8276; *Email*: loarch@uswest.net. *Vermont*:

P.O. Box 1592, Burlington, VT 05402; *Email*: vermont@cpusa.org. *Washington*: P. O. Box 24806, Seattle, WA 98124; *Telephone*: 206-725-1555; *Email*: wacpusa@ wacpusa@attbi.com; *Web site*: http://www. cpusa.org/wa/. *Wisconsin*: P.O. Box 259045, Madison, WI 53725

Concerned Citizens Party of Connecticut

63 Deepwood Drive, Wolcott, CT 06716; *Telephone*: 203-879-0517; *Email*: info@concernedcitizensparty.com; *Web site*: http://www.concernedcitizensparty.com

An affiliate of the national Constitution Party, the Concerned Citizens Party of Connecticut aims to offer candidates and a political platform that directly addresses the party's belief that "the Democratic and Republican parties are indistinguishable and do not represent the best interests of the American people." The party supports prayer in public places, schools, and government institutions; an end to abortions; strong environmental policies; an end to state income taxes; and giving parents more control over the education of their children.

Confederate Party (Confederate National Party)

Email: ConfederateNationalParty@groups.msn.com; *Web site*: http://groups.msn.com/ConfederateNationalParty

Also known as the Confederate States of America, the Confederate Party believes that "the current federal government has become too large, too powerful, and too restrictive of the rights of the citizens... and special interest groups have become too powerful in their influence over elected officials." The party supports the right of States to secede from the Union; English being declared the nation's official language; the withdrawal of the United States from the United Nations and having the U.N. evicted from American soil; abolition of the Federal Reserve Bank; the withdrawal of all U.S. military forces from all foreign nations and territories; abolition of the federal income tax; a limit on the salaries of elected officials and a law that limits their service to two consecutive terms.

Affiliates. *Alabama*: *Email*: ConfederatePartyofAlabama@ groups.msn.com; *Web site*: http://groups.msn.com/ConfederatePartyofAlabama. *Arizona*: *Email*: ConfederatePartyofArizona@groups.

msn.com; *Web site*: http://groups.msn.com/ConfederatePartyofAri-
zona. *Arkansas*: *Email*: ConfederatePartyofArkansas@groups.msn.
com; *Web site*: http://groups.msn.com/ConfederatePartyofArkansas.
California: *Email*: ConfederatePartyofCalifornia@groups.msn.
com; *Web site*: http://groups.msn.com/ConfederatePartyofCalifor-
nia. *Florida*: *Email*: ConfederatePartyofFlorida@groups.msn.com;
Web site: http://groups.msn.com/ConfederatePartyofFlorida. *Georgia*: *Email*: ConfederatePartyofGeorgia@groups.msn.com; *Web site*:
http://groups.msn.com/ConfederatePartyofGeorgia. *Kentucky*: *Email*:
ConfederatePartyofKentucky@groups.msn.com; *Web site*: http://
groups.msn.com/ConfederatePartyofKentucky. *Louisiana*: *Email*:
ConfederatePartyofLouisiana@groups.msn.com; *Web site*: http://
groups.msn.com/ConfederatePartyofLouisiana. *Maryland*: *Email*:
ConfederatePartyofMaryland@groups.msn.com; *Web site*: http://
groups.msn.com/ConfederatePartyofMaryland. *Michigan*: *Email*:
ConfederatePartyofMichigan@groups.msn.com; *Web site*: http://
groups.msn.com/ConfederatePartyofMichigan. *Mississippi*: *Email*:
ConfederatePartyofMississippi@groups.msn.com; *Web site*: http://
groups.msn.com/ConfederatePartyofMississippi. *Missouri*: *Email*:
ConfederatePartyofMissouri@groups.msn.com; *Web site*: http://
groups.msn.com/ConfederatePartyofMissouri. *North Carolina*:*Email*:
ConfederatePartyofNorthCarolina@groups.msn.com; *Web site*: http://
groups.msn.com/ConfederatePartyofNorthCarolina. *Oklahoma*: *Email*:
ConfederatePartyofOklahoma@groups.msn.com; *Web site*: http://
groups.msn.com/ConfederatePartyofOklahoma. *Pennsylvania*:*Email*:
ConfederatePartyofPennsylvania@groups.msn.com; *Web site*: http://
groups.msn.com/ConfederatePartyofPennsylvania. *South Carolina*:
Email: ConfederatePartyofSouthCarolina@groups.msn.com; *Web
site*: http://groups.msn.com/Con-federatePartyofSouthCarolina.
Tennessee: *Email*: ConfederatePartyofTennessee@groups.msn.com;
Web site: http://groups.msn.com/ConfederatePartyofTennessee. *Texas*:
Email: ConfederatePartyofTexas@groups.msn.com; *Web site*: http://
groups.msn.com/ConfederatePartyofTexas. *Virginia*: *Email*: Confed-
eratePartyofVirginia@groups.msn.com; *Web site*: http://groups.
msn.com/ConfederatePartyofVirginia. *West Virginia*: *Email*: Confed-
eratePartyofWestVirginia@groups.msn.com; *Web site*: http://groups.
msn.com/ConfederatePartyofWestVirginia.

Conservative Party of New Jersey (see New Jersey Conservative Party)

Conservative Party of New York State

486 78th Street, Brooklyn, NY 11209; *Telephone*: 718-921-2158; *Fax*: 718-921-5168; 325 Parkview Drive, Schenectady, NY 12303; *Telephone*: 518-356-7882; *Fax*: 518-356-3773; *Email*: cpnys@nycap.rr.com; *Web site*: http://www.cpnys.org

The Conservative Party was formed in 1962 with the goal of "restoring a meaningful choice to the voters of New York State. At that time, the three existing political parties all espoused the liberal philosophy of the welfare state at home and the collectivist ideology abroad." Since its inception, the party has grown to 170,000 registered voters and is dedicated to the traditional American values of individual freedom, individual responsibility and individual effort.

Although the party had enjoyed electoral local and regional success from its beginnings, the party played a significant role in the 1994 election by providing the margin of victory for Governor George E. Pataki when over 325,000 of its members voted for him. The Conservative Party influence surfaced again two years later when its endorsement helped elect two state Supreme Court Justices in the 3rd Judicial District, one in the 9th Judicial District, and six in the 10th Judicial District. The 1999–2000 Legislature included 34 State Senators and 53 Assembly Members with Conservative Party endorsements.

Statewide the Party has forged strong ties to Republicans and Democrats of compatible views and claims a key role in "halting the leftward drift of New York State government." On the national level, the Party is affiliated with the American Conservative Union and acts as the New York branch of the nationwide American conservative movement.

The Party supports a strong military and the development of a strategic nuclear defense system; the expansion of North Atlantic Treaty Organization membership to central European nations as a guard against Russian expansionism in the former Iron Curtain countries; the reduction of the role the federal government plays in the lives of its citizens; a significant reduction in federal government spending; the abolition of the federal Department of Education; cessation of all federal dollars to fund the arts; the end of federal welfare programs; the end of legalized abortion; the right of citizens to own guns; term limits for congressmen and senators of not more than 12 years; and legislating English as the official national language.

Constitution Action Party

P. O. Box 5705, Arlington, VA 22205; *Email*: contact party through its web site; *Web site*: http://www2.ari.net/home/CAP

The Constitution Action Party came into existence primarily due to the "failure of the Democratic and Republican parties to address the needs of American citizens. The CAP intends to become the dominant party in America by uniting traditional values with a program of economic populism." The Party's name denotes its efforts to return the United States to its Constitutional foundation as developed by the country's founding fathers.

The Party supports elimination of the personal income tax; a strong military with a mission toward domestic security rather than acting as the world's policeman; the elimination of all race-based affirmative action programs; the reduction of the role the federal government plays in the life of its citizens; and the end to legalized abortion, which the Party believes is the most important issue in modern-day America.

Constitution Party

23 North Lime Street, Lancaster, PA 17602; *Telephone*: 800-283-8647, 717-390-1993; *Fax*: 717-299-5115; *Email*: contactus@constitution-party.com; *Web site*: http:// www.constitutionparty.net, http://www.constitutionparty.com

The Constitution Party was founded in 1992 initially as the United States Taxpayers Party in New Orleans, Louisiana by a coalition of independent state parties united to limit the powers of the federal government and restoring civil government to the principles on which America was founded, based on the Declaration of Independence and the U.S. Constitution.

In 1992, the party's first presidential candidate, Howard Phillips, was on the ballot in 21 states with his running mate, General Albion Knight Jr. In 1995 it became the fifth political party to be formally recognized by the Federal Election Commission as a national political party. In 1996 the party achieved presidential ballot access in 39 states with Howard Phillips and Herb Titus as its presidential and vice-presidential candidates. In 2000 the Constitution Party achieved presidential ballot access in 41 states and qualified with write-in candidate status in seven others. Additionally that year, the Party fielded over 100 candidates nationwide in a variety of local, state, and federal elections. In the 2004 elections, the Party (with the Michael Peroutka/Chuck Baldwin ticket) was on the ballot in 36 states, qualified for write-in status in eight other states, and garnered 50% more votes than in the previous election.

Howard Phillips, a former Nixon Administration official and Conservative Coalition chairman, founded the U.S. Taxpayers Party in 1992 as a vehicle for commentator (and former Nixon speech writer) Pat Buchanan to use for a possible presidential run. In 1999, the USTP changed its name to the Constitution Party and adopted a self-described Religious Right Platform, pro-life, anti-gun control, anti-tax, anti-immigration, protectionist, anti–New World Order, anti–United Nations, anti-gay rights, anti-welfare, and pro-school prayer. Leaders hoped that the new name would reinforce the Party's image of supporting the U.S. Constitution's provisions and limitations. One of the party's primary goals is to "restore American jurisprudence to its Biblical foundations and to limit the federal government to its Constitutional boundaries."

When Buchanan decided to stay with the Republican Party, Phillips ran as the USTP presidential nominee in 1992 (he received 43,000 votes in 21 states), in 1996 (receiving 185,000 votes in 39 states), and as the Constitution Party nominee in 2000 (he received 98,000 votes in 41 states and qualified as a write-in candidate in seven other states).

In an effort to build its membership base, the Party began fielding local candidates in 1994 but was mostly unsuccessful and has offered very few local candidates since 1998. The party received a brief boost in the media when conservative U.S. Senator Bob Smith, an announced Republican Party Presidential hopeful, briefly left the Grand Old Party to seek the Constitution Party nomination in 2000. However, his campaign lasted only two weeks before he left the Party. The Constitution

Party suffered another setback in 2000 when many of Buchanan's followers launched the nearly identical America First Party.

The party supports abolishing Congressional pensions; an all volunteer military, with no draft and no compulsory government service; a balanced budget amendment; abolishing the Civil Service system; abolishing the Department of Education; the rights of parents to provide for the education of their children in the manner they deem best; abolishing the Department of Energy; the definition of marriage as a union between one man and one woman; the U.S. leaving the United Nations; the right of citizens to bear arms; the elimination of the Food and Drug Administration; phasing out the federal Social Security system; the withdrawal of the United States from the North American Free Trade Agreement, the General Agreement on Tariffs and Trade, and the World Trade Organization; and abolishing federal income taxes and the Internal Revenue Service.

Affiliates. *Alabama*: P.O. Box 1832, Cullman, AL 35056; *Telephone*: 256-796-7374; *Fax*: 256-736-2101; *Email*:chairman@alconstitutionparty.org; *Web site*: http://www.alconstitutionparty.org. *Alaska*: 50615 Shemya Way, Kenai, AK 99611; *Telephone*: 907-776-5898. *Arizona*: 53510 West Candelight Road, Maricopa, AZ 85239; *Telephone*: 520-568-4041; *Email*: rangeo@juno.com; *Web site*: http://www.azconstitutionparty.org. *Arkansas*: 1272 Pace Lane, Pea Ridge, AR 72751; *Telephone*: 479-451-9726; *Email*: chairman@cparkansas.org; *Web site*: http://www.cparkansas.org/. *California*: American Independent Party, 8158 Palm Street, Lemon Grove, CA 91945; *Telephone*: 619-460-4484; *Email*: sdaip@cox.net; *Web site*: http://www.aipca.org/. *Colorado*: American Constitution Party, 7124 Eldridge Court, Arvada, CO 80004; *Telephone*: 303-420-6498; *Email*: embox 1776@aol.com. *Connecticut*: Concerned Citizens Party, 63 Deepwood Drive, Wolcott, CT 06716; *Telephone*: 203-879-0517; *Email*: concernedcitizens@juno.com. *Delaware*: 1610 Ogletown Road, Newark, DE 19711; *Telephone*: 302-737-2949; *Email*: ConstitutionPartyof Delaware@juno.com. *District of Columbia*: 1408 Highland Avenue, Cinnaminson, NJ 08077; *Telephone*: 800-615-8624; *Email*: lowell@ uscom.com. *Florida*: 16874 131st Way North, Jupiter, FL 33478; *Telephone*: 561-741-7592; *Email*: jnlfarm@bellsouth.net; *Web site*: http://www.cpflorida.com/. *Georgia*: P.O. Box 2153, Woodstock, GA

30188; *Telephone*: 770-924-8546; *Email*: ga@constitutionparty.com; *Web site*: http://www.gaconstitutionparty.org/. *Hawaii*: P.O. Box 90863, Honolulu, HI 96835; *Telephone*: 808-383-3715; *Email*: ronneff@hawaii.rr.com; *Web site*: http://www.constitutionparty-ofhawaii.com. *Idaho*: 1162 Morgan Hill, Cocolalla, ID 83813; *Telephone*: 208-265-0258; *Email*: garyas@mindspring.com; *Web site*: http://www.constitutionpartyidaho.com. *Illinois*: 304 Lincolnshire Boulevard, Belleville, IL 62221; *Telephone*: 618-355-0616; *Email*: stufflebeamrc@computstuff.org; *Web site*: http//www.constitution-partyillinois.com/. *Indiana*: 402 West Spruce Street, Princeton, IN 47670; *Telephone*: 812-385-1112; *Email*: contact party through its web site; *Web site*: http://www.freewebs.com/cpindiana. *Iowa*: P.O. Box 62, Randall, IA 50231; *Telephone*: 515-733-9800; *Email*: ia@constitution-party.com. *Kansas*: P.O. Box 483, Wichita, KS 67201; *Telephone*: 316-744-1155; *Email*: ks@constitutionparty.com; *Web site*: http://ks.constitutionparty.com/. *Kentucky*: 9800 Tiverton Way, Louisville, KY 40242; *Telephone*: 502-425-3619; *Email*: Eparker6@iglou.com; *Web site*: http://www.cpky.org/. *Louisiana*: P.O. Box 1092, Gray, LA 70359; *Telephone*: 985-872-5016; *Email*: dtmounts@hotmail.com. *Maine*: 10 Streaked Mountain Road, South Paris, ME 04281; *Telephone*: 207-743-6020; *Email*: stofarm@aol.com. *Maryland*: 12 Woodbine Circle, Elkton, MD 21921; *Telephone*: 410-996-0077; *Email*: mikechastain@comcast.net; *Web site*: http://www.marylandconsti-tutionparty.com/. *Massachusetts*: 83 Turner Road, Townsend, MA 01469; *Telephone*: 978-597-8038; *Email*: chairman@cpoma.org; *Web site*: http://www.cpoma.org. *Michigan*: U.S. Taxpayers Party of Michigan, 600 South Dowling, Westland, MI 48186; *Telephone*: 734-728-0956; *Email*: HalDunn@wowway.com; *Web site*: http://ustax payerspartyofmichigan.com/. *Minnesota*: 14720 285th Avenue, Zimmerman, MN 55398; *Telephone*: 763-754-7827; *Email*: robilj1@aol.com; *Web site*: http://www.cpmn.org/. *Mississippi*: 2738 County Road 406, Okolona, MS 38860; *Telephone*: 662-447-2577; *Email*: lesriley@bellsouth.net; *Web site*: http://www.constitutionpartyMS.com. *Missouri*: 28 Sennawood Drive, Fenton, MO 63026; *Telephone*: 636-349-3243; *Email*: mo@constitutionparty.com; *Web site*: http://www.constitutionpartymo.org. *Montana*: 2212–2nd Avenue South, Great Falls, MT 59405; *Telephone*: 406-727-5924; *Email*: 5martins@

in-tch.com; *Web site*: http://www.cpomt.webhop.org. *Nebraska*: The Nebraska Party, 87288 — 543 Avenue, Wausa, NE 68786; *Telephone*: 402-586-2579; *Email*: information@nebraskaparty.org; *Web site*: http://www.nebraskaparty.org. *Nevada*: Independent American Party of Nevada, 1611 F Street, Sparks, NV 89431; *Telephone*: 775-284-4427; *Email*: info@nevadafamilies.org; *Web site*: http://www.iapn.org/. *New Hampshire*: 5 Couchtown Road, Warner, NH 03894; *Telephone*: 603-456-2316; *Email*: info@nhconstitutionparty.org; *Web site*: http://www.nhconstitutionparty.org. *New Jersey*: 1408 Highland Avenue, Cinnaminson, NJ 08077; *Telephone*: 800-615-8624; *Email*: lowell@uscom.com; *Web site*: http://www.constitutionparty-nj.org/. *New Mexico*: 10804 Lexington Northeast, Albuquerque, NM 87112; *Telephone*: 505-323-1124; *Email*: davebatch@ispwest.com; *Web site*: http://members.ispwest.com/davebatch. *New York*: 444 Whitehall Road, Albany, NY 12208; *Telephone*: 877-571-5479; *Email*: bvdeitz@aol.com; *Web site*: http://www.nyconstitutionparty.com/. *North Carolina*: 801 Hepplewhite Court, Fuquay-Varina, NC 27526; *Telephone*: 919-557-3065; *Email*: cambycam@justice.com; *Web site*: http://www.cpnc.info/. *North Dakota*: 504–14th Street, Southwest, New Salem, ND 58563; *Telephone*: 701-794-8702; *Email*: rhea@westriv.com; *Web site*: http://www.constitutionpartynd.com/. *Ohio*: 4060 Leatherstocking Drive, Columbus, OH 43230; *Telephone*: 877-220-0398; *Email*: info@ohiocp.org; *Web site*: http://www.ohiocp.org/. *Oklahoma*: 4449 East 99th Street, Chandler, OK 74834; *Telephone*: 918-866-2256; *Email*: holmesta@hotmail.com; *Web site*: http://www.freewebs.com/cpoklahoma. *Oregon*: 51163 Banston Road, Scappoose, OR 97056; *Telephone*: 503-543-7312; *Email*: ekstroms@earthlink.net; *Web site*: http://www.constitutionpartyoregon.com/. *Pennsylvania*: P.O. Box 1766, Lancaster, PA 17608; *Telephone*: 717-390-1993; *Email*: jmcnamee@constitutionpartypa.com; *Web site*: http://www.constitutionpartypa.com. *Rhode Island*: 144 Hatchery Road, North Kingston, RI 02852; *Telephone*: 401-295-4122; *Email*: timgoodness@hotmail.com. *South Carolina*: P.O. Box 25055, Greenville, SC 29616; *Telephone*: 864-242-4474; *Email*: scconstitution@bellsouth.net; *Web site*: http://www.dsindex.com/cp/. *South Dakota*: 5909 Bakker Park Drive, Sioux Falls, SD 57106; *Telephone*: 605-361-3094; *Email*: sdakcpchair@sio.midco.net. *Tennessee*: 2586 Hocksett Cove, Ger-

mantown, TN 38139; *Telephone*: 901-624-3884; *Email*: dlc2586@
aol.com; *Web site*: http://www.cpot.org/. *Texas*: P O Box 290730,
Kerrville, TX 78029; *Telephone*: 888-278-3927; *Email*: bryanm@
npn.net; *Web site*: http://www.cptexas.org/. *Utah*: 1799 North Highway 89, Lauton, UT 84040; *Telephone*: 801-544-4056; *Email*: fsht-
bgdjr@hotmail.com; *Web site*: http://www.cputah.org/. *Vermont*: P.O.
Box 1647, Williston, VT 05495; *Telephone*: 802-425-5588; *Email*:
smithfamily@gmavt.net; *Web site*: http://www.constitutionpartyvt.
com/. *Virginia*: 450 Maple Avenue East, Vienna, VA 22180; *Telephone*:
540-675-3308; *Email*: info@constitutionpartyva.com; *Web site*: http://
www.constitutionpartyva.com/. *Washington*: 4610 Bates Road,
Spokane, WA 99206; *Telephone*: 509-928-6910; *Email*: rwpeck@
gbronline.com; *Web site*: http://www.constitutionpartyofwa.com.
West Virginia: P.O. Box 90, Reader, WV 26167; *Telephone*: 304-386-
4431; *Email*: denzil1776@hotmail.com; *Web site*: http://groups.
yahoo.com/group/ConstitutionParty-WV. *Wisconsin*: P.O. Box 994,
Appleton, WI 54912; *Telephone*: 877-2012441, 920-843-1789; *Email*:
chairman@cpow.org; *Web site*: http://www.cpow.org/. *Wyoming*: P.O.
Box 1888, Riverton, WY 82501; *Telephone*: 307-857-6041; *Email*:
wrp@trib.com.

Constitutionalist Party

Email: jmarkels@earthlink.net; *Web site*: http://home.earth-
link.net/~jmarkels/cp.html

A new entity, the Constitutionalist Party came to exist as a
"result of frustration with the current political parties of America
who are not taking the steps necessary to promote the Constitution
and human freedom." The Party believes that "all other political parties ... pay lip service to the following of the Constitution and the
advancement of human freedom while promoting legislation that
does otherwise or they seek to promote change without allowing for
any compromise, which essentially makes change impossible."

The Constitutionalist Party believes that the Republican Party
has reversed its stand on smaller government when it proposes legislation after legislation that gives the government even more control over its citizens' lives, such as the Flag Burning Amendment, the
Patriot Act, and the myriad of proposals the Party has made after the

terrorist attack of September 11, 2001. The CP opposes the Republican Party's use of governmental rules and regulations to control social policy. The CP vigorously opposes the Democratic Party's belief that more government is the answer to every problem faced by citizens in the United States. The Party believes that "the Democrats' dependence on the federal government instead of self-reliance erodes the strength of personal freedom." The CP views the New Deal as the first step towards the decline of self-dependency in America and opposes the Democrats' intents to make these programs even bigger.

The Constitutionalist Party seeks to improve America and preserve the freedom of the people by supporting a close adherence to the Constitution and limiting the power of the federal government over the lives of its citizens. The Party supports abortion but disagrees with the Supreme Court ruling of *Roe v. Wade*, which it views as unconstitutional, believing instead that the issue should be decided by each state; the Constitution's Second Amendment, the right of citizens to bear arms; an end to the death penalty; an end to taxes on personal property; freedom of religion and a strict separation of church and state; a constitutional amendment requiring a balanced budget; an end to the federal "war on drugs"; abolishing the Department of Education; the legalization of marijuana for medical use in every state; abolishing the Bureau of Indian Affairs; a strong military focused on defending America from foreign nations; continued participation in the World Trade Organization; and the withdrawal of the United States from the United Nations.

Cool American Party

Email: contact party through its web site; *Web site*: http://cool-party.freeservers.com

The Cool American Party is a conservative movement started in 1980 by Dr. W.H Gustavious Fresch, who used the Party as an introduction to third party politics to his students at Nebraska Lutheran College in Waco, Nebraska. Its appeal to conservatives moved the Party out of the classroom and into the realm of national politics. However, its growth and influence was short-lived and in 1988 most of its members were lured to leave the party and join the larger George Bush-led Republican Party. Its founder died shortly after the defection of most of his followers. After being dormant for several years, the Party is now revamping its structure and becoming active again. The Cool American Party supports anti-abortion legislation; the right of citizens to own and bear guns; strong illegal immigration laws; an end to welfare; and states' rights.

Creator's Rights Party of Georgia

P.O. Box 1081, Carrollton, GA 30116; *Email*: nhorsley@wechoose life.net; *Web site*: http://www.christiangallery.com/creator.html

The Creator's Rights Party is a Christian-based, conservative organization that believes all rights of the people are derived from God, The Creator. The Party's goal is to restore The Creator's plan for government, which is clearly defined in America's Declaration of Independence and Constitution. The Party believes that today's major political parties and its politicians have totally disregarded God's plan and led America down the wrong path, which The Creator's Party hopes to restore.

As proof of its belief that America has turned away from God's plan, the Party points to several developments, including the legalization of abortion ("the number one problem facing America today"); prayer being outlawed in public schools; doctors being allowed to assist in a patient's death; the police and military being used to enforce tyrannical laws; and homosexuals claiming that God created them to be who they are. Its stance against abortion and the importance this issue holds with the Party is clearly defined in their monthly *Abortion Abolitionist* magazine.

The Party believes that before God's plan for government is totally destroyed, secession of the States will become a reality, and America will cease to exist. The Party is working to avoid this drastic step by helping to reinstate the original principles of the Declaration of Independence and the Constitution, under God's wisdom. If The Creator's will is ignored, then the Party feels that the secession of the States from the United States of America is the only sane choice. The Party feels that American citizens do not want the United States destroyed so the real threat of a state seceding from the Union would cause the majority to address its concerns (such as abortion) and eliminate the problem (make abortion illegal), thereby removing the reason for the state to secede.

D.C. Statehood Green Party

1739 Irving Street NW, Washington, D.C. 20010; *Telephone*: 202-232-1724; *Email*: steeringcommittee@dcstatehoodgreen.org; *Web site*: http://www.dcstatehoodgreen.org

The D.C. Statehood Green Party supports self-determination, both in individuals and in democratic institutions; statehood for the District of Columbia; passage of the Equal Rights Amendment to the Constitution; imposing a legal limit on national campaign periods; a woman's right to abortion; and an end to the death penalty. The Party was founded as the D.C. Statehood Party in 1971, merged with the D.C. Green Party in October 1999, and is affiliated with the Green Party of the United States.

Democratic Farm Labor Party (of Minnesota) (Minnesota DFL)

255 East Plato Blvd, St. Paul, MN 55107; *Telephone*: 800-999-7457, 651-251-6300; *Fax*: 651-251-6325; *Email*: contact party through its web site; *Web site*: http://www.dfl.org

The Democratic Farm Labor Party supports the preservation and protection of farmland through soil conservation; the economic well-being of rural communities through the preservation of small business and family farms; access to farm credit at reasonable terms and interest rates, including temporary relief during economic emergencies; use of agricultural surpluses to alleviate hunger around the world; distinct separation of church and state; voluntary enlistment in the armed services—no draft; decreasing dependence on nuclear power; and a ban on gifts from lobbyists to elected officials.

Democratic Nonpartisan League (North Dakota Democratic Nonpartisan League)

Kennedy Center, 1902 East Divide Avenue, Bismarck, ND 58501; *Telephone:* 701-255-0460; *Fax*: 701-255-7823; *Email*: people@dem-npl.com; *Web site*: http://www.demnpl.com

From its initial statehood until 1915, North Dakota politics was controlled by the Republican Party, which had complete control of the State House, State Senate, and the governor's office. In 1916 a North Dakota group sold $16 memberships and started the Non-Partisan League, which supported small business taxes being paid in six-month increments, a reduction in interest rates, and safer working conditions.

In 1918, the NPL took political control of the North Dakota House and Senate. As years went by, the NPL's control gradually eroded and the Republican money in the primaries was too much to overcome. In 1956, the NPL took a major step and filed its candidates in the Democratic column in the primary election.

Democratic Party

430 South Capitol Street SE, Washington DC 20003; *Telephone*: 202-863-8000; *Email*: contact party through its web site; *Web site*: http://www.democrats.org

The Democratic Party is one of the two major political parties in America and, along with the Republican Party, is the focus of the animus of almost all third political parties in America. The Democratic National Committee is the national party organization for the Democratic Party and was founded by Thomas Jefferson in 1792. Party members were called "Republicans" or "Democratic-Republicans," and in 1830 members adopted the shortened name of "Democrats."

The Party's basic vision is based on the strength and power of economically empowered, socially diverse and politically active Americans in which wealth and social status were not an entitlement to rule. "The common thread of Democratic history, from Thomas Jefferson to Bill Clinton, has been an abiding faith in the judgment of hardworking American families, and a commitment to helping the excluded, the disenfranchised and the poor strengthen our nation by earning themselves a piece of the American Dream. We remember that this great land was sculpted by immigrants and slaves, their children and grandchildren."

An 1870 political cartoon by Thomas Nast called "A Live Jackass Kicking a Dead Lion" symbolized the Democratic Party as a donkey for the first time ever. Since then, the donkey has been widely used as a symbol of the Party, though unlike the Republican elephant, has never been officially adopted as the Party's logo. In the early 20th century, the traditional symbol of the Democratic Party in Midwestern states such as Indiana, Kentucky and Ohio was the rooster, as opposed to the Republican eagle. This symbol still appears on Kentucky and Indiana ballots.

In a quirky turn of events that so often happens in politics, for most of the 20th Century, Missouri Democrats used the Statue of Liberty as their ballot emblem. This meant that when Libertarian candidates received ballot access in Missouri in 1976, they could not use the Statue of Liberty, their national symbol, as the ballot emblem and instead used the Liberty Bell until 1995, when the mule became Missouri's state animal. From 1995 until 2004 there was some confusion on the behalf of voters, as the Democratic ticket was marked with the Statue of Liberty, and it seemed that the Libertarians were using a donkey.

Thomas Jefferson founded the Democratic Party in 1792 as a congressional caucus to fight for the Bill of Rights and against the elitist Federalist Party. In 1798, the "party of the common man" was officially named the Democratic-Republican Party and in 1800 elected Jefferson as the first Democratic President of the United States. Jefferson served two terms and was followed by James Madison in 1808 who strengthened America's armed forces and helped reaffirm American independence by defeating the British in the War of 1812. James Monroe was elected president in 1816 and led the nation through a time commonly known as "The Era of Good Feeling" in which Democratic-Republicans served with little opposition.

The controversial election of John Quincy Adams in 1824 led to a four-way split among Democratic-Republicans and resulted in the emergence of Andrew Jackson as a national leader. The former general formed a highly organized support base, created the national convention process, re-wrote the party platform, and reunified the Democratic Party with his presidential victories in 1828 and 1832. The Party held its first National Convention in 1832 and nominated President Jackson for his second term. In 1844, the National Convention simplified the Party's name to the Democratic Party.

In 1848, the National Convention established the Democratic National Committee, now the longest running political organization in the world. The Convention charged the DNC with the responsibility of promoting "the Democratic cause" between the conventions and preparing for the next convention.

During the 1850s, the Southern wing of the Democratic Party aligned itself with the expansion of slavery in direct opposition to the newly-revamped Republican Party. Democrats in the Northern states opposed slavery, and at the 1860 nominating convention the Party split and nominated two candidates, which resulted in a Democratic loss and the rise of Abraham Lincoln. Among numerous other factors, the Democratic collapse was part of a chain of events that led to the U.S. Civil War.

After the war, the Democrats were a feeble party with little national influence. However, the Party gained strength from Southern resentment to post-war Reconstruction, which coalesced as hostility towards the Republicans. For several decades after Reconstruction ended, the region was known as the "Solid South" because it reliably voted Democratic. The presidential elections from 1876 to 1892 were close, and the Democrats had control of the House of Representatives for most of this period. The Democratic Governor of New York, Grover Cleveland, won the Presidency in 1884 and again in 1892. In 1888 he had won the popular vote but lost the electoral vote.

As the American electorate began to rapidly change at the end of the 19th Century, the Party embraced the immigrants who flooded into cities and industrial centers, built a political base by bringing them into the American mainstream, and helped create the most powerful economic engine in history. Democratic Party leader William Jennings Bryan led a movement of agrarian reformers and supported the right of women's suffrage, the progressive graduated income tax and the direct election of Senators. As America entered the 20th Century, the Democratic Party became dominant in local urban politics.

In 1912, Woodrow Wilson became the first Democratic president of the 20th Century and led the country through World War I, fought for the League of Nations, established the Federal Reserve Board, and passed the first labor and child welfare laws.

The stock market crash of 1929 and the ensuing Great Depression both forced the federal government to take a more active role in the day-to-day lives of Americans and their institutions. The Democrats seized upon this opportunity to expand the powers of the federal government and nominated Franklin Delano Roosevelt for president, who won a landslide victory in 1932. Re-elected in 1936, he found that his federal expansionist plans were being opposed by a coalition of Republicans and conservative Democrats. Fighting this roadblock, Roosevelt focused his so-called New Deal programs on job-creation through public works projects and on social welfare programs such as Social Security. His policies united a diverse group of Democratic voters, the so-called New Deal Coalition, that included labor unions, minorities, liberals, and the traditional base of Southern white voters. This powerful voter base allowed the Democrats to control the government for much of the next 30 years.

Over the next several years, the New Deal Coalition became weakened as more Democratic leaders voiced support for civil rights, which upset the Party's powerful base of Southern Democrats. When Harry Truman's 1948 Democratic National Convention presidential platform supported civil rights and anti-segregation laws, many Southern Democratic delegates deserted the Party and formed the short-lived "Dixiecrats," who were led by Strom Thurmond (who would later join the Republican party).

Truman won re-election and his administration began a serious fight against racism, integrated the military, and oversaw the reconstruction of Europe by establishing the Marshall Plan and the North Atlantic Treaty Organization.

In the 1960s, President John Fitzgerald Kennedy led the vision to put a man on the moon and bring him back safely to Earth. He also created the Peace Corps and negotiated a treaty banning atmospheric testing of nuclear weapons.

While many white Democrats in the "Solid South" continued to drift away from the party, African-American voters, who had traditionally given strong support to the "anti-slave" Republican Party, began shifting their allegiance to the Democratic party due to its New Deal economic opportunities and support for civil rights. The party's complete reversal on civil rights issues came to a startling end when President Lyndon Baines Johnson signed into law the Civil Rights Act of 1964 and the Voting Rights Act. Continuing the Democratic Party ideal of expanding the powers of the federal government into the lives of Americans, he created a series of so-called Great Society programs, such as Medicare.

The effect of the Southern Democrats' abandonment of the party became evident in the 1968 Presidential election when every former Confederate state except Texas voted for either Republican Richard

Nixon or independent George Wallace, a former Southern Democrat. Defeated candidate Vice President Hubert Humphrey garnered most of his electoral votes from the Northern states, which was a dramatic shift from voting trends of just 20 years before.

In 1976, Jimmy Carter was elected president and helped to restore the nation's trust in government following the Watergate scandal of the Nixon administration. One of his crowning achievements was helping to negotiate the historic Camp David peace accords between Egypt and Israel. However, his administration will always be tied to the American hostages that were held in Iran for over a year and his inability to free them. As a final insult, the Iranian government freed the hostages on the very day that Carter was replaced by Ronald Reagan as president. His administration also saw a dramatic rise in interest rates which spurred inflation.

In 1992, Arkansas Governor Bill Clinton was elected the 42nd President of the United States and his administration oversaw a significant economic expansion. The Deficit Reduction Act of 1993, passed by both the House and Senate without a single Republican vote, led to the end of perennial budget deficits. Having inherited a $290 billion deficit in 1992, his last budget was over $200 billion in surplus. The Clinton Administration helped reduce unemployment to its lowest level in decades and saw the lowest crime in a generation. In 1996, Clinton became the first Democratic president reelected since Roosevelt and the Democrats became the first party controlling the White House to gain seats in Congress since 1822. For all his political successes, however, Clinton will always be remembered for having an affair with a White House intern that led to his unsuccessful impeachment.

In the 2000 election, even though Al Gore lost the presidential campaign, Democrats netted four additional Senate seats (they would briefly regain control in 2001), one additional House seat, and one additional gubernatorial seat. However, by 2004 the Party was having troubles, caused by a combination of events, including the terrorist attack on New York's World Trade Center in 2001, deepened political divisions across the country, dealing with a popular war-time president in George Bush, and the seeming inability to develop a national vision for America. The results of their representative problems are evident by the fact that by 2005 the Democrats are the minority party in both the United States Senate and the United States House of Representatives, as well as in governorships and state legislative seats.

Of the two major U.S. political parties, the Democratic Party is to the left of the Republican Party, although its politics are not as consistently leftist as the traditional social democratic and labor parties in much of the rest of the world. Being a national party, by definition, requires consensus building and espousing a wide-appeal program to ensure their candidates get elected and the party has a voice and influence in national politics. However, as a general rule, Democrats support civil rights, progressive taxation, specific gun control measures, reproductive rights, a multilateral foreign policy, a strong environment, public education, the use of social welfare programs to combat unemployment and poverty, and the right of workers to organize in labor unions.

In response to fairly recent events and social trends of the past twenty years or so, the so-called "New Democrat movement" has moved the Democratic agenda more toward a centrist approach, which has garnered the party the wrath of those who feel the Democrats have abandoned their core beliefs. While the party disagrees with this criticism and responds that it is reacting to a changing society, it has suffered unprecedented electoral losses since the late 1990s that have caused many to question its validity and continued longevity as a national party. Along with strong mistrust of the Republican Party, the seemingly changing position of the Democratic Party has been the impetus for the proliferation of the so-called third parties, whose members feel a general disconnect and animus for the two major political organizations.

The Democratic National Committee provides national leadership for the United States Democratic Party and is responsible for developing and promoting the Democratic political platform, coordinating fundraising, and devising election strategy. There are similar committees in every U.S. state and in most counties.

Affiliates. In most states the Party is simply known as the "Democratic Party." However, two of its state Party organizations have slightly different names, the Minnesota Democratic-Farmer-Labor Party and the North Dakota Democratic-NPL Party. *Alabama*:

P.O. Box 950, The Bell Building #700, 207 Montgomery Street, Montgomery, AL 36104; *Telephone*: 800-995-3386, 334-262-2221; *Fax*: 334-262-6474; *Email*: contact party through its web site; *Web site*: http://www.aladems.org. *Alaska*: 2000 East Dowling Boulevard #8, P.O. Box 231230, Anchorage, AK 99523; *Telephone*: 866-258-3050, 907-258-3050; *Fax*: 907-258-1626; *Email*: adp@alaska.net; *Web site*: http://www.alaskademocrats.org. *Arizona*: 2910 North Central Avenue, Phoenix, AZ 85012; *Telephone*: 602-298-4200; *Email*: contact party through its web site; *Web site*: http://www.azdem.org. *Arkansas*: 1300 West Capitol Avenue, Little Rock, AR 72201; *Telephone*: 501-374-2361; *Fax*: 501-376-8409; *Email*: info@arkdems.org; *Web site*: http:// www.arkdems.org. *California*: 1401 21st Street #100, Sacramento, CA 95814; *Telephone*: 916-442-5707; *Fax*: 916-442-5715; *Email*: contact party through its web site; *Web site*: http://www.cadem.org. *Colorado*: 777 Santa Fe Drive, Denver, CO 80204; *Telephone*: 303-623-4762; *Fax*: 303-623-2443; *Email*: info@coloradodems.org; *Web site*: http://www.coloradodems.org. *Connecticut*: 179 Allyn Street #301, Hartford, CT 06103; *Telephone*: 860-560-1775; *Fax*: 860-560-1522; *Email*: contact party through its web site; *Web site*: http://dems.info. *Delaware*: 19 East Commons Boulevard, 2nd Floor, New Castle, DE 19720; P.O. Box 2065, Wilmington, DE 19899; *Telephone*: 800-685-5544, 302-328-9036; *Email*: delaware@deldems.org; *Web site*: http//www.deldems.org. *Florida*: P.O. Box 1758, Tallahassee, FL 32302; 214 South Bronough Street, Tallahassee, FL 32301; *Telephone*: 850-222-3411; *Fax*: 850-222-0916; *Email*: email@fladems.com; *Web site*: http://www.fladems.com. *Georgia*: 1100 Spring Street #710, Atlanta, GA 30309; *Telephone*: 404-870-8201; *Fax*: 404-873-4396; *Email*: contact@georgiaparty.com; *Web site*: http//www.georgiaparty.com. *Hawaii*: 770 Kapi'olani Boulevard #115, Honolulu, HI 96813; *Telephone*: 808-596-2980; *Fax*: 808-596-2985; *Email*: contact party through its web site; *Web site*: http://www.hawaiidemocrats.org. *Idaho*: P.O. Box 445, 988 Longmont #110, Boise, ID 83701; *Telephone*: 800-542-4737, 208-336-1815; *Fax*: 208-336-1817; *Email*: info@idaho-democrats.org; *Web site*: http://www.idaho-democrats.org. *Illinois*: P.O. Box 518, Springfield, IL 62705; *Telephone*: 217-546-7404; *Fax*: 217-546-8847; *Email*: contact party through its web site; *Web site*: http://www.ildems.com. *Indiana*: One North Capitol Avenue #200,

Indianapolis, IN 46204; *Telephone*: 800-223-3387, 317-231-7100; *Email*: contact party through its web site; *Web site*: http://www.indems.org. *Iowa*: 5661 Fleur Drive, Des Moines, IA 50321; *Telephone*: 515-244-7292; *Fax*: 515-244-5051; *Email*: iadem@ iowademocrats.org; *Web site*: http://www.iowademocrats.org.*Kansas*: P.O. Box 1914, Topeka, KS 66601; 700 Southwest Jackson #706, Topeka, KS 66603; *Telephone*: 785-234-0425; *Fax*: 785-234-8420; *Email*: kdp@ksdp.org; *Web site*: http://www.ksdp.org. *Kentucky*: P.O. Box 694, Frankfort, KY 40602; 190 Democrat Drive, Frankfort, KY 40601; *Telephone*: 502-695-4828; *Email*: contact party through its web site; *Web site*: http://www.kydemocrat.com. *Louisiana*: 701 Government Street, Baton Rouge, LA 70802; *Telephone*: 225-336-4155; *Fax*: 225-336-0046; *Email*: info@lademo.org; *Web site*: http:// www.lademo.org. *Maine*: P.O. Box 5258, 12 Spruce Street, Augusta, ME 04332; *Telephone*: 207-622-6233; *Fax*: 207-622-2657; *Email*: contact party through its web site; *Web site*: http://www.maine demos.org. *Maryland*: 188 Main Street #1, Annapolis, MD 21401; *Telephone*: 410-269-8818; *Fax*: 410-280-8882; *Email*: contact party through its web site; *Web site*: http://www.mddems.org. *Massachusetts*: SAR Building, 10 Granite Street, 4th Floor, Quincy, MA 02169; *Telephone*: 617-472-0637; *Fax*: 617-472-4391; *Email*: contact party through its web site; *Web site*: http://www.massdems.org. *Michigan*: 606 Townsend Street, Lansing, MI 48933; *Telephone*: 517-371-5410; *Fax*: 517-371-2056; *Email*: contact party through its web site; *Web site*: http://www.mi-democrats.com. *Minnesota*: Minnesota Democratic-Farm-Labor Party, 255 East Plato Boulevard, St. Paul, MN 55107; *Telephone*: 800-999-7457, 651-251-6300; *Fax*: 651-251-6325; *Email*: contact party through its web site; *Web site*: http:// www.dfl.org. *Mississippi*: 832 North Congress Street, Jackson, MS 39202; P.O. Box 1583, Jackson, MS 39215; *Telephone*: 601-969-2913; *Fax*: 601-354-1599; *Email*: democrats@msdemocrats.net; *Web site*: http://www.msdemocrats.net. *Missouri*: 208 Madison Street, P.O. Box 719, Jefferson City, MO 65102; *Telephone*: 573-636-5241; *Fax*: 573-634-8176; *Email*: contact party through its web site; *Web site*: http://www.missouridems.org. *Montana*: P.O. Box 802, Helena, MT 59624; *Telephone*: 406-442-9520; *Fax*: 406-442-9534; *Email*: contact party through its web site; *Web site*: http://www.montanademocrats.

org. *Nebraska*: 633 South 9th Street #201, Lincoln, NE 68508; *Telephone*: 800-677-7068, 402-434-2180; *Fax*: 402-434-2188; *Email*: info@nebraskademocrats.org; *Web site*: http://www.nebraskademocrats.org. *Nevada*: 1325 East Vegas Valley Drive, Suite C, Las Vegas, NV 89109; *Telephone*: 702-699-7343; *Email*: contact party through its web site; *Web site*: http://www.nvdems.com. *New Hampshire*: 2 1/2 Beacon Street, Concord, NH 03301; *Telephone*: 603-225-6899; *Fax*: 603-225-6797; *Email*: office@nhdp.org; *Web site*: http://www.nhdp.org. *New Jersey*: 194–196 West State Street, Trenton, NJ 08608; *Telephone*: 609-392-3367; *Fax*: 609-396-4778; *Email*: contact party through its web site; *Web site*: http://www.njdems.org. *New Mexico*: 1301 Northeast San Pedro, Albuquerque, NM 87110; *Telephone*: 505-830-3650; *Email*: contact party through its web site; *Web site*: http://www.nmdemocrats.org. *New York*: 60 Madison Avenue, New York, NY 10010; *Telephone*: 212-725-8825; *Fax*: 212-725-8867; *Email*: nydems@nydems.org; *Web site*: http://www.nydems.org. *North Carolina*: 220 Hillsborough Street, Raleigh , NC 27603; *Telephone*: 919-821-2777; *Fax*: 919-821-4778; *Email*: contact party through its web site; *Web site*: http://www.ncdp.org. *North Dakota*: Kennedy Center, 1902 East Divide Avenue, Bismarck, ND 58501; *Telephone*: 701-222-1371; *Fax*: 701-255-7823; *Email*: people@demnpl.com; *Web site*: http://www.demnpl.org. *Ohio*: 271 East State Street, Columbus, OH 43215; *Telephone*: 614-221-6563; *Fax*: 614-221-0721; *Email*: contact party through its web site; *Web site*: http://www.ohiodems.org. *Oklahoma*: George Krumme Center, 4100 North Lincoln Boulevard, Oklahoma City, OK 73105; *Telephone*: 405-427-3366; *Fax*: 405-427-1310; *Email*: odp@okdemocrats.org; *Web site*: http://www.okdemocrats.org. *Oregon*: 232 Northeast 9th Avenue, Portland, OR 97232; *Telephone*: 503-224-8200; *Fax*: 503-224-5335; *Email*: info@dpo.org; *Web site*: http://www.dpo.org. *Pennsylvania*: 510 North Third Street, Harrisburg, PA 17101; *Telephone*: 717-238-9381; *Fax*: 717-233-3472; *Email*: info@padems.com; *Web site*: http://www.padems.com. *Rhode Island*: 249 Roosevelt Avenue #202, Pawtucket, RI 02860; *Telephone*: 401-721-9900; *Fax*: 401-724-5007; *Email*: info@ridemocrats.org; *Web site*: http://www.ridemocrats.org. *South Carolina*: P.O. Box 5965, Columbia, SC 29250; 1529 Hampton Street #200, Columbia, SC 29201; *Telephone*: 800-841-1817, 803-799-7798; *Fax*: 803-765-1692;

Email: contact party through its web site; *Web site*: http://www.scdp.org. *South Dakota*: 207 East Capitol #103, Pierre, SD 57501; *Telephone*: 605-224-1750; *Fax*: 605-224-1759; *Email*: democrats@sddp.org; *Web site*: http://www.sddp.org. *Tennessee*: 223 8th Avenue North #200, Nashville, TN 37203; *Telephone*: 615-327-9779; *Fax*: 615-327-9759; *Email*: headquarters@tndp.org; *Web site*: http://www.tndp.org. *Texas*: 707 Rio Grande Street, Austin, TX 78701; *Telephone*: 512-478-9800; *Fax*: 512-480-2500; *Email*: contact party through its web site; *Web site*: http://www.txdemocrats.org. *Utah*: 455 South 300 East #301, Salt Lake City, UT 84111; *Telephone*: 801-328-1212; *Fax*: 801-328-1238; *Email*: mail@utdemocrats.org; *Web site*: http://www.utdemocrats.org. *Vermont*: P.O. Box 1220, 73 Main Street #36, Montpelier, VT 05601; *Telephone*: 802-229-1783; *Fax*: 802-229-1784; *Email*: contact party through its web site; *Web site*: http://www.vtdemocrats.org. *Virginia*: Capitol Place, 1108 East Main Street, 2nd Floor, Richmond, VA 23219; *Telephone*: 800-322-1144, 804-644-1966; *Fax*: 804-343-3642; *Email*: contact party through its web site; *Web site*: http://www.vademocrats.org. *Washington*: P.O. Box 4027, 616 First Avenue #300, Seattle, WA 98194; *Telephone*: 206-583-0664; *Fax*: 206-583-0301; *Email*: info@wa-democrats.org; *Web site*: http://www.wa-democrats.org. *West Virginia*: 5 Greenbrier Street, Charleston, WV 25311; *Telephone*: 304-342-8121; *Fax*: 304-342-8122; *Email*: wvparty@wvdemocrats.com; *Website*: http://www.wvdemocrats.com. *Wisconsin*: 222 West Washington Avenue #150, Madison, WI 53703; *Telephone*: 608-255-5172; *Fax*: 608-255-8919; *Email*: party@wisdems.org; *Web site*: http://www.wisdems.org. *Wyoming*: 254 North Center Street #205, Casper, WY 82601; *Telephone*: 800-729-3367, 307-473-1457; *Fax*: 307-473-1459; *Email*: wyomingdemocrats@qwest.net; *Web site*: http://www.wyomingdemocrats.com

Democratic Patriotism Party

Email: contact party through its web site; *Web site*: http://www.homestead.com/dpatriotparty/page1.html

The Democratic Patriotism Party supports a woman's right to choose (although the party does not implicitly support abortion); limited gun control, such as the idea that no convicted felon should be able to own a gun; gay rights, gay marriages, and gay adoptions; the death penalty; free education for all citizens, but not private school vouchers; an increase in American oil exploration as well as investigating alternate fuel sources; and assassination of foreign leaders when in the best interest of the United States.

Democratic Socialists Party of America

198 Broadway #700, New York, NY 10038; *Telephone*: 212-727-8610; *Fax*: 212-608-6955; *Email*: dsa@dsausa.org; *Web site*: http://www.dsausa.org/

The Democratic Socialists Party of America is the nation's principal affiliate of the Socialist International, which includes such socialist parties as the Swedish Social Democrats, Canada's New Democratic Party, Nicaragua's Sandinista National Liberation Front, Palestine's Fatah, Israel's Labour Party and Meretz, and the British Labour Party. Party members strive to build a national progressive movement for social change while establishing an openly socialist presence in American communities and politics. The Party also sponsors a youth section, the Young Democratic Socialists, which is comprised of students from colleges and high schools and young people in the work force and is the only U.S. member of the International Union of Socialist Youth, the largest political youth coalition in the world. The DSA disseminates its views through its quarterly publication, *Democratic Left*.

The DSA was created in 1983 from a merger of the Democratic Socialist Organizing Committee (a remnant of the defunct Socialist Party of America) and the New American Movement (a coalition of writers and intellectuals). The Party focuses its efforts at the local level and works with labor unions, community organizations, and campus activists. Some of the Party's most well-known members include AFL-CIO President John Sweeney, feminist Gloria Steinem, actor Ed Asner, author Barbara Ehrenreich, scholar and activist Cornel West, and libertarian socialist Noam Chomsky.

Affiliates. *Alaska*: P.O. Box 70252, Fairbanks, AK 99707; *Telephone*: 907-479-6782; *Fax*: 907-479-9466; *Email*: rtfarris_99708@yahoo.com. *California*: 1256 Monterey Avenue, Berkeley, CA 94707; *Telephone*: 510-524-3247; *Email*: banjo@california.com; 11 Panorama

Drive, San Francisco, CA 94131; *Telephone*: 415-550-1062; *Email*: RossBoylan@stanfordalumni.org; *Web site*: http://home.earthlink. net/~drrboylan/dsa/; P.O. Box 181, Corte Madera, CA 94976; *Telephone*: 415-924-6110; *Email*: juneswan@yahoo.com; P.O. Box 162394, Sacramento, CA 95816; *Telephone*: 916-361-9072; *Email*: campd227@pacbell.net; 5122 Gardena Avenue, San Diego, CA 92110; *Telephone*: 619-276-6023; *Email*: vfranc02@earthlink.net; P.O. Box 17061, Encino, CA 91416; *Telephone*: 818-344-4591; *Email*: dgtollefson @msn.com; 1603 Garden Street, Santa Barbara, CA 93101; *Telephone*: 805-962-2057; *Email*: rflacks@igc.org. *Colorado*: P.O. Box 748, Boulder, CO 80306; *Telephone*: 303-449-2511; *Email*: anders@ spot.Colorado.edu. *Florida*: 3820 Northwest, 10th Floor, Gainesville, FL 32605; *Telephone*: 352-376-7479; *Email*: emilybrowne@yahoo. com. *Illinois*: 1608 North Milwaukee Avenue #403, Chicago, IL 60647; *Telephone*: 773-384-0327; *Email*: chiildsa@chicagodsa.org; *Web site*: http://www.chicagodsa.org. *Indiana*: P.O. Box 361132, Indianapolis, IN 46236; *Telephone*: 317-919-4622; *Email*: indianadsa@netscape.net. *Maine*: 44 Milton Street, Portland, ME 04102; *Telephone*: 207-772-9640; *Email*: hbaker@maine.edu. *Massachusetts*: P.O. Box 51356, Boston, MA 02205; *Telephone*: 617-354-5078; *Email*:chair@dsaboston.org; *Web site*: http://dsaboston.org. *Michigan*: 30115 Ardmore Drive, Farmington Hills, MI 48334; *Telephone*: 248-855-3169; *Email*: dsagreen@aol.com; *Web site*: http://kincaidsite.com/dsa. *Minnesota*: 695 Ottawa Avenue, St. Paul, MN 55107; *Telephone*: 651-224-8262; *Email*: info@twincitiesdsa.org; *Web site*: http://www.twincitiesdsa. org. *New Jersey*: 150 East 33rd Street, Paterson, NJ 07514; *Email*: ssheats@lsnj.org. *New York*: P.O. Box 2056, Albany, NY 12220; *Telephone*: 518-463-5611; *Email*: markalban1@earthlink.net; 206 Eddy Street, Ithaca, NY 14850, *Telephone*: 607-273-3009; *Email*: talt@igc. org; *Web site*: http://talt.home.Igc.org/DSAWeb/; 662 Howard Avenue, West Hempstead, NY 11552; *Email*: markfinkel@aol.com; 240 West 98th Street #14F, New York, NY 10025; *Email*: kdschaeffer517@msn.com. *Ohio*: 2102 Wascana Avenue 2nd Floor, Lakewood, OH 44107; *Email*: bernjanes@aol.com; P.O. Box 10506, Columbus, OH 43201; *Telephone*: 614-267-8517; *Email*: smorgen @juno.com; *Web site*: http://www.dsco.org. *Oregon*: 104 Northeast 72nd Avenue, Portland, OR 97213; *Telephone*: 503-252-6303; *Email*:

rosecity@dsaoregon.igc.org. *Pennsylvania*: P.O. Box 8546, Philadelphia, PA 19101; *Telephone*: 215-351-0151; *Email*: philadsa@earth link.net; 5848 Alderton Street #1, Pittsburth, PA 15217; *Email*: roboshep @aol.com; 19 Spring Lane, Fleetwood, PA 19522; *Email*: lbrsmillar@ earthlink.net. *Virginia*: 104 Diamond Road, Troy, VA 22974; *Telephone*: 434-295-8884; *Email*: ckaplan@virginia.edu. *Washington, D.C./ Northern Virginia*: P.O. Box 33345, Washington, D.C. 20033; *Telephone*: 202-232-2500. *Wisconsin*: P.O. Box 628313, Middleton, WI 53562; *Email*: mdsilber@wisc.edu.

Diamond Party

Email: politics_discussion@hotmail.com; *Web site*: http://www. freewebs.com/politicshome/

The Diamond Party is an independent voters league that takes an active and positive stance towards politics. The Party works for a streamlined government, freer markets, and effective justice. The Diamond Party considers itself moderate or centrist in nature, and most of its members describe themselves as moderate libertarian. While not strictly a political party in the common sense of the word, the Diamond Party is a voters league whose members, for the most part, are registered voters as Democrats, Republicans, Greens, and Libertarians.

The Party is not on any state or national ballot and does not field its own candidates, preferring to endorse candidates from established parties who support its basic platform stance. The Party's platform supports a streamlined federal government, with as much political power as possible exercised at the local level; the government acting as a policy-setting group with audit functions overseeing independent companies and agencies; implementing proportional representation and giving voice to third parties; repealing all executive orders that have no congressional approval; expanding the number of judges on the Supreme Court; creating a Constitutional Panel that would advise Congress and the president on constitutional and legal matters; creating more urban enterprise zones and strengthening the nation's infrastructure; strengthening worker's rights and worker safety laws; reducing agricultural subsidies; eliminating the income tax and replacing it with a national sales tax; eliminating property taxes; ending the war on drugs; eliminating gun control laws; reduced sentences and alternative punishments for non-violent criminals; abolishing the death penalty; maintaining an all-volunteer military; universal health care for children; gay marriages and abolishing all sodomy laws; organized prayer only in private schools, not in public schools; allowing abortion in first trimester only and abolishing partial birth abortions, except when mother's health is threatened; legalize prostitution; increased funding of public libraries; expanding the school year from 180 days to at least 210; increasing the National Aeronautics and Space Administration's budget and expanding space exploration efforts; universal implementation of the metric system; and limiting legal immigration.

Downsize D.C. Foundation

6718 Lenclair Street, Alexandria, VA 22306; *Email*: comments@ downsizedc.org; *Website*: http://www.downsizedc.org/index.shtml; http://www.downsizedc.com

A project of the non-profit American Liberty Foundation, the Downsize D.C. Foundation's primary objective is to decrease the size of the federal government and its influence in the lives of average Americans. The Foundation, which publishes the e-mail newsletter *LibertyWire*, supports opposition to the concepts of a national identity card for all citizens; lowering the federal debt limit; repealing tax funding for national political conventions; reverting most government regulation and oversight back to the states; and eliminating the Internal Revenue Service.

Emigration Party of Nevada

1419C North Boulder Highway, Henderson, NV 89015; *Email*: contact party through its web site; *Web site*: http://www.sendem-back.org

The Emigration Party of Nevada supports stopping all illegal immigration; implementing government controls that would discourage illegal immigrants from coming to America; and the expelling of all illegal immigrants from the country. The Party supports making it a felony under Nevada law for any employer to hire an illegal alien and a bounty of $1,000 to be paid to anyone who turns in such an employer; stopping all state welfare money and medical care to any illegal alien; and sending prisoners back to their country of origin, except for those who have committed capital crimes.

Expansionist Party of the United States

295 Smith Street, Newark, NJ 07106; *Telephone*: 973-416-6151; *Email*: XPUS@aol.com; *Web site*: http://members.aol.com/XPUS

Formed in February 1977 the Expansionist Party of the United States believes that America is too small to sustain a positive role in world events but can expand by accepting new states. The Party supports creating new states out of Puerto Rico, the U.S. Virgin Islands, Guam, American Samoa, the Commonwealth of the Northern Marianas, and bringing Canada into the Union. The Party's long-term goals include generating national expansion by accepting states from all over the world that want to join America, thus eventually creating a democratic world union under the Constitution of the United States.

The XP believes that without expansion the United States will become "just one of many mid-sized countries, incapable of absorbing tens of millions of immigrants, incapable of defending itself against great powers, and incapable of projecting its culture and civilization worldwide." The Party seeks to enlarge not just the United States but also human possibility, for everyone, everywhere. "We want the protections of the U.S. Constitution to extend to everyone, everywhere ... the dynamics of our economy and culture to vitalize and develop the world, all the while heeding the rights of other species in environmentally sensible projects. Expansionism is not just for us, in the present states, but for everyone, everywhere. Expansionism is in everyone's interest."

The Party supports abolishing Civil Service tenure and the idea of a permanent government job for life; amending the Constitution to provide a means to override the Supreme Court; abolishing primary elections and forcing the major political parties to choose their candidates through their own internal processes; requiring all eligible citizens to vote; including a "None of the Above" choice on every ballot for every office and if "None of the Above" gets more votes than any named candidate, every named candidate is defeated and forbidden to run again for that office in that election year; forbidding the wealthy to hold public office; reducing the size of Congressional districts and expanding the number of those elected to Congress to more than 435; the government imposing a maximum of 10% for credit card interest; ending American support for the State of Israel; reducing the military budget to limit its abilities to wage wars around the globe; permanent elimination of the national debt; means-testing Medicare and Social Security and ensuring those services are provided only to those with real needs; barring any corporation that moves its operations outside the United States from any government contracts; providing universal health care; expanding the use of the death penalty for convicted criminals; legal censorship of violence in entertainment; abolishing all civil-rights and anti-discrimination laws that interfere with private property rights and freedom of association; abolishing all Indian nations within the United States; reducing the funding for the National Endowment for the Arts; the Federal Communications Commission reducing the amount of time that television can give over to commercials; and outlawing unnecessary abortions.

Faith & Patience Party

700 Southeast 5th Court, Pompano Beach, FL 33060; *Telephone*: 954-785-0127.

A local political party.

Falconist Party

Email: falconistparty@lycos.com; *Web site*: http://www.falconistparty.us

The Falconist Party supports the political, economic, social, moral, and military rebuilding of America and renewing America's pursuit of her manifest destiny, as defined by the country's Founding Fathers. The Party believes that the "oligarchy of the two-party system and interest groups have contributed to the corruption of our political system, apathy in our citizens, and a bureaucracy that is bloated and ineffective in governing America."

The Falconist Party supports election reform (such as the idea that any candidate and/or party that submits five million signatures to the Federal Election Commission shall be on the ballot across the

Family Values Party of Florida • 77

entire country); consolidating the Departments of Commerce, Labor, and Transportation into the Department of Trades and Industry; merging the Department of the Interior with the Environmental Protection Agency; merge the Department of Energy, and parts of the Department of Agriculture to form the Department of Land; replacing the Departments of the Army, Navy, and Air Force with a Joint Force Defense Headquarters; expanding the number of Supreme Court justices from nine to 15; repealing term limits on all federal offices, including President; prohibiting flag burning; public schools teaching the role that Christianity played in the development of America's history, government, and culture; implementing a $3.00 a gallon tax, with $1.00 each going to the federal government, the state government, and the local government; repealing all personal property, estate, and real estate taxes; replacing the Federal Reserve with a government-owned Bank of the United States, to be operated by the U.S. Treasury Department; replacing Social Security with a national savings-investment plan; ending the practice of paying farmers not to plant their crops; establishing a program of national service and universal military training and requiring that all Americans above the age of 26 serve six to 12 months of military service; a person convicted of three violent crimes being automatically executed; providing educational vouchers to home-schooling parents; building more high schools to reduce high school (and class) size; all immigrants above the age of 18 serving a minimum of one year of military service for basic military and citizenship training; unlimited legal immigration; universal health care; repealing no-fault divorce laws; terminating state lotteries and outlawing gambling; American withdrawal from the United Nations, the World Trade Organization, the North American Free Trade Agreement, and the General Agreement on Tariffs and Trade; funding the colonization of the moon; and offering U.S. statehood to each Canadian province.

Family Values Party of Florida

2006 Woodbury Drive #1C, Cantonment, FL 32533; *Telephone*: 850-968-9817; *Email*: fvparty@aol.com; *Web site*: http://members. aol.com/fvparty/fvparty1

The Family Values Party is a religious-based organization that wants to restore family values to the political arena and to the American home. Based on its religious principles and interpretation of the Bible, the Party supports abolishing alcohol, tobacco, gambling, drugs, and abortions; sending only men who have reached the age of 20 to war; bringing prayer and worship into the public arena and schools; making homosexual acts and homosexual marriages illegal; and outlawing all tattoos.

First United & Independent Party of God
P.O. Box 367, Lake Worth, FL 33460; *Telephone*: 561-714-3787
A local political party

Florida Socialist Workers Party
P.O. Box 380846, Miami, FL 33138; *Telephone*: 305-899-8161
A local political party

Founding Fathers Party
Web site: http://www.foundingfathersparty.net
Founded in 2003, the Founding Fathers Party wants to lead America back to the ideals on which it was formed, as defined by the original Founding Fathers. The Party feels it "is the dream that sits at the core of the Republican Party, but without the "vote getting" double-dealing, socialism, victimism, religion, oppression, corruption, or rampant taxation of the other parties."

Freedom Party
Email: feedback@freedomparty.org; *Web site*: http://www.freedomparty.us
The Freedom Party was formed "to combat the federal government's unresponsive attitude towards its citizens and to reverse the political trend of raising taxes and reducing people's personal choices." The Party feels that the primary agenda of both the Democrats and Republicans is to "limit personal choice by controlling the citizens' bodies, families, monetary spending, jobs, and freedom of expression."

The Freedom Party believes that the "law must be used neither to deprive people of their property, nor to discriminate against them or discourage them from making peaceful personal decisions. The proper function of the law is ... to protect all individuals and their property from physical harm, and to ensure that physical force or threats of physical force are not used to discourage any person from making any peaceful personal decision."

Freedom Restoration Party of New York (see Independent American Party)

Freedom Socialist Party — Revolutionary Feminist Internationalists

4710 University Avenue Northeast #100, Seattle, WA 98105; *Telephone*: 206-985-4621; *Fax*: 206-985-8965; *Email*: fspnatl@igc.org; *Web site*: http://www.socialism.com

The Freedom Socialist Party is a "revolutionary, socialist feminist organization, dedicated to the replacement of capitalist rule by a genuine workers' democracy that will guarantee full economic, social, political, and legal equality to women, people of color, gays, and all who are exploited, oppressed, and repelled by the profit system and its offshoot — imperialism." The Party stresses that global democratic struggles—for national liberation, for race and sex liberation — are intertwined with workers' struggles around the world and can ultimately achieve victory only in conjunction with international socialist revolution.

The Party, which publishes the bi-monthly *Freedom Socialist — the Voice of Revolutionary Feminism*, supports freeing trade unions from the "class-collaborationist bureaucrats and from dependence on the twin political parties of big business"; the struggles of the oppressed minorities against racism; unconditional economic, political, and social equality for Blacks, Chicanos, Asian Americans, Native Americans, and Puerto Ricans, and endorse the demand for self-determination by the Indian and Puerto Rican nations; the collaboration of organizations of people of color with the revolutionary movement as the most realistic and historically validated alternative to the dead ends of separatism or reformist integration; the total emancipation of women on every level of life; equality for lesbians and gay men; and strong environmental protections.

Affiliates. *California*: 2170 West Washington Boulevard, Los Angeles, CA 90018; *Telephone*: 323-732-6416; *Fax*: 323-732-6410; *Email*: lafsprw6@aol.com; New Valencia Hall, 1908 Mission Street, San Francisco, CA 94103; *Telephone*: 415-864-1278; *Fax*: 415-864-0778; *Email*: bafsprw@igc.org. *Florida*: 531 Highland Avenue, Quincy, FL 32308; *Telephone & Fax*: 850-875-4636; *Email*: comradeb@hotmail.com. *New Jersey*: 91 Court Street, #3B, Newark, NJ 07102; *Telephone & Fax*: 973-643-0499. *New York*: 8 Stanwix Street, 2nd Floor, Albany, NY 12209; *Telephone*: 518-433-1388; 113 West 128th Street, New York, NY 10027; *Telephone*: 212-222-0633; *Fax*: 212-222-0839; *Email*: fsprw@nyct.net. *Oregon*: Bread and Roses Center, 819 North Killingsworth Street, Portland, OR 97217; *Telephone*: 503-240-4462; *Fax*: 503-240-4463; *Email*: fsp@igc.org. *Washington*: New Freeway Hall, 5018 South Rainier Avenue, Seattle, WA 98118; *Telephone*: 206-722-2453; *Fax*: 206-723-7691; *Email*: fspseattle@mindspring.com.

Friendly State Party (a New York state affiliate of the Constitution Party)

Fusion Party of America
Email: contact party through its web site; *Web site*: http://members.tripod.com/~fusionparty

Originally founded primarily to support lowering the age of eligibility for federal office, the Fusion Party of America basically acts as a political action organization for young people.

Georgia Centralist Party
Email: contact party through its web site; *Web site*: http://www.geocities.com/capitolhill/1268

The ultimate goal of the Georgia Centralist Party is to "provide funding to candidates that represent the values of middle class America and the ideals important to all citizens, from the grassroots level."

Grassroots Party
Originally launched as a Minnesota-based liberal party, the Grassroots Party advocates the legalization of marijuana, promotes hemp farming, and the establishment of a national system of universal health

care. The Party's basic philosophy is very similar to the Greens, but with a much stronger emphasis on marijuana/hemp legalization issues.

The GRP fielded its first Presidential nominee, Dennis Peron, in 1996, who garnered 5,400 votes. Also in 1996, the Party won permanent "major party" ballot status in Vermont. The Vermont affiliate was initially more libertarian and "states rights" oriented in philosophy than its leftist sister party in Minnesota and the Party's 2000 Presidential nominee, Denny Lane, came from this group. Since 1996, most Minnesota GRP activists jumped to either the Green Party or the Democratic Grassroots Caucus. In 2002, many of the libertarian-leaning Vermont GRP leaders bolted to the Libertarian Party, a move that has returned the Vermont faction to a leftist, marijuana/hemp legalization party. The remnants of the Minnesota GRP disbanded and merged into the Liberal Party of Minnesota in 2002.

Green Mountain Independence Party

Email: contact party through its web site; *Web site*: http://dixienet.org/spatriot/v016n02/members28.htm

The Green Mountain Independence Party wants to act as a challenge to the two major parties and to encourage Vermont citizens to "downsize, de-centralize, de-militarize, localize, and humanize their lives." Another goal of the Party is to remind the federal government that the state has the right to leave the Union (just as it chose to join in 1791).

The Party has also floated the idea that Vermont should join forces with New Hampshire, Maine, and possibly the four Canadian Maritime provinces to create a new nation, which would have the population of Denmark. There is also a belief among some Party members that the state should leave the United States and form its own country.

Green Party (Green Party of the United States)

P.O. Box 57065, Washington, D.C. 20037; 1700 Connecticut Avenue NW #404, Washington, D.C. 20009; *Telephone*: 866-414-7336; 202-319-7191; *Fax*: 202-319-7193; *Email*: info@greenpartyus.org; *Web site*: http://www.gp.org

The Green Party of the United States (officially recognized as the

Green Party National Committee) is a federation of state-based Green Parties and is committed to environmental issues, non-violence, social justice, and grassroots organizing, all without corporate donors. The national party is an active partner with the European Federation of Green Parties and the Federation of Green Parties of the Americas.

The Green Party decision-making body is the Coordinating Committee, which is composed of delegates from each accredited state party. The Party was formed in 2001 as a reincarnation of the older Association of State Green Parties, which had operated from 1996 to 2001. The Party works to promote local state affiliates, which in turn will allow the Party to gain national prominence.

Affiliates. *Alabama*: P. O. Box 7241, Gulf Shores, AL 36547; *Telephone*: 205-951-9608; *Email*: info@alabamagreenparty.org; *Web site*: http://www.alabamagreenparty.org. *Alaska*: P.O. Box 102341, Anchorage, AK 99510; *Telephone*: 907-566-7873; *Email*: greenak@ak.net; *Web site*: http://alaska.greens.org. *Arizona*: P. O. Box 60173, Phoenix, AZ 85082; *Telephone*: 602-417-0213; *Email*: contact party through its web site; *Web site*: http://www.azgp.org. *Arkansas*: P.O. Box 444, Omaha, AR 72662; *Email*: contact party through its web site; *Web site*: http://www.arkgreens.org. *California*: P.O Box 2828, Sacramento, CA 95812; *Telephone*: 916-448-3437; *Email*: gpca@greens.org; *Web site*: http://www.cagreens.org. *Colorado*: P.O. Box 13001, Denver, CO 80201; *Telephone*: 303-575-1631; *Email*: contact party through its web site; *Web site*: http://www.greens.org/colorado. *Connecticut*: P.O. Box 231214, Hartford, CT 06123; *Telephone*: 888-877-8607; *Email*: greens@ctgreens.org; *Web site*: http://www.ctgreens.org. *Delaware*: P.O. Box 6044, Wilmington, DE 19804; *Email*: contact party through its web site; *Web site*: http://gpde.us. *Florida*: P.O. Box 1316, Key West, FL 33041; *Email*: contact party through its web site; *Web site*: http://www.floridagreens.org. *Georgia*: 1083 Northeast Austin Avenue, Atlanta, GA 30307, P.O. Box 5332, Atlanta, GA 31107; *Telephone*: 404-806-0480; *Fax*: 404-806-0584; *Email*: ggp@greens.org; *Web site*: http://www.greens.org/georgia. *Hawaii*: *Email*: Contact party through its web site; *Web site*: http://www.greenhawaii.org. *Idaho*: 1810 West State Street, PMB# 325, Boise, ID 83702; *Telephone*: 208-388-4549; *Email*: idaho@idahogreenparty.org; *Web site*: http://www.idahogreenparty.org. *Illinois*: P.O. Box 623, Urbana, IL

61803; *Telephone*: 312-924-1803; *Email*: info@ilgp.org; *Web site*: http://www.ilgp.org. *Indiana*: P.O. Box 441105, Indianapolis, IN 46244; *Telephone*: 812-824-9115; *Email*: mail@indianagreenparty.org; *Web site*: http://www.indianagreenparty.org. *Iowa*: P.O. Box 2448, Iowa City, IA 52244; *Telephone*: 319-337-7341; *Email*: iowa@greens. org; *Web site*: http://greens.org/iowa. *Kansas*: P.O. Box 1482, Lawrence, KS 66044, *Email*: contact@kansas.greens.org; *Web site*: http://kansas.greens.org. *Kentucky*: *Email*: contact party through its web site; *Web site*: http://www.kygreens.org. *Louisiana*: P.O. Box 531761, New Orleans, LA 70153; *Telephone*: 504-363-1108; *Email*: info@lagreens.org; *Web site*: http://www.lagreens.org. *Maine*: PO Box 309, Brooks, ME 04921; *Telephone*: 207-374-5636; P.O. Box 2046, 283 Water Street #16, Augusta, ME 04338; *Telephone*: 207-623-1919; *Email*: info@mainegreens.org; *Web site*: http://www.mainegreens. org. *Maryland*: P.O. Box 2230, Annapolis, MD 21404; *Email*: contact party through its web site; *Web site*: http://www.mdgreens.org. *Massachusetts*: Green-Rainbow Party, P.O. Box 440353, Somerville, MA 02144; *Telephone*: 978-688-2068; *Email*: office@green-rainbow.orgl *Web site*: http://www.massgreens.org/, http://www.green-rainbow. org. *Michigan*: 548 South Main Street, Ann Arbor, MI 48104; *Telephone*: 734-663-3555; *Email*: contact party through its web site; *Web site*: http://www.migreens.org. *Minnesota*: 621 West Lake Street #205, Minneapolis, MN 55408; *Telephone*: 612-871-4585; *Email*: info@ mngreens.org; *Web site*: http://www.mngreens.org. *Mississippi*: P.O. Box 3564, Jackson, MS 39207; *Telephone*: 601-948-7818; *Email*: greenpartyms@hotmail.com; *Web site*: http://www.greenpartyms.org. *Missouri*: P.O. Box 8094, St. Louis, MO 63156; *Telephone*: 314-664-1199; *Email*: info@mogreens.org; *Web site*: http://www.mogreens.org. *Montana*: 624 North 32nd Street, Billings, MT 59101; *Telephone*: 406-248-3378; *Email*: contact party through its web site; *Web site*: http://www.mtgreens.org. *Nebraska*: P.O. Box 85442, Lincoln, NE 68501; *Email*: contact party through its web site; *Web site*: http://www.nebraska.greens.org. *Nevada*: P.O. Box 11152, Reno, NV 89510; *Telephone*: 775-787-8935; *Email*: info@nevadagreenparty.org; *Web site*: http://www.nevadagreenparty.org. *New Hampshire*: P.O. Box 1589, Concord, NH 03302; *Email*: contact party through its web site; *Web site*: http://www.nhgreens.org. *New Jersey*: P.O. Box 9802,

Trenton, NJ 08650; *Telephone*: 609-278-4467; *Email*: contact party through its web site; *Web site*: http://www.gpnj.org. *New Mexico*: P.O. Box 40281, Albuquerque, NM 87196; *Telephone*: 505-473-3621; *Email*: contact party through its web site; *Web site*: http://www. greenpartynm.org. *New York*: *Email*: contact party through its web site; *Web site*: http://www.gpnys.org. *North Carolina*: *Email*: chair@ ncgreenparty.org; *Web site*: http://www.ncgreenparty.org. *North Dakota*: 1103 East Indiana Avenue, Bismarck, ND 58504; *Telephone*: 701-527-6370; *Email*: myfriend_boddah@hotmail.com. *Ohio*: P.O. Box 754, New Albany, OH 43054; *Email*: contact party through its web site; *Web site*: http://www.ohiogreens.org. *Oklahoma*: P.O. Box 52901, Oklahoma City, OK 73152; *Telephone*: 405-218-1242; *Email*: info@okgreens.org; *Web site*: http://www.okgreens.org. *Oregon*: Pacific Green Party of Oregon, P.O. Box 1606, Eugene, OR 97440; *Telephone*: 503-235-0300; *Email*: info@pacificgreens.org; *Web site*: http://www.pacificgreens.org. *Pennsylvania*: P.O. Box 11962, Harrisburg, PA 17108; *Telephone*: 800-647-4685; *Email*: contact party through its web site; *Web site*: http://www.gpofpa.org. *Rhode Island*: P.O. Box 1151, Providence RI 02901; *Telephone*: 401-490-7602; *Email*: contact party through its web site; *Web site*: http://www. greens.org/ri. *South Carolina*: P.O. Box 5341, Columbia, SC 29250; *Email*: contact party through its web site; *Web site*: http:// www.scgreenparty.org. *South Dakota*: 4502 East 16th Street, Sioux Falls, SD 57110; *Email*: socialanok@aol.com. *Tennessee*: *Email*: contact party through its web site; *Web site*: http://tn.greens.org. *Texas*: 818 West 31st, Houston, TX, 77018; *Email*: txgreens@txgreens. org; *Web site*: http://www.txgreens.org. *Utah*: 2793 East Cherry Lane, Layton, UT 84040; *Telephone*: 801-631-2998; *Email*: gpu@gput.org; *Web site*: http://www.gput.org. *Vermont*: P.O. Box 1413, Montpelier, VT 05602; *Email*: contact party through its web site; *Web site*: http://www.vermontgreens.org. *Virginia*: P.O. Box 7316, Falls Church, VA 22040; *Email*: contact party through its web site; *Web site*: http://www.vagreenparty.org. *Washington*: P.O. Box 17707, Seattle, WA 98107; *Telephone*: 206-781-3848; *Email*: info@wagreens.us; *Web site*: http://www.wagreens.us. *Washington, D.C.*: D.C. Statehood Green Party, 1739 Irving Street NW, Washington, D.C. 20010; *Telephone*: 202-232-1724; *Email*: steeringcommittee@dcstatehoodgreen.

org; *Web site*: http://www.dcstatehoodgreen.org. *West Virginia*: 223 Cedar Run Road, Friendly, WV 26146; *Telephone*: 304-684-2452; *Email*: greens@gpwv.org; *Web site*: http://www.gpwv.org. *Wisconsin*: P.O. Box 1701, Madison, WI 53701; *Telephone*: 608-204-7336; *Email*: contact party through its web site; *Web site*: http://www.wisconsin greenparty.org. *Wyoming*: P.O. Box 1833, Laramie, WY 82073; *Telephone*: 307-755-1606; *Email*: wyoming@gp-us.org

Greens/Green Party USA

P.O. Box 3568, Eureka, CA 95502; *Telephone*: 866-473-3672; *Email*: info@greenparty.org; *Web site*: http://www.greenparty.org/

Founded in 1984, the Greens/Green Party USA is a non-profit membership organization that aims to make the world more democratic, safer, and cleaner. First organized as the Green Committees of Correspondence, the Greens/Green Party USA is the oldest, continuously active Green organization in America and was the group that originated the Green Ten Key Values, which are now accepted by nearly all Greens in the United States. The Ten Key Values point to a new society and way of life based on Ecological Wisdom, Social Justice, Cooperation, and Non-Violence. All membership payments and donations go directly to the Party and not to any candidate or candidate's authorized committee or to direct electoral activity. The Party keeps its members informed through its quarterly newspaper, *Green Politics*.

The G/GPUSA Party believes that "today's industrial society, driven by a market system based only on profit, is rapidly destroying the foundations in nature on which human existence depends, including air, water, soil, forests, plants and animals, and mineral and fuel resources." The Party's Ten Key Values include Grassroots Democracy (increasing public participation at every level of government and to ensure that public representatives are fully accountable to the people who elect them); Ecological Wisdom (supporting a sustainable society that uses resources in such a way that ensures their availability for future generations); Social Justice and Equal Opportunity (ensuring that everyone has the rights and opportunities to benefit equally from the resources provided by society and the environment); Nonviolence (promoting a nonviolent approach to opposing violence-based practices and policies); Decentralization (promoting a restructuring of social, political and economic institutions away from a system controlled by and mostly benefits the powerful few, to a democratic, less bureaucratic system); Community Based Economics (encouraging local communities to promote economic development that assures protection of the environment and workers' rights, citizen participation in planning, and enhancing the neighborhood's quality of life); Feminism (replacing the cultural ethics of domination and control, with more cooperative ways of interacting which respect differences of opinion and gender); Respect for Diversity (the importance to value cultural, ethnic, racial, sexual, religious and spiritual diversity); Personal and Global responsibility (encouraging individuals to improve their personal well being while enhancing ecological balance and social harmony); and Future Focus and Sustainability (promoting actions and policies aimed to long-term goals).

Guns and Dope Party of California

Email: contact party through its web site; *Web site*: http://www. gunsanddope.com

As its name implies, the Guns and Dope Party advocates gun and dope ownership to all citizens who want them, without forcing them onto those not interested. The Party also supports a less centralized state and federal government, more freedom for California citizens, and the legalization of prostitution.

Independence Party of Minnesota

P.O. Box 40495, St Paul, MN 55104; *Telephone*: 651-487-9700; *Fax*: 651-917-7145; *Email*: contact party through its web site; *Web site*: http://www.mnip.org

The history of the Independence Party of Minnesota dates to the 1992 Ross Perot presidential campaign, after which many Perot supporters joined United We Stand America, a non-partisan, non-profit, membership organization, created to lobby for reforms to make government more ethical, accountable and fiscally responsible. UWSA, closely identified with Ross Perot, was essentially a national organization directed from Texas.

UWSA established affiliate organizations in all 50 states and began lobbying for a balanced national budget, campaign finance reform, term limits, and fair international trade policies. Party members insist that in 1994 the basic UWSA proposals became the Republicans' Contract with America, and was the genesis for the Republican Party gaining control of the Senate and the House of Representatives. Simultaneously, other Perot supporters chose to establish a new political party in Minnesota, which would eventually be called the Independence Party of Minnesota.

In September 1995, Perot announced his intention to form a new political party called Citizens to Establish a Reform Party. In Minnesota, the Independence Party decided to join the national Reform Party, and in early 1996 the Reform Party of Minnesota was established. At about the same time, United We Stand America was discontinued and many of its members became affiliated with the Reform Party.

Perot was the 1996 Reform Party USA Presidential candidate and he received 12% of the votes in Minnesota and nine percent across the country. This result, along with the number of votes received by other party candidates for various political offices, gave the party validity and permanent status in the state of Minnesota.

By 1998, after a period of sustained growth, the national Reform Party was recognized by the Federal Election Commission as a major party on the national level. In June 1998, the Reform Party of Minnesota voted to formally affiliate with the Reform Party USA, although there was much dissension between the state and national organizations. In the 1998 election, former Navy Seal and professional wrestler Jesse Ventura surprised the political establishment by winning the Minnesota governor's race while running as a Reform Party candidate.

Differences between the state and national organizations continued and was highlighted by the fact that Ventura's surprise victory was achieved with no financial help from the national party. This friction led to a struggle between Perot and Ventura as the leader of the party. After continuous conflict, Ventura labeled the national Reform Party as "hopelessly dysfunctional" and in March 2000, at his urging, the Reform Party of Minnesota voted to disaffiliate from the RPUSA and return to the Independence Party of Minnesota name. Since that date, the party has not been associated with any national political organization and works as a Minnesota state party only, focusing on getting its candidates elected to statewide and local political offices.

The party supports the idea that all government functions should be conducted at the lowest possible level and works for a less-intrusive government role in the lives of its citizens.

Independence Party of New York

P.O. Box 871, Lindenhurst, NY 11757; *Email*: chair@ipny.org; *Web site*: http://ipny.org

Formed as a reaction to perceived flaws and non responsiveness in the major political parties, the Independence Party of New York supports less intrusive government; creating a statewide political party committed to the elimination of the electoral advantages of incumbency and the creation of a level playing field for the candidates of all political parties; promoting citizen involvement in the electoral process; and restoring fiscally responsible and accountable government. The party believes that the Democrats and Republicans have "collaborated to subvert political liberty to serve their own ambition for pensions, privileges and perks ... and created a mountain of public debt which will eventually crash down upon the lives of our children and grandchildren." Although primarily a state organization, the party believes that the problems facing New York State are also evident at the national level and that the same remedies would work for each.

The party's proposals include automatically registering individuals to vote who have a driver's license, are 18, and who are otherwise qualified to vote; allowing citizens to vote during a period beginning on the Saturday before the traditional Tuesday date for elections and ending on election day; expanding the opportunity for absentee voting; term limits of 12 years for legislative offices and eight years for executive positions; public funding of campaigns and the elimination of Political Action Committee funding of candidates; eliminating all foreign campaign contributions; ending pensions to elected legislative officials; reducing as much government activities as possible and transferring them to private organizations; decreasing federal and state budgets to zero in five years; ending automatic cost of living adjustments for all government programs unless approved by the legislature; supporting a constitutional amendment providing for a mandated balanced federal budget; making it easier to fire civil service employees for cause; allowing line item veto for the Governor and President; eliminating the current welfare system and replacing it with a needs-based program; creating and funding a national science and technology program that will create educational funds for American citizens who study in the sciences, engineering, and mathematics fields; extending the school year and the school day; and reduce the ability of parole boards to release criminals who committed or threatened violence in the commission of their crimes.

Independent America First Party of Tennessee

2370 Patton Hollow Road, Watertown, TN 37184; *Telephone*: 615-237-3521; *Email*: info@AFPTN.org; *Web site*: http://www. afptn.org

Initially affiliated with the Reform Party, in 2001 the Independent America First Party of Tennessee changed its affiliation to the America First Party. In April 2004 the state party disaffiliated itself from any national organization and adopted its current name. The party is working to establish affiliate organizations in all 50 states and aims to be a challenge to the Democratic and Republican parties, both of which the party blames for the problems faced by Americans.

The party supports a 25-year ban on legal immigration and a limit of 250,000 per year after the ban is lifted; ceasing the importation of non–American workers to fill American jobs; using the military to help the U.S. Border Patrol; preserving the sovereignty of America and rejecting the "One World" concept; withdrawing from the United Nations; dissolving the Federal Reserve System; prayer in all public places and government institutions; abolishing the federal Department of Education; repealing Tennessee Code 49-6-1006 mandating the education of children in black history and multiculturalism; abolishing control of the local schools by the Tennessee Department of Education, and restoring all decisions and funding on education to the counties and local communities; nullifying the federal No Child Left Behind legislation and ending the practice of receiving federal funding for local schools; and legislation designating English as the official language of the United States.

Independent American Party (United States Independent American Party)

24224 Joshua Avenue, Desert Lake, CA 93516; *Telephone*: 760-762-9230, 801-420-6920; *Email*: contact@usiap.org; *Web site*: http://www.usiap.org

Established in May 1998, the Independent American Party (also known as the United States Independent American Party) plans to organize and recruit in every state and the District of Columbia. The party aims to "promote respect for life, liberty and property; strong traditional families; patriotism; and individual, state and national sovereignty." The party believes that "to maintain freedom, our political institutions must be founded upon faith in God and moral laws as declared in the Declaration of Independence, the Constitution of the United States and the Bill of Rights."

The party supports protecting the right and control of private property; denying the federal government the power to take from the individual either his life, liberty, or his property except by due process of law; abolishing the Federal Reserve System; introducing Christian principles as the center of American education; America withdrawing from all international agreements and treaties; banning same-sex marriages; a ban on flag burning; a ban on abortions; the right of Americans to own and bear arms; limiting the government's use of eminent domain; abolishing the federal Department of Education; English being designated as the official national language; eliminating the National Endowment for the Arts; abolishing the Internal Revenue Service; eliminating the Environmental Protection Agency; abolishing the U.S. Department of Energy; abolishing the Office of Homeland Security; and the right of U.S. forces to refuse to serve under the command of the United Nations or any other foreign entity.

Affiliates. *Alabama*: P.O. Box 2, Emelle, AL 35459; *Telephone*: 334-712-9851; *Email*: contact party through its web site; *Web site*: http://www.usiap.org/States/AL/AlabamaIndex.html. *Arizona*: 330

West San Pedro Avenue, Gilbert, AZ 85233; *Email*: contact party through its web site; *Web site*: http://www.usiap.org//States/AZ/ArizonaIndex.html. *California*: 24166 Chaparral, Desert Lake, CA 93516; *Telephone*: 866-837-1643; *Email*: contact party through its web site; *Web site*: http://www.usiap.org/States/CA/CaliforniaIndex.html. *Connecticut*: P.O. Box 358, 1000 State Street, Springfield, MA 01109; *Telephone*: 860-428-8090; *Email*: contact party through its web site; *Web site*: http://www.usiap.org/States/CT/ConnecticutIndex.html. *Florida*: 4618 Key Lime Boulevard, Loxahatchee, FL 33470; *Telephone*: 561-795-1335; *Email*: contact party through its web site; *Web site*: http://www.usiap.org/States/FL/FloridaIndex.html. *Georgia*: 12675 Providence Road, Alpharetta, GA 30004; *Telephone & Fax*: 770-521-1229; *Email*: contact party through its web site; *Web site*: http://www.usiap.org/States/GA/GeorgiaIndex.html. *Hawaii*: 227 Ohua Street, Honolulu, HI 96815; *Telephone*: 808-227-2731; *Email*: contact party through its web site; *Web site*: http://www.usiap.org/States/HI/HawaiiIndex.html. *Idaho*: 2800 Cherry Lane, Boise, ID 83705; *Telephone*: 208-424-9018; *Email*: contact party through its web site; *Web site*: http://www.usiap.org/States/ID/IdahoIndex.html. *Illinois*: 2538 Hartfield Drive, Montgomery, IL 60538; *Telephone*: 630-801-1582; *Email*: contact party through its web site; *Web site*: http://www.usiap.org/States/IL/IllinoisIndex.html. *Indiana*: 1004 Main Street, Elwood, IN 46036; *Telephone*: 765-552-0104; *Email*: contact party through its web site; *Web site*: http:// www.usiap.org/States/IN/IndianaIndex.html. *Kansas*: P.O. Box 361, Ottawa, KS 66067; *Telephone*: 913-645-8742; *Email*: contact party through its web site; *Web site*: http://www.usiap.org/States/KS/KansasIndex.html. *Massachusetts*: P.O. Box 665, Holyoke, MA 01041; *Telephone*: 413-536-5387; *Email*: contact party through its web site; *Web site*: http://www.usiap.org/States/MA/Massachusetts.html. *Michigan*: 29 Law Street, Lapeer, MI 48446; *Telephone*: 810-644-2540; *Email*: contact party through its web site; *Web site*: http://www.usiap.org/States/MI/MichiganIndex.html. *Missouri*: *Email*: contact party through its web site; *Web site*: http://www.usiap.org/States/MO/MissouriIndex.html. *Nebraska*: *Email*: contact party through its web site; *Web site*: http://www.usiap.org/States/NB/NebraskaIndex.html. *New York* (Freedom Restoration Party of New York): *Email*: contact party through its web site; *Web site*: http://www.usiap.org/States/ NY/NewYorkIndex.html. *North Carolina*: P.O. Box 475, Glenville, NC 28736; *Email*: contact party through its web site; *Web site*: http://www.usiap.org/States/NC/NorthCarolinaIndex.html. *Oklahoma*, P.O. Box 2903, Oklahoma City, OK 73101; *Telephone*: 405-603-2410; *Email*: contact party through its web site; *Web site*: http://www.usiap.org/States/OK/OklahomaIndex.html. *Pennsylvania*, 129 Batdorf Road, Bernville, PA 19506; *Email*: contact party through its web site; *Web site*: http://www.usiap.org/States/PA/PennsylvaniaIndex.html. *South Dakota*: HC 59 Rock Drive, Custer Highlands, Edgemont, SD 57735; *Email*: contact party through its web site; *Web site*: http://www.usiap.org/States/SD/SouthDakotaIndex.html. *Utah*: 2454 Village Circle, Salt Lake City, UT 84108; *Telephone*: 801-583-0305; *Email*: contact party through its web site; *Web site*: http://www. usiap.org/uiap/index.htm. *Virginia*: 2509 North Quantico Street, Arlington, VA 22207; *Telephone*: 703-338-1756; *Email*: contact party through its web site; *Web site*: http://www.usiap.org/States/VA/VirginiaIndex.html.

Independent American Party of Nevada

P.O. Box 2567, Sparks, NV 90432; *Telephone*: 775-284-4427; *Fax*: 775-356-0727; *Email*: info@iapn.org; *Web site*: http://www.iapn.org

The Independent American Party of Nevada believes that an "independent America is a freer America" and works to keep citizens free from government control. The party supports ending American ties with the United Nations; an end to legalized abortions; enforcing illegal immigration laws and increasing border patrols; withdrawal from the North American Free Trade Agreement, the General Agreement on Tariffs and Trade, and the World Trade Organization; repealing the 1913 Federal Reserve Act; and abolishing income taxes.

Independent Coalition Party

Telephone: 505-873-7627; *Email*: icp@swcp.com; *Web site*: http://www.independentcoalition.org

Based in New Mexico and formed in reaction to the perceived indifference of the two major political parties, the Independent Coalition Party aims to be a unifying source for voters. The party supports better ballot access for independent and minor parties; decriminalization of marijuana drug laws; development of renewable energy and organic farming industries in New Mexico; diversity and decentralization in the public school system; and downsizing the military and its international missions.

Independent Democrats of Florida

525 West 49th Street, Miami, FL 33140; *Telephone*: 305-864-5110. Local political party.

Independent Party

P.O. Box 201951, Yale Station, New Haven, CT 06520; *Email*: contact party through its web site; *Web site*: http://www.yale.edu/ip

Established in 1934 as the Conservative Party of the Yale Political Union, the Independent Party attracts members from all parts of the political spectrum, including libertarians, socialists, totalitarians, anarchists, and mainstream democrats and republicans. The party does not support a single political belief system but encourages debate on all political ideas.

Independent Party of America

236 Derby Downs Drive, Sneads Ferry, NC 28460; *Email*: info@independentpartyofamerica.com; *Web site*: http://www.independentpartyofamerica.com

The Independent Party of America promotes a platform "of true democracy" and tailors its efforts to individual voting districts, supporting candidates who adhere to the IPA political principles. Formed because of the perceived failure of the established two-party system in America, the IPA is working to convince citizens that their vote does count, that changes can be made to the system, and encouraging the idea of direct representation. The IPA focuses its efforts over the internet, taking advantage of its technology and instant accessibility.

Independent Party of Florida

P.O. Box 100, Largo, FL 33779; *Telephone*: 727-585-1111. Local political party.

Industrial Workers of the World Party

P.O. Box 13476, Philadelphia, PA 19101; *Telephone*: 215-222-1905; *Email*: ghq@iww.org; *Web site*: http://www.iww.org

Part of the international IWW movement, the Industrial Workers of the World Party in the United States strives to unite the workers of America to represent them against "management" and the industrial power structure which "takes advantage of workers for its own financial gain." Following the lead of the international organization, the IWW in America believes that the "trade unions foster a state of affairs which allows one set of workers to be pitted against another set of workers in the same industry, thereby helping defeat one another in wage wars. Moreover, the trade unions aid the employing class to mislead the workers into the belief that the working class have interests in common with their employers." Using the slogan "Abolition of the Wage System," the IWW aims to resolve this worker conflict and to represent all workers against management in all industries.

With the goal of organizing a variety of unions into "One Big Union," the IWW organizes industrially rather than by trade and these unions are grouped into six departments that include Agriculture and Fisheries, Mining and Minerals, General Construction, Manufacture and General Production, Transportation and Communication, and Public Service. The IWW's goals, projects, and messages are distributed to its members through its official publication, *The Industrial Worker*, which is published 10 times a year.

Affiliates. *Arizona*: 1205 East Hubble, Phoenix, AZ 85006; *Telephone*: 602-254-4057; *Email*: phoenix@iww.org; *Web site*: http://iww.org/branches/US/AZ. *California*: P.O. Box 91691, Pasadena, CA 91691; *Telephone*: 323-682-4143; P.O. Box 12423, San Diego, CA 92112; P.O. Box 11412, Berkeley, CA 94712; *Telephone*: 510-845-0540; *Email*: bayarea@iww.org; P.O. Box 23008, Santa Barbara, CA 93121; *Telephone*: 209-662-4846; 1327 Baird Road, Santa Rosa, CA 95409; *Telephone*: 707-539-7739; *Email*: contact party through its web site; *Web site*: http://iww.org/branches/US/CA. *Colorado*: 2298 Clay, Denver, CO 80211; *Telephone*: 303-433-1852; *Email*: breadandroses @msn.com; *Web site*: http://iww.org/branches/US/CO. *Florida*: P.O. Box 12311 Pensacola, FL 32591; *Email*: iwwpensacola@yahoo.com;

Web site: http://iww.org/branches/US/FL. *Illinois*: P.O. Box 18387, Chicago, IL 60618; *Telephone & Fax*: 815-550-2018; *Email*: chicago @iww.org; P.O. Box 3658, Joliet, IL 60434; *Telephone*: 815-483-8299; *Email*: joliet@iww.org; P.O. Box 507, Waukegan, IL 60079; *Email*: waukeganiww@iww.org; *Web site*: http://iww.org/branches/US/IL. *Kansas*: 300 West 14th Street, Lawrence KS 66044; *Telephone*: 785-865-1374; *Email*: contact party through its web site; *Web site*: http://iww.org/branches/US/KS. *Maine*: 75 Russell Street, Bath, ME 04530; *Email*: contact party through its web site; *Web site*: http://iww.org/branches/US/ME. *Maryland*: 800 St. Paul Street, Baltimore, MD 21202; *Telephone*: 410-230-0450; *Email*: iww@redem-mas.org; *Web site*: http://iww.org/branches/US/MD. *Massachusetts*: P.O. Box 391724, Cambridge, MA 02139; *Telephone*: 617-469-5162; *Email*: bostgmb@parsons.iww.org; *Web site*: http://iww.org/ branches/US/MA. *Michigan*: 8916 Royce, Sterling Heights, MI 48313; *Telephone*: 810-321-7154; P.O. Box 6629, Grand Rapids, MI 49516; *Email*: griww@earthlink.net; *Web site*: http://iww.org/branches/ US/MI. *Minnesota*: 1522 North 8th Avenue East, Duluth, MN 55805; *Email*: contact party through its web site; *Web site*: http:// iww.org/branches/US/MN. *Missouri*: 5506 Homes Street, Kansas City, MO 64110; *Telephone*: 816-523-3995; *Email*:kansascityiww@iww.org; *Web site*: http://iww.org/branches/US/MO. *Montana*: *Telephone*: 406-490-3869; *Email*: trampiu330@aol.com; *Web site*: http://iww.org/ branches/US/MT. *New Jersey*: P.O. Box 3107, New Brunswick, NJ 08903; *Email*: newbrunsnj@iww.org; *Web site*: http://iww.org/ branches/US/NJ. *New Mexico*: P.O. Box 4352, Albuquerque, NM 87196; *Telephone*: 505-268-1571; *Email*:abq@iww.org; *Web site*: http://iww.org/branches/US/NM. *New York*: P.O. Box 7430, JAF Station, New York, NY 10116; *Email*: iww-nyc@bari.iww.org; P.O. Box 74, Altamont, NY 12009; *Telephone*: 518-861-5617; *Web site*: http:// iww.org/branches/US/NY. *North Carolina*: 1550 Trent Boulevard #Q–4, Greensboro, NC 28560; *Email*: contact party through its web site; *Web site*: http://iww.org/branches/US/NC. *Ohio*: P.O. Box 42233, Cincinnati, OH 45242; *Email*: cincyiww@iww.org; *Web site*: http:// iww.org/branches/US/OH. *Oklahoma*: 6189 West 11th Place, Tulsa, OK 74127; *Telephone*: 918-282-7348; *Email*: contact party through its web site; *Web site*: http://iww.org/branches/US/OK. *Oregon*: P.O.

Box 371, Eugene, OR 97401; *Telephone*: 541-343-7828; *Email*: iwwlu@efn.org; P.O. Box 15005, Portland, OR 97293; 616 East Burnside Street, Portland, OR 97214; *Telephone*: 503-231-5488; *Email*: pdx@iww.org; *Web site*: http://iww.org/branches/US/OR. *Pennsylvania*: P.O. Box 796, Lancaster, PA 17608, *Telephone*: 610-358-9496; *Email*: papercranepress@erols.com; P.O. Box 42777, Philadelphia, PA 19101; *Telephone*: 215-222-1905; *Email*: phillyiww@iww.org; 139 Rossmore Street, East Pittsburgh, PA 15112; *Email*: pittsburghiww@ yahoo.com; *Web site*: http://iww.org/branches/US/PA. *Texas*: P.O. Box 650011, Austin, TX 78765; *Telephone*: 512-467-7360; *Email*: delgin@io.com; *Web site*: http://iww.org/branches/US/TX. *Utah*: P.O. Box 520835, Salt Lake City, UT 84152; *Telephone*: 801-485-1969; *Email*: slcgmb@iww.org; *Web site*: http://iww.org/branches/US/UT. *Washington*: P.O. Box 5464, Tacoma, WA 98415; P.O. Box 2775, Olympia, WA 98507; *Telephone*: 360-705-0567; *Email*: olywobs@ riseup.net; 1122 East Pike Street #1142, Seattle, WA 98122; *Telephone*: 206-931-3745; *Email*: disruptive@yahoo.com; *Web site*: http://iww.org/branches/US/WA. *Wisconsin*: P.O. Box 2442, Madison, WI 53703; 1334 Williamson Street, Madison, WI 53703; *Telephone*: 608-255-1800; P.O. Box 3010, Madison, WI 53704; *Telephone*: 773-255-5412; *Email*: baltimored1@yahoo.com; 1019 Williamson Street #B, Madison, WI 53703; *Telephone*: 608-262-9036; 100 South Baldwin Street, Madison, WI 53703; *Telephone*: 608-204-9011; P.O. Box 07632, Milwaukee, WI 53207; *Email*: contact party through its web site; *Web site*: http:// iww.org/branches/ US/WI.

Internet Party

Email: info@theinternetparty.org; *Web site*: http://www.theinternetparty.org

While not a political party in the traditional sense, the Internet Party (physically located near Philadelphia, Pennsylvania) aims to use the power of public voice, through its internet site, to return control of the government to the people. A new organization, the party basically conducts daily on-line polling on specific topics and distributes the results to its members, various political organizations, and other interested institutions.

Jeffersonian Party

Email: ReplyFrom-Jeffersonian@yahoo.com; *Web site*: http://www.JeffersonianParty.com

Reconstituted in 2000, the Jeffersonian Party promotes more personal freedom and less intrusive federal government. The party supports elimination of all federal laws, programs, and agencies not specifically authorized by the U.S. Constitution; elimination of the progressive income tax; terminating U.S. membership in the United Nations; the right of citizens to own and bear arms; and holding a Constitutional Amendment Convention every 20 years.

The original Jeffersonian Party was founded by Thomas Jefferson in 1792 as a congressional caucus in support of the Bill of Rights. In 1800, Jefferson was elected President of the United States, becoming the first of three Jeffersonian Presidents (followed by James Madison and James Monroe), who held the presidency for 24 consecutive years. The election of John Quincy Adams in 1824 led to inter-party friction and a temporary dissolution of the party.

In 2000, nearly 175 years after its dissolution, the party re-emerged as a voice for states rights and constitutional adherence. It's mission is to promote candidates for the U.S. House and Senate who support and adhere to the founding principles of Thomas Jefferson, which have been derived from his writings and speeches.

Knights Party

P.O. Box 2222, Harrison, AR 72601; *Telephone*: 870-427-3414; *Email*: asktheknights@hotmail.com; *Web site*: http://www.kkk.com

The Knights Party considers itself the "Political Voice of White Christian America" and proclaims "Equal Rights for All, Special Privileges for None." The party has had a controversial past that has, at times, caused it to lose members and popular support.

The Knights of the Ku Klux Klan was founded in Louisiana in 1956 and probably enjoyed its greatest public face when its leader, David Duke, surprised the political establishment when he received more than 700,000 votes during his run for Louisiana governor in the 1980s. Being a controversial and charismatic leader, Duke opened the closed world of the Klan by allowing media access to public Klan rallies and by engaging in national interview programs.

Using the slogan "White Pride, World Wide," the Knights Party is working to build a nationwide grass roots movement of "White Christian men, women, and children who support a return of White Christians to government." Under the leadership of Thomas Robb, associates and supporters nationwide have been working to move The Knights to center stage of American politics. Those who join the party get a free subscription to its monthly newsletter, *The Crusader*.

The party supports recognizing that America was founded as a White nation; repealing the North American Free Trade Agreement and the General Agreement on Tariffs and Trade treaties; putting American interest first in all foreign policy matters; ceasing all foreign aid; cutting off trade with countries that refuse to establish strict environmental laws; abolishing all discriminatory affirmative action programs; using the military to patrol America's borders for illegal aliens; abolishing all anti-gun laws and encouraging every adult to own a weapon; outlawing the purchase of American property and industry by foreign corporations and investors; repealing the Federal Reserve Act; encouraging private and home-schooling; creating a single, flat-rate income tax; outlawing abortion except to save the mother's life or in case of rape or incest; the death penalty for those convicted of molestation and rape; a national law against the practice of homosexuality; drug testing for welfare recipients; and the voluntary repatriation of everyone not satisfied with living under White Christian rules of conduct back to the native lands of their people.

The Ku Klux Klan came into existence at the end of the Civil War during a period called "Black Reconstruction," during which the freedom and recognition of Black citizens began to emerge. Feeling under siege from Northern-based policies forced upon it against its will, there was a strong and coordinated backlash from the South and a growing resentment against the Black race. From this conflict arose the KKK with its anti–Black, anti-government, pro–White southern men — beliefs that attracted attention and followers. During the past decades, like-minded social and political interests coalesced and evolved into a variety of so-called "White Power" parties, including the Knights Party.

Since its inception, the party has been the target of government investigations, media scrutiny and public protests. The party insists it has learned from its past excesses and has re-organized itself to better address its political concerns.

La Raza Unida (Partido Nacional La Raza Unida)

P.O. Box 13, San Fernando, CA 91340; *Telephone & Fax*: 818-365-6534; *Email*: info@LaRazaUnida.com, partido_nacional@yahoo.com; *Web site*: http://www.larazaunida.com/; http://www.pnlru.org

During the 1960s, Chicano field workers, long taken advantage of by US–based company owners and an entrenched political system, realized they needed to organize in order improve their financial status. In 1969, the concept behind La Raza Unida spread throughout the Southwest, along with other emerging Chicano political organizations. In various areas, the party emerged and focused on different issues, depending on the local circumstances. Starting in the San Francisco Bay Area, the party adopted a militant line and organized behind united working class issues. Simultaneously, in Colorado, La Raza Unida rose to power within La Crusada Por Justicia, under the leadership of Corky Gonzales. In Texas, the party focused on electing Chicanos to various Boards of Education and City Councils. And in New Mexico, the organization worked to combine the Nationalist line of Corky Gonzales and the election of Raza officials. In 1972, La Raza Unida held its first National Convention and elected José Angel Gutiérrez National Chair.

The party, through internal strife and changes caused by social events, has evolved into an independent community-based force that is dedicated to the betterment of its people and consists of student groups, agencies, mainstream political organizations, and independent community action groups.

The party supports a reduced hourly work week; renewable energy sources and low pollution resources; tuition-free higher education; universal health care; a reduced military with less international missions; free television and radio time for all candidates during election periods; and eliminating the idea of illegal aliens, with all those arriving in the United States having full rights upon arrival.

Affiliates. *Arizona*: P.O. Box 44144, Tucson, AZ 85733; *Telephone*: 520-909-6615; *Email*: nemakm53@msn.com. *California*: P.O.

Box 4265, Chula Vista, CA 91909; *Telephone:* 619-987-8063; *Fax:* 619-934-4561; *Email:* pnlrusd@hotmail.com. *New Mexico:* P.O. Box 40376, Albuquerque, NM 87196; *Telephone:* 505-255-9312; *Email:* pnlrunm@yahoo.com.

Labor Party

P.O. Box 53177, Washington, D.C. 20009; *Telephone:* 202-234-5190; *Fax:* 202-234-5266; *Email:* info@thelaborparty.org, lp@thelaborparty.org; *Web site:* http://www.thelaborparty.org

Believing that both the Democratic and Republican parties have "failed the working people," the Labor Party formed as a liberal organization created in 1996 by a group of labor unions, including the United Mine Workers, the Longshoremen, American Federation of Government Employees, and the California Nurses Association. In 1998 the party endorsed its first state and federal candidates but has, since then, remained uninvolved in electoral politics.

The party is national in scope and includes state parties, chapters and local committees, all of which organize members, promote party-related activities, and elect delegates to Labor Party conventions. The convention is the supreme governing body of the Labor Party and has final authority in all matters of national policy, program and constitution.

Between conventions, the National Council is the governing body with full authority to issue policy statements in the name of the Labor Party. The National Council is made up of representatives of the major affiliating unions and worker-supportive organizations, Labor Party chapter representatives and individuals who represent constituencies not otherwise adequately represented. The National Organizer directs the Labor Party's activities on a day-to-day basis.

The party's primary effort is promoting its 16-point Call for Economic Justice program, which includes amending the constitution to guarantee everyone a job at a living wage; paying laid-off workers two months' severance for every year of service; restoring workers' rights to organize, bargain, and strike; ending bigotry ("an injury to one is an injury to all"); guaranteeing universal access to quality health care; a 32-hour, four-day work week with 20 paid vacation days a year ("more time for family and the community"); protecting families (with paid family leave, flexible working schedules, affordable child and elder care, and minimum pensions); ensuring quality public education to all; stopping corporate abuse of trade (moving jobs to the source of the cheapest labor and ignoring labor and environmental standards that interfere with profits); ending corporate welfare by eliminating tax breaks and government subsidies); making the wealthy pay their fare share of taxes; revitalizing the public sector (strengthening the Occupational Safety and Health Administration, enforcing strict environmental protection laws, rebuilding the nation's infrastructure, and expanding local mass transportation); ending corporate domination of elections; building a transition movement to protect jobs and the environment; enforcing safety and health regulations in the workplace; and re-claiming the workplace through job design, use of technology, and development of needed skills.

The Debs-Jones-Douglass Institute is the non-profit educational and cultural arm of the Labor Party and is named for labor leaders Eugene V. Debs, Mother Jones, and Frederick Douglass. The Institute's mission is to assist in the establishment of a society in which equality of opportunity and citizenship is assured, through providing education using the fullest range of methods, curricula and delivery systems. The work of DJDI includes educational and cultural projects on health care, higher education, occupational health and safety and genetics.

Affiliates. *Arizona*: P.O. Box 1147, Tucson, AZ 85702; *Telephone*: 502-885-7673. *California*: P.O. Box 8266, Berkeley, CA 94707; *Telephone*: 510-273-9219; P.O. Box 40637, San Francisco, CA 94140; *Telephone*: 650-355-5329; P.O. Box 26446, Los Angeles, CA 90026; *Telephone*: 323-662-8228; 101 Race Street, San Jose, CA 95126; *Telephone*: 408-993-8217. *Connecticut*: P.O. Box 340, Kensington, CT 06037; *Telephone*: 860-251-6030. *Florida*: 1720 Northeast 75th Street, Gainesville, FL 32641; *Telephone*: 352-378-5655. *Illinois*: 37 South Ashland Avenue, Chicago, IL 60607; *Telephone*: 312-829-8300, 651-451-2102; P.O. Box 803226, Chicago, IL 60680; *Telephone*: 312-409-0038. *Iowa*: 1413 Franklin Street, Iowa City, IA 52240; *Telephone*: 319-354-4834. *Maine*: P.O. Box 4777, Portland, ME 04112; *Telephone*: 207-871-0218. *Massachusetts*: 26 Eddy Street, Waltham, MA 02453;

Telephone: 781-647-9350; P.O. Box 15446, Boston, MA 02215; *Telephone*: 617-547-6484. *Michigan*: P.O. Box 39192, Redford, MI 48239; *Telephone*: 248-788-6528. *Minnesota*: P.O. Box 2512, Inver Grove Heights, MN 55076; *Telephone*: 651-451-2102; *Email*: aenglish@igc.org. *Missouri*: P.O. Box 30127, Kansas City, MO 64112; *Telephone*: 816-753-1672. *New Jersey*: 243 Livingston Avenue, New Brunswick, NJ 08901; *Telephone*: 732-418-1721. *New Mexico*: P.O. Box 12546, Albuquerque, NM 87195; *Telephone*: 505-296-5485. *New York*: c/o AFSCME Local 215, 75 Varick Street, New York, NY 10013; 43 Madonna Lake Road, Cropseyville, NY 12052; *Telephone*: 518-279-3749. *Ohio*: P.O. Box 6414, P.O. Box 5652, Cleveland, OH 44101; *Telephone*: 216-382-4597. *Oregon*: P.O. Box 4731, Portland, OR 97208; *Telephone*: 503-757-8907; 298 Garfield Street, Ashland, OR 97520; *Telephone*: 541-482-6988. *Pennsylvania*: P.O. Box 34142, Philadelphia, PA 19101; *Telephone*: 215-743-4379; P.O. Box 1547, Bethlehem, PA 18018; *Telephone*: 610-865-7920; *Email*: megl001@moravian.edu; 100 North Bellefield Avenue, Pittsburgh, PA 15213; *Telephone*: 412-682-3327. *Utah*: 1160 South Denver Street, Suite D, Salt Lake City, UT 84111; *Telephone*: 801-891-6700. *Vermont*: c/o UE Local 221, P.O. Box 593, Burlington, VT 05402; *Telephone*: 802-658-6788. *Washington*: P.O. Box 94684, Seattle, WA 98124; *Telephone*: 206-382-5712. *Washington, D.C.*: 2909 Parker Avenue, Wheaton, MD 20902; *Telephone*: 301-942-0071.

League for the Revolutionary Party/Communist Organization for the Fourth International

P.O. Box 1936, Murray Hill Station, New York, NY 10156; *Telephone*: 212-330-9017; *Email*: lrpcofi@earthlink.net; *Web site*: http://www.lrp-cofi.org; P.O. Box 204, 1924 West Montrose, Chicago, IL 60613; *Telephone*: 773-463-1340.

Using the slogan "Re-create the Fourth International," the League for the Revolutionary Party is dedicated to the restoration of authentic Marxism and the political independence of the working class throughout the world. The party is joined in this effort by adherents to the Communist Organization for the Fourth International. The LRP aims to resurrect the method of Trotsky's Transitional Program and supports all struggles of the workers and oppressed, while fighting for class-wide demands that point to the need for socialist revolution.

In 2003, the Communist Organization for the Fourth International adopted a new fundamental statement of its revolutionary Marxist world view and expanded its founding Political Resolution, which is the COFI document that lays out its goals. This updated version details plans for expanding a working-class revolutionary party in the post–September 11 world.

The new document develops the party's understanding of the collapse of Stalinism and the decay of Social Democratic reformism and "Third World" nationalism. It also expands the party's analysis and program for the struggle in important areas of revolutionary work, from trade unions to the fight against racism, with new attention to the fight against rising anti–Arabism and anti–Semitism.

The document's overall theme is the task of re-creating the Fourth International, the authentic Marxist, Leninist and Trotskyist World Party of Socialist Revolution. It emphasizes that just as only the working class can overthrow capitalism, it is also true that only the working class can build the revolutionary party leadership it requires. The document also reinforces the party's condemnation of middle-class "Marxists," the so-called "condescending saviors," who claim that the working class is incapable of coming to communist self-consciousness and who proclaim the need for the enlightened intellectuals to lead the struggle against capitalism.

The party realizes that the specter of communism does not haunt the world today and recognizes that in recent decades the working class around the world has risen up time and again against the murderous and exploitative rule of capitalism. But since the Bolshevik revolution of 1917, its struggles have not led to the creation of new revolutionary workers' states, much less communism. The COFI believes that "the working class does not need ... more middle-class and bureaucratic condescending saviors ... they have been a big part of the problem and not the solution. The reason our class has not been able to take power has been the absence of a genuine proletarian leadership. The COFI fights for the renewal of that class-conscious Bolshevik leadership ... and stands for the resurrection of the theory and practice of authentic revolutionary Marxism."

The party believes that "the building of COFI is vital to the struggle of creating a classless world ... and that the fundamental principles of Bolshevik-Leninism ... have been gutted and turned to their opposite by most of the organizations that claim to carry its banner ... and that elementary communist principles have been abandoned. The abandonment of genuine Marxism was not the result of some evil conspiracy; it was the consequence of betrayals of a class character."

The basic principles of COFI include the idea that capitalism is the most advanced form of class society and is based on the extraction of surplus value through wage labor; capitalism will be recognized as the last class society in history; due to its monopolistic nature, capitalism has ceased to develop the productive forces needed to sustain itself; capitalism in decay accelerates nationalism and militarization to divert and repress the class struggle and exacerbates every social division to keep the working class divided; and racism, originally used to justify slavery in the Western hemisphere, has became an instrument to create and defend imperialist domination of the Third World. The LRP believes that these "flaws of capitalism" will eventually spell the doom of the class society and will inherently lead to the worldwide establishment of a true Marxist world.

The LRP/COFI traces its heritage to the Communist League and First International of Marx and Engels; the Second International and, after 1900, its revolutionary wings led by Lenin and Luxemburg; the Russian revolution and the Third International of Lenin and Trotsky; the Left Opposition, International Communist League and Fourth International; and the fight led by Trotsky against middle-class influences in the Fourth International. Today the revolutionary banner is carried by COFI.

COFI's resurrection of Marxist theory and practice began in 1972 and led to the founding of the Revolutionary Socialist League in 1973 and the League for the Revolutionary Party in 1976. Its views are derived from the first four Congresses of the Third International and the documents and struggles of the Communist Left Opposition and the Fourth International. The LRP publishes the *Proletarian Revolution* magazine eight times a year.

Left Party

Email: contact party through its web site; *Web site*:
http://www.leftparty.org

The Left Party works at developing a revolutionary socialist
organization of workers, the oppressed, and youth. The party believes
that a revolution that does not result in greater democratic guaran-
tees for the oppressed of society is doomed to failure. The party supports internationalism and anti-imperialism; strong environmental
policies; no military intervention outside the United States; abolition of the World Bank; repealing of the Patriot Act; abolishment of
the death penalty; legalization of prostitution; full rights for immigrants, including the right to vote; cancellation of the national debt;
a 30-hour work week; free education for all, from preschool to college; free health care; the right to vote extended to 16-year-olds; and
no prison terms for non-violent crime.

Legal Party

P.O. Box 33, Tarpon Springs, FL 34688; *Email*: contact party
through its web site; *Web site*: http://www.members.tripod.com/
legal_party

The Legal Party considers itself a "virtual-political-entity" and
was established to return the government of the United States back
to the people and out of the hands of so-called "licensed attorneys."
The party believes that for the past 60 years or so, so-called "licensed
attorneys" have usurped all three branches of government that, by
1999, has developed into an entity meant to solely serve the "privileged class," all while the lawyers charge monopolistic fees of $300.00
per hour. The party supports an end to this usurpation and seeks to
restore power back to the people.

The party supports the idea of removing licensed attorneys from
all activities, seizing their property, and closing all law schools; no
government employee shall make a wage that is greater than the lowest hourly wage paid in the private sector; government employee pen-
sion plans can be no greater that the lowest retirement plan in the
private sector; abolishing the Internal Revenue Service; for every 100
government employees (at all levels) there shall be 10 elected citizens
to monitor their activities; free health care for all; an end to forced

integration at all levels of government; free education (at all levels) for all; and no citizen ever loses their right to vote.

Liberal Party of New York

P.O. Box 140849, Staten Island, NY 10314; *Email*: lpweb@liberalparty.org; *Web site*: http://www.liberalparty.org

Spawned from the American Labor Party and founded in 1944 by leftist-leaning supporters of Franklin Roosevelt who were dissatisfied with both the Democratic and Republican parties, the Liberal Party of New York State is the longest existing third party in the history of the United States. When the American Labor Party became perceived as being too influenced by communist supporters who supported Henry Wallace's presidential bid, top leaders left and formed the Liberal Party, which endorsed Harry Truman in 1948. The party nominates and endorses candidates for a variety of offices on the basis of merit, independence, and progressive viewpoints, regardless of party affiliations, including past Liberal Party nominees such as Averell Harriman, Mario Cuomo, Jacob Javits, Robert Kennedy, Daniel Patrick Moynihan, Fiorello LaGuardia, and John Lindsay.

In 1944, the Liberal Party began making plans to expand nationally under the leadership of former Republican presidential candidate Wendell Willkie, who had left the Republican Party over philosophical differences. However, the sudden death of Willkie left the party without a nationally-recognized leader and its expansion plans were halted.

In the 1940s and 1950s, the Liberal Party supported rent control and consumer protection legislation for the state. In the 1960s, the party sponsored a legal suit in the United States Supreme Court for congressional reapportionment, one immediate result of which was the election of Shirley Chisholm, the nation's first African-American congresswoman.

The Liberal Party supports a woman's right to choose abortion; universal health care; abolishing the practice of funding private and parochial schools with taxpayer dollars; life imprisonment without parole legislation (the party oppose the death penalty); every citizen being forced to participate in the electoral process; and a complete overhaul of the state's educational system to better meet the needs of its students.

The Liberal Party has declined in influence since the 1980 election and its 1998 candidate for governor (Betsy McCaughey Ross) garnered less than two percent of the vote. After receiving relatively few votes in the 2002 election, the party lost its state recognition and ceased operations at the state level. Currently, the party's main obstacle in its attempt to revive its state-wide operations and influence is the growing popularity of the Working Families Party, which has garnered strong labor union support.

Liberal Progress Party

Email: TheLiberalProgressParty@yahoo.com; *Web site*: http://www.geocities.com/theliberalprogressparty

The goal of the Liberal Progress Party is to challenge the national conservative political agenda it sees as becoming a majority influence in America. The party believes that "it should not be the policy of the United States to preemptively strike nations to further conservative political goals." The party supports legalizing and taxing drugs ("due to the fact that the war on drugs has been completely ineffectual"); reducing the deficit and paying off the national debt; legalizing same-sex marriages; stopping drilling in the Alaskan National Wildlife Refuge; universal health coverage; and abolishing the death penalty.

Libertarian National Socialist Green Party

Email: media@nazi.org; *Web site*: http://www.nazi.org

The creation of the Libertarian National Socialist Green Party was due directly to its founding members' discontent with the direction taken by both the Democratic and Republican parties to address the nation's problems. The party disagrees with the fundamental principles of globalism and internationalism and, when created, used Green and Libertarian ideas to accent forgotten tenets of Nationalism. The platform of the Libertarian National Socialist Green Party supports making the government more responsive to its citizens while maintaining the ability for civil growth through collective effort. The party is nationalistic in nature and believes all problems should be addressed from an American point of view.

The party supports ending all no-knock warrants and government monitoring of American citizens; federal subsidizing of individual living costs to liberate creativity; decriminalize all behavior which affects only one person; federal funding to equalize public schooling; use military forces to rebuild damaged inner cities; declare English and German as the nation's official languages; free public transportation operating 24 hours a day as an alternative to driving cars; forced separation of mixed-race couples; ending all government benefits to non-citizens; stopping the World Bank's policy of making unsupported Third-World loans; imposing a value-added tax on all trade transacted within the United States; and taxing all synagogues, churches, and mosques, and recognizing them as a foreign power within America's borders.

The party formed by incorporating various aspects, beliefs and tenets from the Green Party, the Libertarian Party, various Anarchist and Socialist groups, and some of the European Pagan movements. Its point of view focuses on ideals shared by most environmental movements and their ideological ancestor, Adolf Hitler's National Socialist German Worker's Party, which was active from 1933 to 1945.

Libertarian Party (National Libertarian Party)

2600 Virginia Avenue, NW, #100, Washington, D.C. 20037; *Telephone*: 202-333-0008; *Fax*: 202-333-0072; *Email*: hq@lp.org; *Web site*: http://www.lp.org

Formed in 1971 in response to the perceived failure of the Democratic and Republican parties to serve the interests of the American people, the Libertarian Party stresses America's heritage of freedom; individual liberty and personal responsibility; a free-market economy; and a foreign policy of non-intervention, peace, and free trade. It is currently the third largest political party in the United States.

The party supports reducing the size and power of government; reducing all taxes; encouraging commerce free from government intrusion; removing the government playing an intrusive role in the lives of its citizens; ending the war on drugs; the right of citizens to keep and bear arms; keeping the military an all-volunteer force; same-sex unions; a constitutional amendment requiring government budgets be balanced by cutting expenditures and not by raising taxes; the ending of all government subsidies; a complete separation of education and state; the elimination of the Occupational Safety and Health Administration; replacing Social Security with a private, voluntary system; the withdrawal of the United States from the World Bank and the International Monetary Fund; the repeal of all laws regulating or prohibiting gambling; the repeal of the Racketeer Influenced and Corrupt Organizations Act; the repeal of all laws interfering with the right to commit suicide; the repeal of all laws that establish criminal or civil penalties for the use of drugs; eliminating all restrictions on immigration; abolishing the Department of Agriculture; repealing federal inheritance taxes; repealing of the Occupational Safety and Health Act; abolishing the Civil Service system; and the privatization of the National Aeronautics and Space Administration.

Party timeline: (1971) Libertarian Party is founded; (1972) vice presidential candidate Tonie Nathan becomes the first woman in U.S. history to receive an electoral vote; (1978) Dick Randolph of Alaska becomes the first elected Libertarian state legislator; (1979) permanent ballot status is achieved in California when more than 80,000 voters register Libertarian; (1980) presidential candidate Ed Clark appears on the ballot in all 50 states, the District of Columbia, and Guam, and receives almost one million votes; the party gains attention as a serious political entity; (1984) on the ballot in 39 states, David Bergland and Jim Lewis come in third in the race for President for the first time in the LP's history; Bergland publishes *Libertarianism in One Lesson*, a campaign book that eventually sells over 75,000 copies, and is still used today as an introductory text; (1986) Ray Cullen, candidate for Treasurer in California, gets 570,000 votes, largest vote total ever for a third party candidate in California; (1987) Libertarians are elected to every seat on the city council in Big Water, Utah; former U.S. Congressman Ron Paul resigns from the Republican Party and joins the LP and later runs as the party's presidential candidate; and (1996) the LP becomes the first third party in American history to earn ballot status in all 50 states two presidential elections in a row.

Affiliates. *Alabama*: 2330 Highland Avenue, Birmingham, AL 35205; *Telephone*: 205-328-8683; *Fax*: 205-322-1848; *Email*: contact party through its web site; *Web site*: http://www.al.lp.org. *Alaska*: PMB 373, 205 East Dimond Boulevard, Anchorage, AK 99515; *Telephone*: 907-566-1235; *Email*: contact party through its web site; *Web* *site*: http//www.ak.lp.org. *Arizona*: 4802 East Ray Road #23–255. Phoenix, AZ 85044; *Telephone*: 602-248-8425; *Fax*: 602-532-7777; *Email*: contact party through its web site; *Web site*: http://www. azlp.org. *Arkansas*: P.O. Box 15214, Little Rock, AR 72231; *Telephone*: 501-745-6341; *Email*: contact party through its web site; *Web site*: http://www.lpar.org. *California*: 14547 Titus Street #214, Panorama City, CA 91402; *Telephone*: 877-884-1776, 818-782-8400; *Fax*: 818-782-8488; *Email*: media@ca.lp.org; *Web site*: http://www.ca.lp.org. *Colorado*: 1425 Brentwood Street #18, Lakewood, CO 80214; *Telephone*: 303-837-9393; *Fax*: 303-329-0498; *Email*: statechair@lpcolorado.org; *Web site*: http://www.lpcolorado.org. *Connecticut*: P.O. Box 2501, Middletown, CT 06457; *Telephone*: 866-296-2888, 860-585-5857; *Email*: liberty@lpct.org; *Web site*: http://www.lpct.org. *Delaware*: P.O. Box 1472, Dover, DE 19903; *Telephone*: 302-659-1920; *Email*: chair@de.lp.org; *Web site*: http://www.de.lp.org. *Washington, D.C.*: P.O. Box 65803, Washington, D.C. 20035; *Telephone*: 202-636-4277; *Email*: info@lp-dc.org; *Web site*: http://www.lp-dc.org. *Florida*: P.O. Box 3012, Winter Park, FL 32790; *Telephone*: 800-478-0555, 386-749-9498; *Fax*: 386-749-1917; *Email*: contact party through its web site; *Web site*: http://www.lpf.org. *Georgia*: 1874 Piedmont Road #590–E, Atlanta, GA 30324; *Telephone*: 404-888-9468; *Fax*: 404-874-8339; *Email*: executive.director@ga.lp.org; *Web site*: http://www. lpgeorgia.com. *Hawaii*: 625 Keawe Street, Honolulu, HI 96813; *Telephone & Fax*: 808-537-3078; *Email*: contact party through its web site; *Web site*: http://www.hi.lp.org. *Idaho*: P.O. Box 895, Nampa, ID 83653; *Telephone*: 208-442-9590; *Email*: contact party through its web site; *Web site*: http://www.lpidaho.com. *Illinois*: 2808 West War Memorial Drive #E, Peoria, IL 61615; *Telephone*: 800-735-1776; *Fax*: 309-213-2474; *Email*: director@lpillinois.org; *Web site*: http:// www.il.lp.org. *Indiana*: 156 East Market Street #405, Indianapolis, IN 46204; *Telephone*: 800-388-1776, 317-920-1994; *Email*: lpinhq@ lpin.org; *Web site*: http://www.lpin.org. *Iowa*: P.O. Box 7256, Des Moines, IA 50309; *Telephone*: 800-655-5742; *Email*: lpiachair @mchsi.com; *Web site*: http://www.lpia.org. *Kansas*: P.O. Box 2456, Wichita, KS 67201; *Telephone*: 800-335-1776; *Email*: chair@lpks.org; *Web site*: http//www.lpks.org. *Kentucky*: 719 Talon Place, Louisville, KY 40223; *Telephone*: 888-595-4276; *Email*: contact party through its web site; *Web site*: http:// www.ky.lp.org. *Louisiana*: P.O. Box 66301, Baton Rouge, LA 70896; *Telephone*: 318-346-9326; *Email*: contact party through its web site; *Web site*: http://www.la.lp.org. *Maine*: P.O. Box 2020, Biddeford, ME 04005; *Telephone*: 207-780-1776; *Fax*: 207-846-0900; *Email*: contact party through its web site; *Web site*: http://www.lpme.org. *Maryland*: P.O. Box 1128, Bel Air, MD 21014; *Telephone*: 800-657-1776; *Fax*: 410-838-1043; *Email*: director@md. lp.org; *Web site*: http://www.md.lp.org. *Massachusetts*: PMB #276, 203 Washington Street, Salem, MA 01970; *Telephone*: 800-564-6576; *Email*: contact party through its web site; *Web site*: http://www. lpma.org. *Michigan*: 913 West Holmes Road, Lansing, MI 48910; P.O. Box 27065, Lansing, MI 48924; *Telephone*: 888-373-3669; *Email*: chair@lpmich.org; *Web site*: http://www.lpmich.org. *Minnesota*: 799 Raymond Avenue, St. Paul, MN 55114; *Telephone*: 800-788-2660, 651-646-8980; *Email*: info@lpmn.org; *Web site*: http://www.lpmn.org. *Mississippi*: 1625 East County Line Road #200–145, Jackson, MS 39211; *Email*: mail@mslp.org; *Web site*: http://www. concentric.net/ ~acausey/LP/lphome.htm. *Missouri*: P.O. Box 78623, St. Louis, MO 63178; *Telephone*: 877-868-3487; *Email*: info@lpmo.org; *Web site*: http:// www.lpmo.org. *Montana*: P.O. Box 4803, Missoula, MT 59806; *Telephone*: 406-721-9020; *Email*: contact party through its web site; *Web site*: http://www.mtlp.org. *Nebraska*: 3201 South 32nd Avenue, Omaha, NE 68105; *Telephone*: 402-827-1668; *Email*: chair@lpne.org; *Web site*: http://www.lpne.org. *Nevada*: P.O. Box 94554, Las Vegas, NV 89193; *Telephone*: 775-626-1776; *Email*: contact party through its web site; *Web site*: http://www.lpnevada.org. *New Hampshire*: P.O. Box 5293, Manchester, NH 03108; *Telephone*: 800-559-5764, 603-431-1618; *Email*: info@lpnh.org; Web site: http://www.lpnh.org. *New Jersey*: P.O. Box 56, Tennent, NJ 07763; *Telephone*: 800-201-6557; *Email*: contact party through its web site; *Web site*: http://www. njlp.org. *New Mexico*: PMB 182, 1380 Southeast Rio Rancho Boulevard, Rio Rancho, NM 87124; *Telephone*: 505-378-8025; *Email*: contact party through its web site; *Web site*: http://www.lpnm.org. *New York*: P.O. Box 728, Bellport, NY 11713; *Telephone*: 516-767-4688, 516-767-4688; *Email*: contact party through its web site; *Web site*: http://ny.lp.org. *North Carolina*: 1821 Hillandale Road, Box 1B-253, Durham, NC 27705; *Telephone*: 919-286-0152; *Email*: info@lpnc.org, director@lpnc.org; *Web site*: http://www.lpnc.org. *North Dakota*: *Email*: contact party through its web site; *Web site*: http://www.ndlp.org. *Ohio*: 700 Morse Road #208, Columbus, OH 43214; *Telephone*: 800-669-6542, 614-547-0290; *Fax*: 877-496-9010; *Email*: hq@lpo.org; *Web site*: http://www.lpo.org. *Oklahoma*: P.O. Box 14042, Tulsa, OK 74139; *Telephone*: 800-353-2887; *Email*: contact party through its web site; *Web site*: http://www.oklp.org. *Oregon*: 12602 Southwest Farmington Road, Beaverton, OR 97005; *Telephone*: 800-829-1992, 503-924-5991; *Fax*: 503-640-8717; *Email*: chair@lporegon.org; *Web site*: http://www.lporegon.org. *Pennsylvania*: 3863 Union Deposit Road #223, Harrisburg, PA 17109; *Telephone*: 800-774-4487; *Email*: info@lppa.org, chair@lppa.org; *Web site*: http://www.lppa.org. *Rhode Island*: Box 603159, Providence, RI 02906; *Email*: contact party through its web site; *Web site*: http://www.rilp.org. *South Carolina*: P.O. Box 7767, Myrtle Beach, SC 29572; *Telephone*: 843-267-0045; *Fax*: 843-650-5809; *Email*: chairman@sclibertarians.org; *Web site*: http://www.sclibertarians.org. *South Dakota*: P.O. Box 9341, Rapid City, SD 57709; *Email*: contact party through its web site; *Web site*: http://www.sdlp.us. *Tennessee*: P.O. Box 2361, Cookeville, TN 38502; *Telephone*: 888-960-1776; *Fax*: 423-448-6341; *Email*: contact party through its web site; *Web site*: http://lptn.net. *Texas*: P.O. Box 56426, Houston, TX 77256; *Telephone*: 800-422-1776; *Email*: director@lptexas.org; *Web site*: http://www.tx.lp.org. *Utah*: P.O. Box 526025, Salt Lake City, UT 84152; *Telephone*: 800-280-7900, 801-534-8872; *Email*: lpuexec@aol.com; *Web site*: http://www.lputah.org. *Vermont*: P.O. Box 5475, Burlington, VT 05402; *Telephone*: 800-682-1776; *Email*: contact party through its web site; *Web site*: http://www.vtlp.org. *Virginia*: 4201 Wilson Boulevard #110–164, Arlington, VA 22203; *Telephone*: 800-619-1776; *Email*: chair@lpva.com; *Web site*: http://www.lpva.com. *Washington*: P.O. Box 7118, Bellevue, WA 98008; *Telephone*: 800-353-1776, 425-641-8247; *Fax*: 425-641-9085; *Email*: contact party through its web site; *Web site*: http://www.lpws.org. *West Virginia*: P.O. Box 75423, Charleston, WV 25375; *Telephone*: 800-524-5798; P.O. Box 4058, Star City, WV 26504; *Email*: contact party through its web site; *Web site*: http://www.lpwv.org. *Wisconsin*: P.O. Box 20815, Greenfield, WI 53220; *Telephone*: 800-236-9236; *Email*: contact@lpwi.org, chair@lpwi.org; *Web site*: http://www.lpwi.org. *Wyoming*: 653 Washakie, Lander, WY 82520; *Email*: contact party through its web site; *Web site*: http://www.wyolp.org.

Liberty Union Party of Vermont

787 Western Avenue, Brattleboro VT 05301; *Telephone*: 802-257-7250; *Email*: libunion@sover.net; *Web site*: http://www.libertyunion.windham.vt.us/index.html

Founded in June 1970, the Liberty Union Party of Vermont was a major socialist third party in Vermont that believed the government is responsible for providing the security, health, and survival of its citizens. Initially, the party fielded numerous candidates for statewide elections and enjoyed a period of success in the southern part of the state. However, without much activity, the party lost its major party status in 1978 when it failed to garner five percent of the total votes cast in a state election. The party is now regrouping its efforts to make a comeback and currently supports universal free health care; free education at all levels; and the decommission of all nuclear power plants.

Light Party

20 Sunnyside Avenue #A–156, Mill Valley, CA 94941; *Telephone*: 415-381-4061; *Fax*: 415-381-2084; *Email*: freedom@lightparty.com; *Web site*: http://www.lightparty.com

Operated within the non-profit San Francisco Medical Research Foundation, the Light Party was established in 1984 as the Human Ecology Party and mainly focuses on health, spirituality, and environmental issues. The party strives to serve as a beacon of light and wisdom (thus the name) that supports individuals taking greater responsibility in improving the quality of life for themselves, their community, their nation and the world.

The party administers the National Political Awareness Test that asks candidates which items they will support if elected, but not which items they will oppose. The Light Party believes that voters are more concerned with, and attuned to, what a candidate supports, not what they will oppose. The NPAT covers a variety of issues, including abortion; budget priorities; alternative energy; taxes; defense spending; nuclear disarmament; campaign finance and government reform; crime; drugs; education; employment and affirmative action; environment and energy; gun control; health care; immigration; international aid; international policy and trade; national security; social security; technology and communications; welfare; and poverty programs.

The party considers its members a synthesis of the Republican, Democratic, Libertarian and Green Parties and maintains a goal to create "Health, Peace and Freedom For All." The party's platform includes the idea that "the strength of our nation is directly proportional to the health of our people;" the "freedom of choice tax" allows citizens to selectively fund various programs and projects they feel serve the common good and simultaneously supports the idea of a simplified flat tax plan; creating a "green" tax on all environmentally unsustainable industries (such as oil, gas, herbicides, pesticides, nuclear, logging, and timber); the restructuring of Third World debt; the use of technology to create a sustainable, global, solar hydrogen/hemp based economy; the abolition of all nuclear weapons; supports a Palestinian State and a United Nations resolution declaring the city of Jerusalem as an International City of Peace; transforming Alcatraz Island in the San Francisco Bay into The Global Peace Center; and creating a National Initiative for Democracy that will restore constitutional government and citizens rights back to the people.

Make Marijuana Legal Party of Vermont

Email: contact party through its web site; *Web site*: http://www.webspawner.com/users/makemarijuanalegal

The Make Marijuana Legal Party of Vermont "is not trying to convert anyone into a marijuana user, but is trying to convert marijuana users into voters." The primary goal of the party is to make marijuana possession and use legal to all citizens of the state over the age of 18.

Marijuana Party (Pot Party)

P.O. Box 970, Paradise, CA 95967; *Email*: contact party through its web site; *Web site*: http://www.pot-party.com

Founded in 1995 and closely affiliated with the U.S. Marijuana Party, the Marijuana Party (more commonly called the Pot Party) works to legalize marijuana growth, possession, and use. An additional goal of the party includes implementing proportional representation to ensure majority rule. Talk show host Marcus Denoon became the founder and leader of the Pot Party and ran as its presidential candidate in 1996.

Marijuana Reform Party of New York

P.O. 420, Grand Central Station, New York, NY 10163; *Telephone*: 212-370-1835; *Email*: contact party through its web site; *Web site*: http://www.marijuanareform.org

The Marijuana Reform Party of New York was established to "provide a vehicle for political action for New Yorkers who support medical marijuana and for those who want to end the criminal prohibition of marijuana." While the New York constitution does not have a provision for voter-driven ballot initiatives, the state does encourage the formation of independent, small political parties, many focused on single issues, such as the Marijuana Reform Party.

The Marijuana Reform Party of New York evolved from Thomas Leighton's campaign for Borough President of Manhattan in 1997. Using the tag line "Marijuana Greens," Leighton got three percent of the vote with a total campaign budget of only $500.00 and finished a surprising third, while defeating four other candidates from established third parties. Encouraged by these results, his campaign team decided to build on the unexpected success and formed a single-issue political party dedicated to ending marijuana prohibition.

In the following years the party was not able to match this early success but decided to continue working as a minor political party, spurred on partly by the significant increase in low-level marijuana arrests in New York City. While their 1998 campaign failed to achieve its main goal of attaining 50,000 votes (thus qualifying as an official political party), it did bring together a group of concerned citizens willing to work for change in the marijuana laws of New York, and ultimately ending the so-called War on Drugs.

The party advocates the implementation of a new marijuana policy for New York based on the program introduced in the Netherlands, where Dutch policy treats drug addiction as a public health problem rather than as a criminal justice problem. The policy works to separate the market in marijuana from that of more dangerous drugs, such as cocaine and heroin, by allowing for the legal sale and use of small amounts of cannabis in licensed shops. This policy has reduced the exposure of the relatively large numbers of marijuana users to the smaller population of hard drug users and concentrates police resources on the more serious and violent traffickers of cocaine and heroin.

Some of the party's beliefs include adults who choose to use marijuana in the privacy of their own homes should not be subject to civil or criminal sanctions; children should not use marijuana and should be provided drug education; the growth, distribution and use of marijuana should be controlled through a system of regulation and taxation; medical marijuana should be readily available to those who need it; drug addiction should be dealt with through treatment and prevention, rather than police and prisons; no parent should lose custody of their children for merely using marijuana unless such drug use was part of a larger documented pattern of neglect or abuse; all pre-employment drug testing for marijuana should be eliminated and that no person should be deprived of employment for off-the-job marijuana use; no one should be arrested in New York for merely smoking marijuana; the abolition of mandatory minimum sentencing for drug-related offenses; the government should not have the right to seize homes, cars, or any other assets of those convicted of marijuana-related offenses; and no one should be denied any government benefit, entitlement, aid or loan because of a conviction for any offense involving marijuana.

Maryland South Party

Email: mdgreyrider@aol.com; *Web site*: http://members.aol.com/mdgreyrider

The first Southern National Congress (which led to the formation of the Maryland South Party) met in Montgomery, Alabama in 2005 to "provide a renewed voice to those Southern citizens effectively disenfranchised by today's political system that does not serve the cause of liberty, justice, domestic tranquility, or national defense; but rather operates in the selfish interests of a regime inimical to the South and her people ... the SNC wants to establish itself as a permanent forum for the expression of distinct Southern interests, Southern grievances, and Southern solutions...."

Minnesota Democratic-Farmer-Labor Party

255 East Plato Boulevard, St. Paul, MN 55107; *Telephone*: 800-999-7457, 651-251-6300; *Fax*: 651-251-6325; *Email*: contact party through its web site; *Web site*: http://www.dfl.org

Affiliated with the Democratic Party, the Minnesota Democratic-Farmer-Labor Party believes "the family farm is the keystone of our society and must be preserved." The party supports the preservation and protection of farmland through soil conservation and sound sustainable ecological practices; the economic well-being of rural communities through the preservation of small business and family farms and fair prices for agricultural products; access to farm credit at reasonable terms and interest rates, including temporary relief during economic emergencies; use of agricultural surpluses to alleviate hunger in the United States and around the world; community reinvestment to promote local business and home ownership; regulation of interstate businesses, especially banks, to prevent adverse effects on locally owned businesses and banks; the all-volunteer military (no draft); increased use of renewable energy sources and decreasing dependence on nuclear power and oil; a ban on gifts from lobbyists to elected officials; nationally funded, community-based comprehensive and affordable health care for all; Israel's right to exist within secure borders and Palestinian rights to self-determination; mandatory sentencing of drug dealers; abolition of capital punishment; taxing agricultural lands on the basis of production value rather than market value; and exempting senior citizens from paying property taxes if their income does not exceed 125% of the poverty level and they live in single family homes.

Mountain Party of West Virginia (West Virginia Mountain Party)

RR 1, Box 108, Ripley, WV 25271; *Telephone*: 304-372-1455; *Email*: contact party through its web site; *Web site*: http://www.mtparty.org

The Mountain Party was created as a direct result of Denise Giardina's 2000 gubernatorial campaign. Under West Virginia election laws, a political party is a group or organization whose candidate for governor gets at least one percent of the vote in the most recent general election, which she accomplished. The party's platform is based on clean air, water, and land; responsible mining and logging practices; economic fairness and an end to corporate welfare; small community schools and limits on busing; universal health care; and campaign finance reform.

Multicapitalist Party

Email: contact party through its web site; *Web site*: http://www.oicu2.com/afc

The Multicapitalist Party advocates multicapitalism, basically a financially-driven platform designed to offer freedom and equal prosperity. The party does not intend to get involved in moral legislation (drugs, sex, abortion, criminal punishment, and more), which it feels does not belong in the hands of elected officials but rather in the hands of citizenry by direct democratic vote. The party operates as a "Mole Party" that stealthily places its members in the midst of existing parties and call themselves "Moderate Democrats" or "New Republicans."

Multicapitalism sets limits for capital successes, which allows the less fortunate a chance to fill voids created in the marketplace. Under this theory, banks, for instance, would be limited in their individual expansion to ensure the existence of numerous smaller financial institutions. Chain stores would also be limited in their financial reach, which would allow for the presence of more "mom and pop" stores throughout America.

The Multicapitalist Party was formed in 1994 and its original members covered liberals and conservatives. The party is secretive by nature and its members do not openly write political opinions or divulge membership lists. Its goal is to infiltrate existing parties and to disseminate its views and work toward its political goals.

The party supports deregulation of telephone and power companies; a national tax and the abolishment of the Internal Revenue Service; blocking federal grants to the states for social programs; and anti-trust regulations to level the playing field to allow all the opportunity to financial success.

National Alliance

P.O. Box 90, Hillsboro, WV 24946; *Telephone*: 304-653-2091; *Fax*: 304-653-4690; *Email*: contact alliance through its web site; *Web site*: http://www.natvan.com

A White nationalist organization, the National Alliance stands for a comprehensive view of life and reviews all areas of interest from a world view. It aims to work on long-term goals and unlike the Democrats or Republicans, the Alliance prides itself on not initiating goals "in reaction to current social, racial, or economic problems." The Alliance sees itself as a "part of Nature, subject to Nature's law, and recognizes the inequalities which arise as natural consequences of the evolutionary process and which are essential to progress in every sphere of life." Its members "accept our responsibilities as Aryan men and women to strive for the advancement of our race in the service of Life."

The National Alliance was organized in 1974 with many of its initial members coming from the National Youth Alliance, which had been founded in 1970 in Virginia by Dr. William Pierce. Although the ideologies of the two organizations were identical, membership in the National Youth Alliance had been restricted to those under 30 years of age, and the group had focused its efforts to college and university campuses. Forming the National Alliance broadened the appeal of the NYA to include White members of all ages, occupations, and backgrounds.

In reaction to what it felt was a coordinated effort by various Jewish organizations, among others, to destroy White society in the 1970s, the National Youth Alliance had adopted a militant, confrontational stance in opposition to these groups. The name of the group's first periodical, the tabloid *ATTACK!*, reflected this stance and its articles reinforced its militant positions. During this period, the NYA conducted street demonstrations denouncing the communists, Jews, and other avowed enemies of White America and also the federal government which tolerated and even encouraged this opposition.

Realizing that the NYA was too small to make a significant long-term difference in its fight for White survival, members recognized the need for a more long-term approach, and the formation of a larger organization, in order to "win the final battle for survival." To reflect this evolving mood, the National Alliance changed the name of its periodical from *ATTACK!* to *National Vanguard* in 1978, with a corresponding change in the political stridency of its articles.

In 1978 a group of members interested in the religious/spiritual aspects of the National Alliance's work organized the Cosmotheist Community Church just as the membership growth of the Alliance increased. Its growth was short-lived however, as the Alliance suffered a decline in membership levels during the Reagan presidential years. Decreasing membership translated into a lower national profile and the group's move from Washington, D.C. to rural West Virginia in 1985.

In 1987 the National Alliance's publishing arm, National Vanguard Books, was reorganized as a separate entity, and began offering audio cassettes in 1991. This entity publishes works by its members and leaders and is the main focal point for getting the Alliance's message out to the public. In December 1991, the Alliance began broadcasting its message worldwide via shortwave radio with its weekly program, *American Dissident Voices*. In 1992 a number of AM radio stations in the United States began carrying the party's program.

By 1989 the social and political climate in America was changing significantly and the Alliance's membership roles began to increase in reaction to "White American's realizing that their country was headed to the brink of dissolution and ruin and that the politicians in Washington were unwilling and unable to avert disaster." Since the late 1980s membership has remained steady.

The goals of the National Alliance include White Living Space (where the White Race can breed and grow away from the influence of multiculturalism; which means White schools, White residential neighborhoods and recreation areas, White workplaces, White farms, and an absence of non–Whites); an Aryan Society (creation and sustainment of White of societies that are based on Aryan values); a Responsible Government (defined as a government completely committed to the service of the White race with no non–Aryan influence); a New Educational System (one that serves three purposes: passing White cultural, intellectual, and spiritual heritage from generation to generation; teaching skills and techniques; and guiding the character development of individuals from childhood to adulthood); and an Economic Policy

Based on Racial Principles (a system that allows individuals to succeed in proportion to their capability and energy, but which, in contrast to capitalism, does not allow them to engage in socially or racially harmful activity, such as stifling competition or importing non–White labor).

Affiliates. *Alabama*: P.O. Box 241753, Montgomery, AL 36124; *Telephone*: 800-886-0242. *Arizona*: 13413 North 35th Avenue, Phoenix, AZ 85029; *Telephone*: 602-595-5175. *Arkansas*: P.O. Box 203, Lincoln, AR 72744; *Email*: info@natallar.com; *Web site*: http://www.natallar.com. *California*: P.O Box 82161, Bakersfield, CA 93380; *Telephone*: 661-387-1910; P.O. Box 215771, Sacramento, CA 95821; *Telephone*: 916-486-5588; *Email*: SactoAlliance@hotmail.com; P.O. Box 7831, Van Nuys, CA 91409; *Telephone*: 818-895-1314; *Web site*: http://www.natallca.com; Riverside, *Telephone*: 951-789-4215. *Colorado*: P.O. Box 2752, Denver, CO 80201; *Telephone*: 303-273-5523; P.O. Box 2125, Colorado Springs, CO 80901; *Telephone*: 719-522-4409; *Email*: nacsprings@yahoo.com; *Web site*: http://www.natallco.com. *Georgia*: P.O. Box 6398, Savannah, GA 31414; *Email*: contact party through its web site; *Web site*: http://www.natallga.org. *Illinois*: P.O. Box 553, Downers Grove, IL 60515; *Telephone*: 630-929-3130; *Email*: natallchicago@hotmail.com; *Web site*: http://www.natallchicago.com. *Indiana*: P.O. Box 421074, Indianapolis, IN 46242; *Email*: indianapolis@natallindy.com; *Web site*: http://www.natallindy.com. *Kentucky*: *Telephone*: 800-220-8154; *Email*: natall_louisville@yahoo.com. *Louisiana*: *Telephone*: 800-488-1364; *Email*: info@nalouisiana.com; *Web site*: http://www.nalouisiana.com. *Maryland*: P.O Box 43433, Baltimore, MD 21236; *Telephone*: 410-813-4017; *Email*: maryland@natallmd.com; *Web site*: http://www.natallmd.com. *Massachusetts*: P.O. Box 423, Hathorne, MA 01937; *Telephone*: 617-389-9139; *Email*: contact party through its web site; *Web site*: http://www.natallboston.com. *Michigan*: P.O. Box 700502, Plymouth, MI 48170; *Telephone*: 734-786-7603; Traverse City, *Telephone*: 231-922-1989; *Email*: contact party through its web site; *Web site*: http://www.natallmi.com. *Minnesota*: P.O. Box 21335, Columbia Heights, MN 55421; *Telephone*: 612-782-7130. *Mississippi*: Southaven, *Telephone*: 662-796-9852. *Nebraska*: P.O. Box 34034, Omaha, NE 68134; *Telephone*: 402-978-4829; *Email*: omaha@natallneb.com; *Web* *site*: http://www.natallneb.com. *Nevada*: P.O. Box 15151, Las Vegas, NV 89114; *Telephone*: 702-320-4885; *Email*: info@lasvegasnationalalliance.com; *Web site*: http://www.lasvegasna.com. *New Jersey*: P.O. Box 956, Hewitt, NJ 07421; *Telephone*: 973-697-1011; *Email*: unitleader@natallnj.com; *Web site*: http://www.natallnj.com. *New York*: P.O. Box 184, West Hurley, NY 12491; *Telephone*: 212-978-3919; *Email*: midhud@natallhv.com; 1436 Altamont Avenue, PMB #176, Schenectady, NY 12303; *Email*: albanyna@natallhv.com; 2604 Elmwood Avenue, PMB #118, Rochester, NY 14618; *Email*: rochesterna@natallwny.com; *Web site*: http://www.natallwny.com. *North Carolina*: Benson, *Telephone*: 919-207-2047; Raleigh, *Telephone*: 919-785-0600; 43 Sheep Rock Road, Snow Camp, NC 27349; *Telephone*: 919-742-2438. *Ohio*: Cleveland, *Telephone*: 440-230-2450. *Tennessee*: Memphis, *Telephone*: 901-205-0575. *Texas*: Dallas/Ft. Worth, *Telephone*: 817-355-4774. *Utah*: P.O. Box 71752, Salt Lake City, UT 84171; *Telephone*: 801-264-5554; *Email*: contact party through its web site; *Web site*: http://www.utahna.com. *Washington*: Seattle, *Telephone*: 360-633-1045; *Email*: seattlewa@hotmail.com; *Web site*: http://www.natallwa.com. *West Virginia*: P.O. Box 90, Hillsboro, WV 24946; *Telephone*: 304-653-4600. *Wyoming*: P.O. Box 381, Douglas, WY 82633; *Telephone*: 800-201-9547; *Email*: natallwy@yahoo.com; *Web site*: http://www.natallwy.com.

National Barking Spider Resurgence Party

493 South Youngfield Court #304, Lakewood CO 80228; *Email*: nbsrparty2008@yahoo.com; *Web site*: http://www.outofthinair. homestead.com/nbsrparty.html

Using the slogan "Don't Drink and Vote," the humorous National Barking Spider Resurgence Party was formed in 1999 after the untimely death of comedian Pat Paulsen, a repeat independent candidate for the presidency of the United States, and the end of the comic strip *Bloom County/Outland* in newspapers. The party's name is derived from the slang term "barking spider," which refers to audible flatulence, a sure sign of an election year. Today's party is determined to encourage triple coupon Saturdays and ballots even a child can understand.

The party was founded by Mike Bay to fill the legacy held by Pat

Paulsen in providing an outsider perspective on insider politics. He named the party the National Barking Spider Resurgence Party in honor of the comic strip's irreverent perspective on American politics.

The party supports a flat tax (and firing all tax lawyers); clean air and clean water policies; the use of methane gas as an alternative energy source; the purchase of at least $25.00 annually on Girl Scout cookies, preferably Thin Mints; eliminating the national Department of Education and returning school control to the states; and meatloaf.

National Disability Party of the USA

Email: contact party through its web site; *Web site*: http://www.disabilityparty.com

Established in February 2000, the National Disability Party of the USA was created by a group of people with disabilities who wanted to make changes in how the government treated them and other handicapped citizens. The Party supports the Americans with Disabilities Act, Individuals with Disabilities Education Act, and the Rehabilitation Act. The principal motivation of the National Disability Party is to "treat all persons (disabled or not) with dignity in every aspect of daily life."

National Socialist Movement (America's Nazi Party)

P.O. Box 580669, Minneapolis, MN 55458; *Telephone*: 651-659-6307; *Email*: nsmcommander@hotmail.com; *Web site*: http://2www.nsm88.com

Formed in 1974, the National Socialist Movement demands the "union of all Whites into a greater America on the basis of the right of national self-determination... equality of rights for the American people in its dealings with other nations ... and the revocation of the United Nations, the North Atlantic Treaty Organization, the World Bank, the North American Free Trade Agreement, the World Trade Organization, and the International Monetary Fund."

The party believes that "the United States has the right to seize other lands and territory in order to feed Americans and to settle surplus population ... only members of the nation may be citizens of the state and only those of pure White blood may be members of the nation ... non-citizens may live in America only as guests and must be subject to laws for aliens ... no Jews or homosexuals may be a member of the nation."

The party supports the deportation of non-citizens if it becomes impossible to feed citizens; preventing non–White immigration; the peaceful or forceful emigration of all non–Whites currently living in America; the abolition of incomes unearned by work; the confiscation of all war profits; discontinuing taxes on things of life's necessity (food, clothing, shelter, and medicine); the abolition of rent and taxes on all property; prohibition of abortion except in cases of rape, incest, race-mixing, or mental retardation; the right of citizens to bear arms; the idea that no non–American newspapers may appear without the express permission of the State; and the creation of a strong central national government.

Affiliates. *Alabama*: *Email*: contact party through its web site; *Web site*: http://www.nsm88.com/units/alabama.html. *Alaska*: *Email*: contact party through its web site; *Web site*: http://www.nsm88. com/units/alaska.html. *Arizona*: *Email*: contact party through its web site; *Web site*: http://www.nsm88.com/units/arizona.html. *Arkansas*: P.O. Box 10973, Conway, AR. 72034; *Telephone*: 501-697-2586; *Email*: nsmarkansas@ansempire.net; *Web site*: http://www.nsm88.com/ units/arkansas.html. *California*: P.O. Box 423918, San Francisco, CA 94142; *Telephone*: 415-346-1231; P.O. Box 3087, Oceanside, CA 92051; *Email*: nsm88_socal_unitleader@yahoo.com; *Web site*: http://www. nsm88.com/units/california.html. *Colorado*: *Email*: coloradofacist@ yahoo.com; *Web site*: http://www.nsm88.com/units/colorado.html. *Connecticut*: contact party through its web site; *Web site*: http://www. nsm88.com/units/connecticut.html. *Delaware*: *Email*: nsmdelaware@ yahoo.com; *Web site*: http://www.nsm88.com/units/delaware.html. *Florida*: *Email*: contact party through its web site; *Web site*: http://www.nsm88.com/units/florida.html. *Georgia*: *Email*: nsmgeorgia@hotmail.com; *Web site*: http://www.nsm88.com/units/ georgia.html. *Hawaii*: *Email*: contact party through its web site; *Web site*: http://www.nsm88.com/units/hawaii.html. *Idaho*: P.O. Box 906, Athol, ID 83801; *Email*: nsmidah088@yahoo.com; *Web site*: http://www.nsm88.com/units/idaho.html. *Illinois*: P.O. Box 7204, Villa Park, IL. 60181; *Email*: chitownbrown88@yahoo.com; *Web site*: http://www.nsm88.com/units/illinois.html. *Indiana*: P.O. Box 410,

Wakarusa, IN 46573; *Telephone*: 574-862-1765; P.O. Box 2, Lebanon, IN 46052; *Email*: nsm_fortwayne@hotmail.com; *Web site*: http://www.nsm88.com/units/ indiana.html. *Iowa*: *Email*: i_am_naziskin@yahoo.com; *Web site*: http://www.nsm88.com/units/iowa.html. *Kansas*: P.O. Box 95, Scandia, KS 66966, P.O. Box 2384, Hutchinson, KS 67504; *Telephone*: 620-921-0194; *Email*: nsmkansascity@hotmail.com; *Web site*: http://www.nsm88.com/units/kansas.html. *Kentucky*: *Email*: contact party through its web site; *Web site*: http://www.nsm88.com/units/kentucky.html. *Louisiana*: *Email*: nsmwarrior-louisiana@yahoo.com; *Web site*: http://www.nsm88.com/units/louisiana.html. *Maine*: *Email*: contact party through its web site; *Web site*: http://www.nsm88.com/units/maine.html. *Maryland*: *Email*: contact party through its web site; *Web site*: http://www.nsm88.com/units/maryland.html. *Massachusetts*: *Email*: nsmboston@hotmail.com; *Web site*: http://www.nsmne.net; http://www.nsm88.com/units/massachusetts.html. *Michigan*: P.O. Box 1042, Cadillac, MI 49601; *Email*: nsmmichigan@hotmail.com; *Web site*: http://www.nsmmichigan.us. *Minnesota*: P.O. Box 580669, Minneapolis, MN 55458; *Telephone*: 651-659-6307; *Email*: nsmcommander@hotmail.com; *Web site*: http://www.nsm88.com/units/minnesota.html. *Mississippi*: *Email*: contact party through its web site; *Web site*: http://www.nsm88.com/units/mississippi.html. *Missouri*: *Email*: contact party through its web site; *Web site*: http://www.nsm88.com/units/missouri.html. *Montana*: *Email*: contact party through its web site; *Web site*: http://www.nsm88.com/units/montana.html. *Nebraska*, *Email*: contact party through its web site; *Web site*: http://www.nsm88.com/units/nebraska.html. *Nevada*, P.O. Box 81841, Las Vegas NV 89180; *Email*: vegas1488@hotmail.com; *Web site*: http://www.nsm88.com/units/nevada.html. *New Hampshire*, *Email*: contact party through its web site; *Web site*: http://www.nsm88.com/units/newhampshire.html. *New Jersey*, P.O. Box 2101, Livingston, NJ 07039; *Email*: whitetiger1724@earthlink.net; *Web site*: http://www.nsm88.com/units/newjersey.html. *New Mexico*, *Email*: brownshirt882000@yahoo.com; *Web site*: http://www.nsm88.com/units/newmexico.html. *New York*: *Email*: contact party through its web site; *Web site*: http://www.nsm88.com/units/newyork.html. *North Carolina*, P.O. Box 9212, Greensboro, NC 27429; *Telephone*: 651-659-6307; *Email*:

contact party through its web site; *Web site*: http://www.nsm88.
com/com/units/ncarolina.html. *North Dakota*: *Email*: contact party
through its web site; *Web site*: http://www.nsm88.com/units/
northdakota.html. *Ohio*, P.O. Box 435, Lakewood, OH 44107; *Telephone*: 937-286-6984; P.O. Box 181, Covington, OH. 45318; *Email*:
nsmwestoh@earthlink.net; *Web site*: http://www.nsm88.com/units/
ohio.html. *Oklahoma*, P.O. Box 8226, Tulsa, OK 74101; *Telephone*:
580-873-9906; *Email*: nsoklahoma@arbuckleonline.com; *Web site*:
http://www.nsm88.com/units/oklahoma.html. *Oregon*, P.O. Box 2177,
Eugene, OR 97402; *Email*: contact party through its web site; *Web
site*: http://www.nsm88.com/units/oregon.html. *Pennsylvania*, P.O.
Box 5250, Bethlehem, PA 18015; P.O. Box 39214, Philadelphia, PA
19136; P.O. Box 101, Myerstown, PA 17067; *Email*: nsmberkspa@hot-
mail.com; *Web site*: http://www.nsm88.com/units/pennsylvania.html.
Rhode Island: *Email*: contact party through its web site; *Web site*:
http://www.nsm88.com/units/rhodeisland.html. *South Carolina*, P.O.
Box 239, Enoree, SC 29335; *Email*: contact party through its web site;
Web site: http://www.nsm88.com/units/scarolina.html. *South Dakota*:
Email: nsmsouthdakota@yahoo.com; *Web site*: http://www.nsm88.
com/units/southdakota.html. *Tennessee*: *Email*: contact party through
its web site; *Web site*: http://www.nsm88.com/units/tennessee.html.
Texas: *Email*: contact party through its web site; *Web site*: http://
www.nsm88.com/units/texas.html. *Utah*: *Email*: contact party
through its web site; *Web site*: http://www.nsm88.com/units/
utah.html. *Vermont*: *Email*: contact party through its web site; *Web
site*: http://www.nsm88.com/units/vermont.html. *Virginia*, P.O. Box
493, Harrisonburg, VA 22803; *Email*: nsmvirginia@hotmail.com; *Web
site*: http://www.nsm88.com/units/virginia.html; http://www.wes-
pawner.com/users/virginia88/index.html. *Washington*, *Email*: wash-
ingtonnsm88@yahoo.com; *Web site*: http://www.nsm88.com/
units/washington.html. *West Virginia*, P.O. Box 147, Romney, WV
26757; *Email*: nsmwv@yahoo.com; *Web site*: http://www.nsm88.com/
units/westvirginia.html. *Wisconsin*: *Email*: contact party through its
web site; *Web site*: http://www.nsm88.com/units/wisconsin.
html. *Wyoming*: *Email*: contact party through its web site; *Web site*:
http://www.nsm88.com/units/wyoming.html

National Socialist White People's Party

Eastpointe, MI; *Email*: contact party through its web site; *Web site*: http://www.nswpp.org

Originally called the American Nazi Party, the National Socialist White People's Party was created by George Lincoln Rockwell (a former naval officer and cartoonist) in Arlington, Virginia in 1959 with the main goal of developing Nazism in America. The party evolved from the Committee to Free America from Jewish Domination, an earlier Rockwell organization, changed its name from the American Nazi Party in 1967, and is modeled after the German Nazi Party, including uniforms and armbands with swastikas.

The party believes that "the Aryan race is under attack worldwide and that there exists a very real possibility that White people may vanish from the face of the earth altogether if something is not done to halt, and then to roll back, the advancing tide of liberalism and racial mixing which liberal democracy has brought about." After years of dormancy, the party is being re-launched along the lines of Rockwell's legacy and is based in Eastpointe, Michigan.

Nationalist Workers Party (Knights of Freedom)

Email: kof_ss_command@hotmail.com;*Web site*: http://www.members.tripod.com/ANP_KOF/AAP.html

The Nationalist Workers Party (Knights Of Freedom) is a political organization for members of the White Race and promotes racial pride and the advancement of the white race.

Native American Party

24338 El Toro Road # E111, Laguna Woods, CA 92637; *Email*: ChiefJack4Prez@www.msnusers.com; *Web site*: http://www.msnusers.com/Chiefjack4Prez/nativeamericanparty.msnw

The Native American Party represents and sponsors Native Americans, the original inhabitants of the country. Among other issues, the party supports a smaller, less centralized government.

Natural Law Party (see United States Peace Government)

Nebraska Party

87288 543rd Avenue, Wausa, NE 68786; *Telephone*: 402-586-2579; *Email*: information@nebraskaparty.org; *Web site*: http://www.nebraskaparty.org

Feeling that the major political parties are out of touch with the average American, the Nebraska Party was established to "restore economic prosperity to all Nebraskans, to restore the Christian Principles of our Forefathers, and to get the Government back in the hands of the people." The party is founded on the principles of the Democrat-Republican Party, which was established in the early 1800s by Thomas Jefferson and represents the working people (labor), family farmers, small business and, senior citizens. The party supports smaller government (at all levels); the abolition of affirmative action programs; the abolition of abortion; and that the responsibility of the government is to support the Christian principles of the nation's forefathers.

Neo Whig Party

P.O. Box 3244, St. George, UT 84790; *Telephone*: 435-673-0251; *Email*: info@neowhig.org; *Web site*: http://www.neowhig.org

A party with a sense of humor, the Neo Whig Party supports the elimination of the income tax, to be replaced with the jack-ass tax; a mandatory death penalty for those who draw graffiti; the idea that the Geneva Convention does not apply to Muslims or the French; use the owl as the party's symbol because they believe its members are smarter than everyone else; judges and lawyers must wear white wigs at all times, even in the shower; fat women are prohibited from wearing low-riders and belly shirts; every town with a population of over 400 must have at least one Starbucks, preferably two; all flight attendants must be female, under the age of 30, unmarried and Swedish; Rhode Island, Massachusetts and Vermont to lose statehood and revert to colony status; speed limits and parking meters to be prohibited by constitutional amendment; "What, Me Worry?" to replace E Pluribus Unum as national motto; John Wayne to replace President Franklin Roosevelt on the dime; Operation Self-Esteem — free breast implants for all women smaller than 40D; all beer, wine and liquor containers will be required to sport labels extolling the health benefits of daily adult beverage consumption; Operation

Latino Outreach — bull-fighting will be legalized in all 50 states; the State of the Union Address will be given in Latin, and U.S. senators will be required to wear togas when they are in the Senate chambers.

The Neo-Whig Manifesto includes such observations as the combined IQ of Hollywood is less than the total number of teeth of three randomly selected West Virginians; political correctness is a polite expression for Stalinism; vegetarians are basically evil people; high culture is better than pop culture; rap is not music; people who don't like jazz are communists and/or perverts; the death penalty is good and its use should be extended, perhaps to overdue library books or spammers; the designated hitter rule is an abomination and should be eliminated from the American League; soccer is a sissy sport; and Groundhog Day should be a national holiday.

Netocratic Party

Email: contact party through its web site; *Web site*: http://www. guerrillacampaign.com/netocrats.htm

Netocratic Party members believe that "Republicans are crooks, the Democrats are bribed, and every other party is run by flakes and that every new political movement turns out to serve someone else's agenda or has some other fatal flaw that prevents you from supporting it."

The party opposes electronic eavesdropping by governments for the purposes of political blackmail, economic espionage and the suppression of dissent; condemns the persistent ignorance and greed which have led humanity to the brink of global environmental catastrophe; demands immediate action to attempt to limit the human suffering and economic losses which will occur because of climate change; opposes prohibition and the militarization of the "War on Drugs"; advocates sobriety, opposes drug and alcohol abuse, and supports a massive increase in funding for prevention and rehabilitation programs; supports universal health care; supports the creation of a 21st century global information sharing alliance to exploit recent advances in space, nano-, bio-, and other technologies; and supports educational reform worldwide to help the spread of knowledge via the internet.

New American Independent Party

Email: info@newamericanindependent.com; *Web site*: http://
www.newamericanindependent.com/index.html

Launched in 2004 in Wayne, Pennsylvania, the New American
Independent Party came into existence as an alternative to the current two-party system, which its founders believe "are not addressing the issues important to America and its citizens, including illegal
immigration, dependence on foreign oil, the outsourcing of American jobs, and the poor state of the public school system."

The party supports electoral reform (increasing voter participation and ending obstacles for independent and third-party candidates); participating in fair trade agreements, rather than free trade
agreements, in order to decrease the nation's trade deficits, ending
the North American Free Trade Agreement and the Central American Free Trade Agreement; ending outsourcing of American jobs;
using military troops to help protect and patrol America's borders;
better protecting America's nuclear power plants, trains, and dams
from terrorist attacks; taking a more neutral stance on the Israeli-
Palestinian conflict and re-evaluating the amount of military aid
given to Israel; investing in research for alternative fuel sources and
ending America's heavy reliance on foreign oil; ending the nation's
"Neo-Conservative Agenda" and stop the government from trying to
shape the world in America's image; strictly enforcing current illegal immigration laws while creating incentives for immigrants to
work in the established legal process to become U.S. citizens; a clearly-
defined separation of church and state while recognizing the importance religion plays in the history of the United States and in the lives
of its citizens; resolving any flaws in the current Social Security program, but not allowing for private accounts; health care for all citizens and allowing for the importation of cheaper drugs from Canada;
fully funding education at all levels for all Americans, but ending
private school vouchers; ceasing teaching the "standardized test" to
students and focus instead on real-word needs; state and federal balanced budget amendments to their respective constitutions; working to save "family farms" and controlling farming conglomerates;
the right of citizens to own and bear arms and advocate harsher
penalties for those who use weapons while committing crimes; releas-

ing from jail non-violent offenders and re-directing their sentences to public service programs that would benefit local communities; and harsher punishment for individuals convicted of animal cruelty or abuse.

New Black Panther Party

Telephone: 888-317-0688; *Email*: newpantherparty@aol.com; *Web site*: http://www.newblackpanther.com

The New Black Panther Party believes in "power in the hands of the people, wealth in the hands of the people, and arms in the hands of the people." The party wants Black America to have the right of self-determination (including a separate state or territory solely for Black citizens) and the same access to jobs and wealth as does "White America."

The 10-point program of the New Black Panther Party includes freedom and the ability to determine the destiny of local communities and the Black Nation; full employment for the Black Nation; tax exemption (as long as the Black Nation does not share the same opportunities as White America), an end to the robbery of the Black Nation by Capitalists, an end to the capitalistic domination of Africa, and repatriations for past offenses; decent housing, free health-care, and an end to the trafficking of drugs targeted at Black America; an educational system that shares and defines the role of Black America in the history of the United States; military exemption for all Black men and women; an end to police harassment, brutality, and murder of Black Americans along with the creation of community-based Black self-defense groups; freeing all Black men and women from international, military, federal, state, county, and city jails and prisons; ensuring that all Black men and women who are brought to trial be judged by a jury of their peers from Black communities; and an end to the racist death penalty as it is applied to Black and oppressed people in the United States.

New England Freedom Association

P.O. Box 841, Nutting Lake, MA 01865; *Email*: contact association through its web site; *Web site*: http://www.geocities.com/free-newengland

The New England Freedom Association is the first political organization to represent the people of the New England area (also called the Atlantic Northeast) and aims to address their concerns and to call for greater freedom and autonomy, if not yet outright independence. The NEFA (which includes the states of Connecticut, Maine, Massachusetts, New Hampshire, Rhode Island, and Vermont) believes that "our geography ... environment ... rich vibrant culture, and the way we view life and society dictates that we are unique from that to the rest of the United States" and are worthy of being their own nation. The Association also believes the United States has become too powerful and increasingly oppressive throughout the world and within its own borders.

The basic goal of NEFA is to achieve greater sovereignty, if not outright independence, for New England from the U.S. federal government and creating the Republic of New England. Once the Republic is formed, the NEFA would then support returning governmental authority to the counties and cities; privatizing as many government services as possible and streamlining the rest of its functions; eliminating jail time for all victimless crimes; eliminating the Electoral College; withdrawing from the North Atlantic Treaty Organization and possibly the United Nations; establishing embassies and consulates around the world; creating a Department of Native Affairs that will address the needs and issues of all tribes; ending deficit budgets; abolishing the Internal Revenue Service; abolishing vice laws regarding prostitution and gambling; abolishing the death penalty; private medical providers and plans (no universal health care); repealing all taxes on income or property; and dissolving all government agencies concerned with transportation (the Department of Transportation, the Interstate Commerce Commission, the Federal Aviation Administration, the National Transportation Safety Board, the Coast Guard, and the Federal Maritime Commission).

New England National Party (see New England Freedom Association)

New Federalist Party

5383 Apache Trail, Harrison, MI 48625; *Email*: contact party through its web site; *Web site*: http://www.geocities.com/new_feder-alists/index.html

Reacting to the perceived inability of the Democratic or Republican parties to address issues important to many Americans, the New Federalist Party, initially focused in the northeastern states, was founded in 2001 and focuses its efforts through regional affiliates. Based on the themes of the original Federalist Party (created in 1787 by Alexander Hamilton), the New Federalist Party's tenets include a strict stance on abortion and promoting the importance of public education.

The party supports the preservation of the environment for its use by mankind and for a strong Environmental Protection Agency; stopping the drilling in the Arctic National Wildlife Refuge; a strong national government; strict enforcement of current gun laws; using any national surplus to pay off the national debt; a strong military and maintaining current spending levels; stopping Anti Ballistic Missile testing; the Federal Communications Commission and its oversight of network television; a reduction in the dependency on foreign oil and investigation into alternative energy sources; a ban on abortion; and a strong public education system, including an end to school vouchers.

New Jersey Conservative Party

15 Terrace Road, Boonton, NJ 07005; *Telephone*: 732-349-9910; *Email*: info@njcp.org, njcpsst@earthlink.net; *Web site*: http://www.njconservativeparty.org; http://www.njcp.org

Founded in 1992, the New Jersey Conservative Party supports the proposed Federal Marriage Amendment to the United States Constitution, restricting the appellate jurisdiction of all federal courts, and the removal of federal judges who refuse to enforce the law as written. The primary goals of the NJCP are to make the government more accountable to the people and to downsize its scope and size.

The party supports citizen candidates and not professional politicians to run for elective office; having the financial records of all government institutions available to all citizens through local libraries; term limits for the New Jersey Legislature; a law that limits New Jersey officials from holding only one elective office simultaneously; ending mandatory paid family leave; laws prohibiting using public money for political campaigns; privatization of government services; limiting the annual growth of property taxes to either 3% or the rate of inflation, whichever is less; ending property taxes being used for schools; school vouchers; the death penalty for murder; the closure of the New Jersey Department of Environmental Protection and Energy and the elimination of the Pinelands Commission; a ban on partial-birth abortions and ending human cloning and embryonic stem cell research; the right of citizens to bear arms; English being mandated as the "official" language of New Jersey; abolishing public pensions and benefits for part time elected officials; and withdrawal of the United States from the United Nations.

New Jersey Independents

P.O. Box 86, Hackensack, NJ 07602; *Telephone*: 201-487-3748; *Email*: nji_1@netzero.com; *Web site*: http://njind.org

Founded in the early 1990s, the New Jersey Independents is affiliated with the North Jersey Independent Alliance. NJI runs and/or supports independent candidates who support the party's platform, which includes an end to foreign policies based on global military supremacy; universal health care; a women's right to choose medical procedures concerning her body; strong environmental policies; a graduated income tax; campaign finance reform; and an end to the two-party system.

New Jersey Lesbian and Gay Coalition

P.O. Box 11335, New Brunswick, NJ 08906; *Telephone*: 732-828-6772; *Email*: mail@njlgc.org; *Web site*: http://www.njlgc.org

The non-profit New Jersey Lesbian and Gay Coalition, along with the Personal Liberty Fund, supports fighting discrimination based on sexual/affectional orientation or gender identification and enhancing the quality of lives of lesbian, gay, bisexual, transgendered, and intersexed people in New Jersey. The Personal Liberty Fund is a non-profit association of individuals, groups and businesses committed to helping lesbian, gay, bisexual, and transgender people in the state.

In 1972, interested individuals and groups met at Rutgers University to form a clearinghouse for lesbian and gay events that eventually led to adopting the name New Jersey Lesbian and Gay Coalition. Some of the groups represented at this initial meeting included the Rutgers University Student Homophile League (now called BiGLARU: Bisexual, Gay and Lesbian Alliance at Rutgers University), the Gay Activists Alliance of New Jersey, the Gay Activist Alliance in Morris County, the William Paterson College Gay Alliance, the Daughters of Bilitis, the Fairleigh Dickinson Student Homophile League, the Gay Activists Alliance of Jersey City, and the Gay Alliance of Princeton.

Dormant for a few years, the Coalition reappeared in 1975 with a call for lesbian and gay organizations around the state to organize an educational conference at Rutgers. This gathering was well received and a second conference followed in 1976. During the late 1970s the Coalition turned away from its initial education-related goals and became more politically-oriented in nature and played a major role in the 1979 March on Washington for Lesbian and Gay Rights. Another major factor that pushed the Coalition to become more politically active was a bill sponsored by State Senator Joseph Maressa of Camden County that would identify sodomy as a crime. The Coalition joined forces with other like-minded organizations and elected individuals to help convince the senator to withdraw his bill.

This success emboldened the Coalition's political activities and led it to fight other laws aimed against the gay community. In 1982 the group drafted legislation aimed to amend the New Jersey Law Against Discrimination so that it would include sexual orientation as one of the grounds upon which it would be illegal to discriminate in housing, employment, education, public accommodations and the provision of state services. From this experience, the Coalition began focusing more and more of its efforts on using political strategies to obtain its goals. In the 1980s, the Coalition led the educational and political efforts to spread the word about AIDS and to encourage the disease be treated as a health problem, not as a political issue.

At the end of 1983, the Coalition created its tax-exempt, legal defense and education arm, The Personal Liberty Fund, with the primary goal of securing private, philanthropic, and government funding for the work it was doing on researching Acquired Immune Deficiency Syndrome, education, and other related legal issues. The

PLF hired a series of AIDS Education Coordinators and promoted the "Frisky Not Risky" safer-sex campaign. The Fund worked with gay and non-gay groups to raise public awareness of AIDS and to foster non-discrimination for persons afflicted with the disease. The PLF also provided legal advice and representation in various court cases.

Since this start, the two organizations have continued their fight for gay rights and have been involved in numerous original and creative events, such as the first New Jersey Lesbian and Gay Pride Parade, Festival, Rally and Concert held in Asbury Park.

New Party

88 Third Avenue #313, Brooklyn, NY 11217; *Telephone*: 800-200-1294; *Email*: inforequest@newparty.org; *Web site*: http://www. newparty.org

The New Party is an umbrella organization for grassroots political groups working to "break the stranglehold that corporate money and corporate media have over our political process." The party's long-term strategy is to change states' election rules to allow fusion voting, a method of voting that allows minor parties to have their own ballot line with which they can either endorse their own candidates or endorse the candidates of other parties. Through fusion, minor parties don't have to compete in the winner-take-all two-party system and can avoid "spoiling" by throwing an election to the most conservative candidate by splitting the votes that might go to two more progressive candidates.

New Progressive Party of Wisconsin (affiliated with the New Party)

New Union Party

1821 University Avenue, #S116, St. Paul, MN 55104; *Email*: nup@minn.Net; *Web site*: http://www1.minn.net/~nup

The New Union Party shares with all Socialist organizations a theoretical foundation in the writings of Karl Marx and Friedrich Engels. The party's ideological roots lie in the revolutionary labor movement of the United States between 1890 to 1914. Although the

NUP advocates political and social revolution, it is committed to "lawful activities to overthrow the capitalist economic system."

The party believes that economic, social and environmental problems cannot be solved under capitalism; socialism is not state control from the top down but, instead, is a stateless workplace democracy built from the bottom up; and a union of all workers provides the economic power needed to fight the corporations of today in order to manage production for human needs instead of profits for tomorrow.

The New Union Party is comprised of men and women who are committed to building a rank-and-file working-class movement for fundamental social change. The NUP's goal is to replace the current competitive, class-divided system of capitalism with the cooperative industrial community, called economic democracy. The New Union Party was founded in 1980, after existing since 1974 as a group called The New Unionists. While the party remains based in Minnesota, its goal is to develop into a national organization.

No Political Affiliation Party of Florida

901 Ironwood Court, Marco Island, FL 34145; *Telephone*: 239-394-8336.

A local political party.

One Earth Party (of Iowa)

Email: contact party through its web site; *Web site*: http://www.oneearthparty.org

The One Earth Party aims to unite everyone ("we are all one on this planet") in a common cause of solving the world's problems. The party believes that all life forms have value and that the planet's natural resources must be protected for the value of all. The One Earth Party is an international, social, economic, political, problem solving association of concerned citizens of earth.

The party believes that "One Earth" should mean that all people, goods, money and ideas can move freely between nations without barriers, quotas, taxes, subsidies, discrimination, or infringement on personal and civil rights; the merging of all international policing units into one organization; that all national governments move to the same set of standards of democracy where each adult of 18 has the right to vote; where national, state and local governments are not allowed to carry debts or trade deficits for more than two current years without the direct approval of a majority of voters; and that English is declared the official language of science, business and government interactions.

The party supports the right of law-abiding citizens to own and bear arms; outlawing capital punishment by 2010; destroying all weapons of destruction, nuclear weapons, bombers, missiles, submarines, aircraft carriers, and land and personnel mines by 2020; withdrawing all military troops from foreign lands; implementing a 32-hour workweek; limiting elective service to 12 years at any level; schools charging fees for special services, such as bus transportation, music, and sports activities; phasing out Social Security by 2040; phasing out all medical benefits by the federal and state governments by 2040; and phasing out all social and corporate welfare subsidies by 2010.

Pacifist Party (see United States Pacifist Party)

Pansexual Peace Party

Email: eris@neosoft.com; *Web site*: http://members.tripod.com/Hail_Eris/eris/PPPP/homey.htm

The Pansexual Peace Party operates according to Discordian disorganizational principles and has no clearly-defined hierarchical structure. The party supports stopping the War on Drugs and decreasing the prison population, especially of non-violent offenders; repealing all criminal laws related to victimless crimes; abolishing capital punishment; the legalization of hemp as a viable agricultural crop; a women's right to choose whether she want to have an abortion or not; zero population growth; the development of alternative energy sources; renaming the Department of Defense the War Department; and an all-volunteer army (no draft).

Parliament Party (see U.S. Parliamentary Party)

Party X

Email: contact party through its web site; *Web site*: http://www.party-x.org

With the belief that "it's not the Republicans against the Democrats, it's the politicians against the people," Party X aims to bring voters back into the political process and to reign in government control and influence over the lives of its citizens. According to Party X, one of the primary problems with politics today is the idea of the "career politician" who, over the years, has lost touch with the average American and is too insular to understand the problems citizens face in today's world. Party X does not view itself as a traditional political party but instead describes itself as "an organization of like-minded people who are concerned for this nation and their children's future." The "X" in Party X represents all citizens and the idea that its members do not want to be labeled or politically categorized. The party subscribes to a political ideology called "Ethicism."

Believing that today's political system is entirely controlled by the Democrats and Republicans, the party works to return the election system to the people and out of the hands of career politicians and special interest groups. The party believes that all ballots need to be controlled by the federal government as it is unconstitutional for each state to determine who can and who cannot run for President; no vote must ever be wasted and the federal government must force states to use an Instant Run-off type of ballot so votes are not wasted and people do not feel like they are forced to vote for the lesser of two evils; and presidential debates must be controlled by the federal government, not the Republicans and Democrats, and all candidates on the ballot will be included in all debates.

Party X encourages average Americans to run for political office, at all levels of government, and to "reverse the damage done by career politicians." The party does not use the word politician, because of all the negative connotations that word inspires, but instead prefers the terms Statesmen and Stateswomen.

Party Y

Email: info@party-y.org; *Web site*: http://www.party-y.org

Party Y is a coalition of young American leaders who joined together in 2002 to launch a new independent political youth party dedicated to meeting the needs of America's under–30 population. Party Y does not consider itself a traditional third party, but instead refers to itself as an internet/media-based virtual party designed to use available technology to link up young voters with equally young political candidates around the country. Party Y does not adhere to any single political philosophy and welcomes all young Americans under the age of 30 as party members and aspiring political candidates.

Party Y plans to create a marketing campaign aimed at developing young candidates to run for Congress; endorse and promote these candidates through an independent political youth party dedicated to meeting the needs of America's under–30 population; introduce a 100% in-party democratic process that allows young voters to call-in or vote online to select Party Y–endorsed candidates and define Party Y's official platform; create a reality television program to audition potential candidates around the country and allow viewers and celebrity judges to select the winners; package this reality television program as a traveling political road show, driving from town to town (school to school), auditioning local talent and enrolling new members; provide 10 representatives from around the country with start-up funds and media resources to run their own congressional campaigns (the television program will track their progress); after candidates are actually elected, the program will cover their activities while in office; get colleges, high schools and youth organizations involved in the Party Y campaign by hosting political road shows; and through these successes, sow the seeds of tomorrow's leaders.

Peace & Freedom Party (California Peace & Freedom Party)

P.O. Box 24764, Oakland, CA 94623; *Telephone*: 510-465-9414; P.O. Box 741270, Los Angeles, CA 90004; *Telephone*: 323-759-9737; *Email*: alameda@peaceandfreedom.org; *Web site*: http://www.peace-andfreedom.org

Founded in Ann Arbor, Michigan in 1967 as a left-wing organization opposed to the Vietnam War, the Peace & Freedom Party (commonly called the California Peace & Freedom Party) reached its peak in 1968 when it nominated Black Panther leader Eldridge Cleaver for President. Although a convicted felon, Cleaver carried nearly 37,000 votes. He became a Reagan Republican in the early 1980s, a crack addict in the late 1980s, and an environmental activist in the late 1990s .

Well-known baby doctor Benjamin Spock, a self-described leftist and staunch opponent of the Vietnam War, was the PFP Presidential nominee in 1972. Since then, the small party has largely been dominated by "battling factions of Marxist-Leninists (aligned with the Workers World Party), Trotskyists, and non-communist left-wing activists."

Today the PFP's activities are mainly focused in California, where it prints the party's newspaper, *The Partisan*. In 1996, the PFP successfully blocked an attempt by the Workers World Party to capture its presidential nomination (and a California ballot spot) for their party's nominee. In a sign of the party's serious decline in support, the PFP's poor showing in the 1998 statewide elections caused the party to lose its California ballot status. It was unable to regain official ballot status by successive failed petition attempts for the 2000 and 2002 elections. However, the PFP finally regained its ballot status in 2003 and currently fields candidates for Congress and other political offices.

The party supports collective ownership and democratic management of industry and natural resources; affirmative action programs to combat past and present racial, national, and gender discrimination; doubling the minimum wage and a 30-hour workweek; an end to international U.S. military intervention; working class people, including their right to organize and to strike; universal health care; strong environmental laws; abolishing the North American Free Trade Agreement, the General Agreement on Tariffs and Trade, and the World Trade Organization; the elimination of all nuclear, chemical, and biological weapons; withdrawal of military forces from all foreign lands; abolishing the Central Intelligence Agency, the National Security Agency, and the Agency for International Development, and other agencies that interfere in other countries' internal affairs; abolishing the death penalty; and free public transportation.

People's Party

Email: contact party through its web site; *Web site*: http://www.angelfire.com/ny4/tpp

Feeling that the two major parties in today's political arena are not representing Americans, the People's Party aims to work for returning control of the government back to the people and out of the hands of career politicians and special-interest groups.

Personal Choice Party of Utah

856 East 100 South #2, Salt Lake City, UT 84102; *Telephone & Fax*: 801-533-8658; *Email*: contact@personalchoice.org; *Web site*: http://www.personalchoice.org

After many years of grassroots work, the Personal Choice Party of Utah was officially formed in 2004 and promotes the idea of less government and the opportunity for more personal choice for the average citizen. The party's immediate plans are to build an organization that will allow it to garner at least 2% of the votes in statewide elections, thus assuring itself of ballot status. The long-term goal of the party is to create state affiliates and then to introduce the party's plans on a global basis.

The party (which uses the Smiley Face as its official emblem) supports less government interference in the lives of its citizens; each individual determining for himself/herself what path to follow for personal happiness; and the only true and legal purpose of the government is to protect the equal inalienable rights of all citizens.

Poé Party of Hawaii

3524 Campbell Avenue, Honolulu, HI 96815
A local political party.

Populist Party USA

Email: populistusa@yahoo.com; *Web site*: http://www.angelfire.com/alt/populistusa

The Populist Party USA strives to renew public interest and participation in America's political arena. The party believes that the Constitution and the political system as designed work well but that currently both have been undermined by professional politicians and special-interest groups. The party supports a limit on the amount of money each political party receives; term limit of 12 years established for each house of Congress to ensure that career politicians, who lose touch with the average citizen and who lose a sense of accountability, are not created; increasing the number of seats in the House of

Representatives to 870, to increase representation (the founding fathers envisioned one representative for every 8000 people; Congress now has one representative for every 600,000 people); reducing the overall tax rate to 20%; instituting a balance budget requirement with any excess funds being used to pay down the national debt; maintaining farm subsidies; research into genetically-altered crops; a strong Social Security system and forbidding the government from using its funds for other purposes; Medicare and Medicaid, but not a universal health care system; an overhaul of the national welfare system to weed out abuse; banning abortion; banning gay marriages; reducing all federal funding for the arts; increased funding for education at all levels; and research into alternative fuel sources.

A relatively new and currently small political party, Populist Party USA is building a grassroots organization with the intent to field local, and then national, candidates.

Pot Party (see Marijuana Party)

Progressive Dane

P.O. Box 1222, Madison, WI 53703; *Telephone*: 608-257-4985; *Email*: office@prodane.org; *Web site*: http://www.prodane.org

Progressive Dane is a progressive political party in Dane County, Wisconsin and believes that ordinary citizens should control public policies at the community and national levels. The party supports tax justice, improved social services, equality in public education, affordable housing, and public transportation. Progressive Dane helps community members organize around issues that are important to them and also works at the grassroots level to elect progressive political candidates.

The party believes that powerful monied interests have corrupted both the Democratic and Republican parties and that the only solution to existing problems is to address them at the community level. Progressive Dane seeks to ally progressive activists and community organizations to form a powerful, united, and independent force in electoral politics and non-electoral struggles.

The party supports a system of progressive local taxation based on the ability to pay and to meet local needs; an end to corporate property tax exemptions; an end to state-imposed caps on local spending; expanding and improving local programs of economic and social aid and protection; greater community participation in establishing local laws and social programs; using locally-owned firms when awarding city contracts; strong environmental programs; expanded use of city powers to contain urban sprawl and preserving the local environment; efficient public transportation that is accessible and affordable to all and believe the city should encourage use of public transportation; flexible zoning policies in order to promote affordable housing alternatives; the right of city employees to join unions; banning pre-employment drug testing of prospective city employees and oppose drug testing of current city employees without probable cause; public financing of municipal elections; making all computerized campaign finance records fully and immediately accessible to the public through the internet and through designated terminals at the city-county building and Madison Public Library branches; extending local voting rights to non-citizens; a living wage rate of 112% of the federal poverty line for a family of four, annually indexed to inflation, which reflects the higher cost of living in the city if Madison; requiring businesses receiving economic subsidies to pay their employees a living wage plus health insurance; formal citizen oversight of the police; and treating drug-related issues as a public health rather than a law enforcement concern.

Progressive Labor Party

P.O. Box 808, Brooklyn, NY 11202; *Telephone*: 718-630-9440, 212-2550-3959; *Fax*: 212-255-0685; *Email*: plp@plp.org; *Web site*: http://www.plp.org

The Progressive Labor Party believes that communism is the only system that will address the needs of all citizens. The PLP aims to be a "mass party, not a cadre elite." The communist organization of society requires the active commitment of its members in order for the system to succeed. In general, communism supports abolishing nationalism; creating a one-working-class-one party world; abolishing racism by building multi-racial unity and internationalism; abolishing sexism; a no money society (no wages, with people working together based on their commitment to each other and to building a communist society); and the workers running every aspect of society. Like all communist organizations, the Progressive Labor Party believes that all citizens must be communist organizers for the system to work and that communism can be won only through armed struggle by masses of workers, soldiers, students and other interested parties to destroy the dictatorship of the capitalist class and set up communism-dictatorship of the working class.

The PLP is a self-described militant, Stalinist-style communist party dedicated to bringing about a world-wide, armed, communist revolution. Because the party denounces all elections as frauds, the PLP does not intend to field any candidates for public office.

Progressive Libertarian Party (of Florida)

11985 Southern Boulevard #168, Royal Palm Beach, FL 33411.
A local political party.

Progressive Party of Missouri

P.O. Box 33106, Kansas City, MO 64114; *Telephone*: 800-456-7891, 816-942-3081; *Email*: info@ppmo.org; *Web site*: http://www.ppmo.org

A state affiliate of the Green Party of the United States, the Progressive Party of Missouri has adopted the attitude of "thinking globally and acting locally" and is an organization of "grassroots activists, environmentalists, advocates for social justice, and concerned citizens who believe that we can make a difference." The party strives to eliminate corporate-dominated, money-driven politics and is committed to "bringing Progressive values and processes to politics and decision-making in Missouri."

The Progressive Party of Missouri was first organized in 2001 in Columbia, Missouri by a group of citizens from around the state who wanted a political alternative to existing parties. The party adheres to tenets of the Green Party of the United States and is organized as a network of local chapters and county committees. The party's mission includes participating in electoral and legislative activities; participating in social movements related to Green value-oriented issues; and securing and maintaining ballot status according to the laws of Missouri.

Progressive ProAction Party

114 Caroline Street, Plymouth WI 53073; *Email*: joeglitter1@hotmail.com; *Web site*: http://www.proactionparty.cafeprogressive.com

Using the tagline "Taking Back the Government for the People," the goal of the Progressive ProAction Party is to unite progressive-minded people and organizations into a grassroots organization dedicated to changing the way government operates. The party strives to "compete for state and local elections across America and to contribute to the growing third party movement currently seizing the attention of the American people."

Taking the view that the current two-party dominated political system benefits only the rich, the party wants to return governmental power back to the people, as envisioned by the founding fathers. The party supports making Health Maintenance Organizations liable for negligent decisions in patient care; ensuring patient access to specialists, prescription drugs, emergency care and treatments at a doctor's request, not an HMO's; allowing free choice of doctors and hospitals; using any national surplus to strengthen and modernize Medicare and Medicaid; mandating birth control education and availability and making free contraceptives available to high school and college students; instituting a cap on college tuition fees; requiring students to receive foreign language education from kindergarten through high school and introducing a more culturally diverse curriculum; eliminating all federal money or government support for private schools; eliminating the cap on Supplemental Security Income taxes; creating stricter anti-monopoly laws; disbanding the Federal Reserve Board; ending U.S. membership and participation in the World Trade Organization and the International Monetary Fund; ending military involvement in all other countries and converting the troops into a defensive armed force; eliminating all nuclear war heads; disbanding the Central Intelligence Agency; independence for Puerto Rico; ending estate taxes on farms and farm land; banning genetically-engineered food products; legalizing hemp farming for paper, rope, and fuel; ending law enforcement racial profiling policies; eliminating all privatization of prisons and prison labor; banning the death penalty; ending the war on drugs and sending drug offenders to rehabilitation centers, not jail; reinstating voting rights for felons; establishing limits on the amount of money a political candidate and party can accept; banning Political Action Committees from contributing to parties and candidates; declaring Election Day a paid national holiday to allow easier access for voting; giving third parties easier ballot access; establishing term limits and instituting an election process for supreme court justices; increasing funding for the Occupational Safety and Health Administration; freezing expansion of all off-reservation casinos and gaming establishments; and establishing strict nutrition guidelines for school lunch programs.

Prohibition Party

P.O. Box 2635, Denver, CO 80201; 10105 West 17th Place, Lakewood, CO 80215; *Telephone*: 303-237-4947; *Email*: earldodge@dodgeoffice.net; *Web site*: http://www.prohibition.org

Established in 1869, the Prohibition Party's original goal was encouraging the prohibition of the manufacture and sale of alcoholic beverages and illegal drugs. While maintaining its original goals, today's party has expanded its vision to include advocating a smaller federal government; banning abortion; the application of Biblical principles to government; and returning all illegal immigrants to their own lands.

Additionally, the party supports banning commercial gambling; banning homosexual marriages; prayer and Bible reading in schools; reverting government authority back to the states; abolishing the federal Department of Education; establishing laws making it easier for third party candidates to qualify for ballot access; lowering taxes and passing a balanced budget amendment to the Constitution; a systematic retirement of the national debt; eliminating the Federal Reserve Bank and withdrawal from the World Bank; enforcing laws prohibiting strikes by federal employees; ending farm subsidies for corporations; the right of citizens to own and bear arms; tax exemptions for all religious institutions; using Social Security funds only for their intended purpose and not for any other government spending requirement; ending all welfare assistance to illegal aliens; reduce legal immigration quotas; and increasing financial support for the National Aeronautics and Space Administration.

Reform Party of the USA

P.O. Box 126437, Ft. Worth, TX 76126; *Telephone:* 817-249-2751; *Fax:* 817-249-5201; *Email:* info@reformparty.org; *Web site:* http://www.reformparty.org

Seeking to rid the federal government of the two-party system and the financial influence of special-interest groups, the Reform Party of the USA aims to "completely overhaul the current political system, decrease the size and power of the federal goverment, and to return political power back to the states and the people."

The Reform Party supports making it illegal for government officials to accept any donations from for-profit businesses; the Federal Communications Commission reserving 20% of the airwaves and broadband resources for public services, including public television, and campaign coverage of local, state, and national elections; ending all trips or junkets paid for by special-interest groups; providing Congress and White House officials the same retirement plans and health care as the average citizen; passing a balanced budget amendment to the Constitution; giving the President line-item veto; reducing the cost of campaigns by shortening the election cycle; voting on Saturdays and Sundays, not Tuesdays, so working people can get to the polls; replacing the Electoral College process for electing the President with a direct vote from the citizens so that every vote counts; limiting Congressional fund-raising to only voters in their district and Senate fund-raising to only voters in their state; limiting House of Representative members to three terms and Senate members to two terms; requiring all tax increases be approved by the people in the next federal election after the proposal has been presented; and prohibiting former elected and appointed officials from ever taking money from foreign governments or foreign interests or from working as foreign lobbyists.

Affiliates. *Alabama: Email:* contact party through its web site; *Web site:* http://www.al.reformparty.org. *Alaska: Email:* contact party through its web site; *Web site:* http://www.ak.reformparty.org. *Arizona:* P.O. Box 5782, Scottsdale, AZ 85261; *Telephone:* 480-391-0821; *Email:* reform@AmeriRoots.com; *Web site:* http://www.rpaz.us. *Arkansas: Email:* contact party through its web site; *Web site:* http://www.ar.reformparty.org. *California: Email:* contact party through its web site; *Web site*: http://www.reformpartyofcalifornia.org. *Colorado*: P.O. Box 622036, Littleton, CO 80162; *Email*: contact party through its web site; *Web site*: http://www.co.reformparty.org. *Connecticut*: *Email*: contact party through its web site; *Web site*: http://www.ct.reformparty.org. *Delaware*: *Email*: contact party through its web site; *Web site*: http://www.de.reformparty.org. *District of Columbia*: *Email*: contact party through its web site; *Web site*: http://www.dc.reformparty.org. *Florida*: P.O. Box 435, Oldsmar, FL 34677; *Telephone*: 813-855-1213; *Fax*: 813-855-1426; *Email*: contact party through its web site; *Web site*: http://www.rpfla.org. *Georgia*: *Email*: contact party through its web site; *Web site*: http://www.ga.reformparty.org. *Hawaii*: *Email*: contact party through its web site; *Web site*: http://www.reformparty.org/StatesContacts/hi.html. *Idaho*: *Email*: contact party through its web site; *Web site*: http://www.id.reformparty.org. *Illinois*: 1255 North Sandburg Terrace, Chicago, IL 60610; *Telephone*: 312-266-7431; *Fax*: 312-266-7644; *Email*: real@rpil-ilrp.com; *Web site*: http://www.reformpartyillinois.com. *Indiana*: *Email*: reformind@aol.com; *Web site*: http://www.in.reformparty.org. *Iowa*: 1246 Edgington Avenue, Eldora, IA 50627; *Telephone*: 641-939-3803; *Email*: contact party through its web site; *Web site*: http://www.ia.reformparty.org. *Kansas*: *Email*: contact party through its web site; *Web site*: http://www.votekansas.org. *Kentucky*: *Email*: contact party through its web site; *Web site*: http://www.ky.reformparty.org. *Louisiana*: *Email*: contact party through its web site; *Web site*: http://www.la.reformparty.org. *Maine*: *Email*: contact party through its web site; *Web site*: http://www.me.reformparty.org. *Maryland*: *Email*: contact party through its web site; *Web site*: http://www.md.reformparty.org. *Massachusetts*: *Email*: contact party through its web site; *Web site*: http://www.ma.reformparty.org.*Michigan*: P.O. Box 141, Wyandotte, MI 48192; *Telephone*: 734-624-5651; *Email*: contact party through its web site; *Web site*: http://www.reformpartyofmichigan.org. *Minnesota*: P.O. Box 1, Newport, MN 55055; *Telephone*: 651-459-4996; *Fax*: 612-827-5110; *Email*: reformparty1@netscape.net; *Web site*: http://www.mn.reformparty.org. *Mississippi*: *Email*: contact party through its web site; *Web site*: http://www.mississippiwebsite.com/reformparty.htm. *Missouri*: 8000 Ward Parkway Plaza, Kansas City, MO 64114; *Telephone*: 816-268-

4646; *Email*: contact party through its web site; *Web site*: http://www.mo.reformparty.org. *Montana*: *Email*: contact party through its web site; *Web site*: http://www.mt.reformparty.org. *Nebraska*: *Email*: contact party through its web site; *Web site*: http://www.spo-rpusa.org/nebraska. *Nevada*: *Email*: contact party through its web site; *Web site*: http://www.nv.reformparty.org. *New Hampshire*: *Email*: contact party through its web site; *Web site*: http://www.nh.reformparty.org. *New Jersey*: 201 Lincoln Boulevard, Middlesex NJ 08846; *Email*: contact party through its web site; *Web site*: http://www.nj.reformparty.org. *New Mexico*: 2924 Northeast Espanola Street, Albuquerque, NM 87110; *Email*: contact party through its web site; *Web site*: http://newmexicorp.us. *New York*: *Email*: contact party through its web site; *Web site*: http://www.spo-rpusa.org/NewYork. *North Carolina*: *Email*: contact party through its web site; *Web site*: http://www.nc.reformparty.org. *North Dakota*: *Email*: contact party through its web site; *Web site*: http://www.nd.reformparty.org. *Ohio*: *Email*: contact party through its web site; *Web site*: http://www.reformohio.org. *Oklahoma*: P.O. Box 773, Tipton, Oklahoma 73570; *Telephone*: 580-667-5774; *Email*: refrm60m@pldi.net; *Web site*: http://www.reformpartyofoklahoma.org. *Oregon*: *Email*: contact party through its web site; *Web site*: http://www.or.reformparty.org. *Pennsylvania*: *Email*: contact party through its web site; *Web site*: http://www.pa.reformparty.org. *Rhode Island*: P.O. Box 41342, Providence, RI 02940; *Telephone*: 401-728-9699; *Email*: contact party through its web site; *Web site*: http://www.ri.reformparty.org. *South Carolina*: *Email*: contact party through its web site; *Web site*: http://www.sc.reformparty.org. *South Dakota*: *Email*: Contact Party through its web site; *Web site*: http://www.sd.reformparty.org. *Tennessee*: *Email*: contact party through its web site; *Web site*: http://www.tn.reformparty.org. *Texas*: 18935 Atasca Oaks Drive, Kingwood, TX 77346: *Telephone*: 281-852-2928; *Email*: chairman@texasreformparty.org; *Web site*: http://www.texasreformparty.org. *Utah*: *Email*: contact party through its web site; *Web site*: http://www.ut.reformparty.org. *Vermont*: *Email*: contact party through its web site; *Web site*: http://www.vt.reformparty.org. *Virginia*: P.O. Box 123, Fieldale, Virginia 24089; *Telephone*: 276-673-1186; *Email*: contact party through its web site; *Web site*: http://www.va.reformparty.org. *Washington*: 1242 State Avenue, Suite I, PMB 347, Marysville, WA 98270; *Telephone*: 509-775-0799; *Email*: contact party through its web site; *Web site*: http://www.wa.reformparty.org. *West Virginia*: *Email*: contact party through its web site; *Web site*: http://www.wv.reformparty.org. *Wisconsin*: *Email*: contact party through its web site; *Web site*: http://www.wi.reformparty.org. *Wyoming*: *Email*: contact party through its web site; *Web site*: http://www.wy.reformparty.org.

Republican Moderate Party of Alaska

P.O. Box 233809, Anchorage, AK 99523; *Telephone*: 907-344-4514; *Fax*: 907-349-1735; *Email*: questions@rmp.com; *Web site*: http://republicanmoderates.com

Formed in 1986 by Ray Metcalfe to "oppose the political hijacking of the Republican Party by the Religious Right," the Republican Moderate Party is a third-party organization not affiliated with the state's Republican Party. The party supports open primary elections, combating the influence of the Religious Right, and establishing a higher standard for openness and honesty in Alaska's political arena. The party is the only minor party to have ever elected a candidate to Alaska's State Senate. Shortly after forming the party, Metcalfe was sued by a group of Religious Right leaders of the Republican Party for creating a political organization using the term "Republican" without their permission. He won in Superior Court and the Republican Party chose not to appeal.

Leaning towards Libertarianism, Republican Moderates "favor an open, tolerant government and are best described as moderately conservative on fiscal issues and moderately liberal on social issues." The party supports smaller government with less control of its citizens' lives and strong right to privacy laws.

Republican Party

Republican National Committee, 310 First Street SE, Washington, D.C. 20003; *Telephone*: 202-863-8500; *Fax*: 202-863-8820; *Email*: info@gop.com; *Web site*: http://www.rnc.org

The Republican Party was established in the early 1850s by antislavery activists and those who believed that government should grant western lands to settlers free of charge. At the time, the Free Soil Party was insisting that all men had a natural right to the soil and was demanding that the government grant land to settlers free of charge. Additionally, the Conscience Whigs, a so-called "radical faction" of the Whig Party based in the North, alienated their Southern supporters by adopting an anti-slavery position. Adding to the instability, the Kansas-Nebraska Act was passed, which allowed territories to determine whether slavery would be legal within its borders, basically nullifying the principles of the Missouri Compromise, and creating a schism within the Democratic Party.

Alvan Bovay took advantage of the political turmoil of the times and united factions from the Free Soil Party, the Conscience Whigs, and the anti Kansas-Nebraska Act Democrats in a meeting in Ripon, Wisconsin, in which he helped establish a new political party. Realizing that the party needed a unifying name, he chose Republican because it was simple, synonymous with equality, and alluded to the earlier popular party of Democratic-Republicans, founded by Thomas Jefferson. In July 1854, in Jackson, Michigan, the Republican Party formally organized itself by holding its first convention, adopting a platform, and nominating a full slate of candidates for state offices. Other states soon followed and the first Republican candidate for president, John C. Frémont, was nominated for the 1856 race, using the slogan, "Free soil, free labor, free speech, free men, Fremont." Although considered a minor third party candidate (the Democrats and Whigs being the majority parties of the day), Frémont was able to garner 33% of the vote and, building on this success, four years later, Abraham Lincoln became the first Republican to win the White House.

Although most remembered for the Civil War and his assassination, the Lincoln Administration had multiple accomplishments, including the establishment of the Department of Agriculture, the creation of the Bureau of Internal Revenue, and the formulation of a national banking system. Lincoln also passed the Homestead Act, which offered public land grants, just as had been proposed by the Free Soil Party.

After years of unrest between the North and South, the Civil War erupted in 1861 and lasted four years. Against the advice of his cabinet, Lincoln signed the Emancipation Proclamation that freed the slaves and the Republican Party worked to pass the 13th Amendment (outlawing slavery), the 14th Amendment (guaranteeing equal protection under the law), and the 15th Amendment (securing voting rights for African-Americans). Many historians have presented the argument that one reason for the Republican support of freeing the slaves and securing them voting rights was to wrestle Democratic power from the Southern states. While definitely a political possibility, the idea was surely unpopular in its time and has had political and social ramifications in the United States up to the present day.

In 1896, Republicans were the first major party to favor women's suffrage and later played a role in securing women the right to vote. When the 19th Amendment was passed (securing voting rights for women), 26 of the 36 state legislatures that ratified it were under Republican control. In 1917, the first woman elected to Congress was a Republican, Jeanette Rankin from Montana.

Presidential power during most of the late 19th and early 20th centuries was held by Republicans while the Democrats and Franklin Roosevelt dominated American politics in the 1930s and 1940s. For 28 of the 40 years from 1952 through 1992, the White House was under Republican control, with Presidents Eisenhower, Nixon, Ford, Reagan and Bush. After eight years of Bill Clinton in the White House, in 2000 the Republicans again regained control of the White House by electing George W. Bush to two terms.

The national structure of the party starts with the Republican National Committee. Each state has its own Republican State Committee and each neighborhood has a precinct captain. The party's basic tenet is that individuals, not the government, are best suited to make decisions on how best to live their lives and run their local communities. The official symbol of the Republican Party is the elephant, which dates back to the mid-term election of 1874. During this time, the Democratic party was trying to convince voters that Republican President Ulysses Grant would seek an unprecedented third term. *Harper's Weekly* cartoonist Thomas Nast depicted a Democratic jackass trying to scare a Republican elephant, and both symbols stuck and became associated with their respective parties. For many years, the party has been known as the "G.O.P." commonly thought to stand for "Grand Old Party." However, many historians say the original acronym dates back to 1875 and originally stood for "Gallant Old Party," which more reflected the tenor of the times.

With the election of Abraham Lincoln in 1860, the Republican Party firmly established itself as a major party that would occupy the White House for 60 of the next 100 years. Theodore Roosevelt became president in 1901, upon McKinley's assassination, and began establishing a standard Republican tenet of competition in a free market, which was a relatively new political concept at the time. In 1903, Roosevelt became involved with foreign policy, supporting revolutionaries who formed the Republic of Panama. His actions in Panama resulted in the treaty that permitted construction of the Panama Canal. In 1905, Roosevelt, who popularized the West African phrase "Speak softly and carry a big stick" to explain his view on foreign policy, successfully negotiated the Treaty of Portsmouth, ending the conflict between Russia and Japan. Roosevelt's accomplishments as a peacemaker earned him the honor of being the first American to receive the Nobel Peace Prize. In 1906, after reading Upton Sinclair's *The Jungle*, Roosevelt encouraged Congress to pass laws concerning meat inspection and food and drug legislation. Two years later he placed 150 million acres of forest land into federal reserves and organized a National Conservation Conference. He was also responsible for creating the Department of Labor.

Deciding not to run for a third term, Roosevelt was succeeded by Republican president William Taft. In spite of its presidential success, discord grew within the Republican Party and in the 1912 election Teddy Roosevelt, dissatisfied with Taft's policies, led his supporters on the "Bull Moose" ticket against the president. This splitting of the Republican Party led to the election of Democratic president Woodrow Wilson.

When Wilson ran for re-election in 1916, he promised to keep the United States out of World War I, but shortly after winning a second term, America took a leading role in the war. This, among other factors, led to the Republicans winning control of Congress in 1918 and a waning of Wilson's popular support. During the so-called Roaring Twenties, three successive Republican presidential administrations kept government small and controlled taxes (Warren G.

Harding: 1921–1925; Calvin Coolidge: 1925–1929; and Herbert Hoover: 1929–1933).

The 1929 Wall Street crash was a disaster for the Republicans and basically ended President Hoover's political career as he became intricately linked to the Great Depression. Despite his creation of the home-loan banks and the Reconstruction Finance Corporation in an attempt to save the American financial structures, Hoover's anti–Depression efforts went unheeded as people turned to the Democrats for a "New Deal." Under Franklin Roosevelt's New Deal and Democratic control, the federal government gained power and size while deficit spending rose as a result of increased government involvement in the economy.

The Republicans basically were out of power until 1946 when the party regained control of both the House and the Senate. The party continued to make gains and in 1952 its candidate, war hero Dwight Eisenhower, became the first Republican president in 25 years. During his two terms in office, Eisenhower established the Interstate Highway System, continued America's strong space exploration program, and in 1953 he appointed a woman, Oveta Culp Hobby, as the first secretary of his newly created Department of Health, Education and Welfare. His administration also used the National Guard to enforce the 1954 *Brown vs. Board of Education* Supreme Court decision that declared "separate but equal" school accommodations unconstitutional. He also completed formal integration of African Americans into the armed forces.

The Republican Party lost in the 1960 election to John Kennedy and in 1964 to Lyndon Johnson. During much of the turbulent sixties the Republicans were out of political power. That changed in 1968 when Richard Nixon defeated Hubert Humphrey. Nixon opened relations with mainland China; oversaw the end of the Vietnam War; began a policy of detente with Russia, which led to the signing of the Anti-Ballistic Missile and other arms control treaties; removed the dollar from the gold standard; and passed the Clean Air Act.

Nixon won a landslide victory in 1972, carrying every state except Massachusetts, but saw his Vice President, Spiro Agnew, resign in 1973 while under investigation for corruption during his term in the 1960s as county executive of Baltimore County, Maryland. President

Nixon appointed House Republican Leader Gerald Ford to the vice presidency and when Nixon became the first-ever President to resign in the wake of the Watergate scandal in 1974, Ford assumed the presidency, selecting former Governor Nelson Rockefeller as his vice president. For the first time in America's history, the country was led by an unelected President and Vice President.

With the specter of Watergate still clearly in the public conscience, Ford used his administration to regain the political faith of the American people. This period saw a cut in taxes; a reduction in size and power of the federal government; and an increase in the role played by state and local government entities. Ford's short-term administration, and Republican presidential power, ended in 1976 with the election of Jimmy Carter.

In 1980 Ronald Reagan won the presidential election by promising a reduced federal bureaucracy and a transfer of some federal functions to the states. While appealing to a basic conservative corps of supporters, he was also able to attract a broad range of voters due to his easygoing and reassuring manner. His sense of humor lightened the pessimism then pervading America and served him well early in his administration when he was shot by John Hinckley, Jr.

During Reagan's first term, he selected Sandra Day O'Connor as the first female Supreme Court justice; chose Elizabeth Dole as the first female secretary of transportation; Jean Kirkpatrick as the first female U.S. representative to the United Nations; and Margaret Heckler as the secretary of health and human services. It was the first time in America's history that three women served concurrently in a president's Cabinet. In his 1984 re-election, President Reagan received the largest Republican landslide victory in history and his diplomacy, along with his successor George Bush, helped bring about the fall of the Berlin Wall and an end to communism. Often called "The Great Communicator," Reagan has been named by some historians as one of America's greatest presidents.

Succeeding a very popular president in 1988, George Bush laid the ground work for nuclear disarmament, free trade, peace in the Middle East, and strengthening the North Atlantic Treaty Organization. His greatest challenge was bringing peace and maintaining the force of law in the Persian Gulf when Iraq invaded Kuwait. He brought together a coalition of allies to defeat Iraq and to restore peace in the region. His popularity soared after Operation Desert Storm and there was a renewed faith in America's political and military power.

Surprisingly he was not able to convert his popularity into another presidential term as his administration was blamed for a worldwide economic slowdown triggered by the collapse of the Soviet Union and the transition of the global economy from an industrial to a high-technology base. His war-time popularity was not able to help him as Americans voted their pocketbook and elected former Arkansas governor Bill Clinton to the presidency.

In 1993, the party began concentrating on organizing its grass-roots voter base while reinforcing its claimed traditional Republican principles of personal freedom and smaller government. House Republican members and candidates created the "Contract With America," an agenda of 10 specific pieces of legislation based on stated Republican principles of individual liberty, economic opportunity, limited and effective government, personal responsibility and strong security. More than 365 candidates signed the Contract to bring fundamental change to how the House of Representatives operated. The idea was a hit with American voters and in 1994 they gave the Republicans control of the House and Senate for the first time in 40 years.

With the election of George W. Bush in 2000, Republicans held the trifecta of political power: the Presidency, the House of Representatives, and the Senate. Along with Bush's election and re-election in 2004 came a rise in the political conservative movement that significantly altered the American political landscape and led to Republican majorities in the country's Governor's offices and numerous local positions.

Affiliates. *Alabama*: P.O. Box 55628, Birmingham, AL 35255; 2019 Highland Avenue, Birmingham, AL 35205; *Telephone*: 205-212-5900; *Fax*: 205-212-5910; *Email*: algop@algop.org; *Web site*: http://www.algop.org. *Alaska*: 1001 West Fireweed Lane, Anchorage, AK 99503; *Telephone*: 907-276-4467; *Fax*: 907-276-0425; *Email*: rpa@alaskarepublicans.com; *Web site*: http://www.alaskarepublicans.com. *Arizona*: 3501 North 24th Street, Phoenix, AZ 85016; *Telephone*: 602-957-7770; *Fax*: 602-224-0932; *Email*: info@azgop.org; *Web site*: http://www.azgop.org. *Arkansas*: 1201 West 6th Street, Little Rock, AR

72201; *Telephone*: 501-372-7301; *Fax*: 501-372-1656; *Email*: info@ arkansasgop.org; *Web site*: http://www.arkansasgop.org. *California*: 1903 West Magnolia Boulevard, Burbank, CA 91506; *Telephone*: 818-841-5210; *Fax*: 818-841-6668; *Email*: contact party through its web site; *Web site*: http://www.cagop.org. *Colorado*: 1777 South Harrison Street #100, Denver, CO 80210; *Telephone*: 800-236-3769, 303-758-3333; *Fax*: 303-753-4611; *Email*: contact party through its web site; *Web site*: http://www.cologop.org. *Connecticut*: 97 Elm Street, Hartford, CT 06106; *Telephone*: 860-547-0589; *Fax*: 860-278-8563; *Email*: contact party through its web site; *Web site*: http://www.ctgop.org. *Delaware*: 3301 Lancaster Avenue #4B. Wilmington, DE 19805; *Telephone*: 302-651-0260; *Fax*: 302-651-0270; *Email*: contact party through its web site; *Web site*: http://www.delawaregop.com. *District of Columbia*: 1275 K Street NW #102, Washington, D.C. 20005; *Telephone*: 202-289-8005; *Fax*: 202-289-2197; *Email*: contact party through its web site; *Web site*: http://dcgop.com. *Florida*: 420 East Jefferson Street, P.O. Box 311, Tallahassee, FL 32301; *Telephone*: 850-222-7920; *Fax*: 850-681-0184; *Email*: contact party through its web site; *Web site*: http://www.rpof.org. *Georgia*: P.O. Box 550008, Atlanta, GA 30355; *Telephone*: 404-257-5559; *Fax*: 404-257-0779; *Email*: info@gagop.org; *Web site*: http://www.gagop.org. *Hawaii*: 725 Kapiolani Boulevard #C–105, Honolulu, HI 96813; *Telephone*: 808-593-8180; *Fax*: 808-593-7742; *Email*: headquarters@gophawaii.com; *Web site*: http://www.gophawaii.com. *Idaho*: Box 2267, Boise, ID 83701; *Telephone*: 866-343-6405, 208-343-6405; *Fax*: 208-343-6414; *Email*: contact party through its web site; *Web site*: http://www.idgop.org. *Illinois*: 205 West Randolph #1245, Chicago, IL 60606; *Telephone*: 312-201-9000; *Fax*: 312-201-0181; P.O. Box 78, Springfield, IL 62705; *Telephone*: 217-525-0011; *Fax*: 217-753-4712; *Email*: contact party through its web site; *Web site*: http://www.ilgop.org. *Indiana*: 47 South Meridian Street, 2nd Floor, Indianapolis, IN 46204; *Telephone*: 317-635-7561; *Fax*: 317-632-8510; *Email*: newsroom@indgop.org; *Web site*: http://www.indgop.org. *Iowa*: 621 East Ninth Street, Des Moines, IA 50309; *Telephone*: 515-282-8105; *Fax*: 515-282-9019; *Email*: iowagop@iowagop.org; *Web site*: http://www.iowagop.org. *Kansas*: 2025 Southwest Gage Boulevard, Topeka, KS 66604; *Telephone*: 785-234-3456; *Fax*: 785-228-0353; *Email*: spoor@ksgop.org;

Web site: http://www.ksgop.org. *Kentucky*: P.O. Box 1068, 105 West 3rd Street, Frankfort, KY 40602; *Telephone*: 502-875-5130; *Fax*: 502-223-5625; *Email*: kygop@rpk.org; *Web site*: http://www.rpk.org. *Louisiana*: 7916 Wrenwood Boulevard, Suite E, Baton Rouge, LA 70804; *Telephone*: 225-928-2998; *Fax*: 225-928-2969; *Email*: http://www.lagop.com/contact/contact.html; *Web site*: http://www.lagop.com. *Maine*: 9 Higgins Street, Augusta, ME 04330; *Telephone*: 207-622-6247; *Fax*: 207-623-5322; *Email*: megop@ime.net; *Web site*: http://www.mainegop.com. *Maryland*: 15 West Street, Annapolis, MD 21401; *Telephone*: 410-269-0113; *Fax*: 410-269-5937; *Email*: press@mdgop.org; *Web site*: http://www.mdgop.org. *Massachusetts*: 85 Merrimac Street #400, Boston, MA 02114; *Telephone*: 617-523-5005; *Fax*: 617-523-6311; *Email*: info@massgop.com; *Web site*: http://www.massgop.com. *Michigan*: 2121 East Grand River Avenue, Lansing, MI 48912; *Telephone*: 517-487-5413; *Fax*: 517-487-0090; *Email*: contact party through its web site; *Web site*: http://www.migop.org. *Minnesota*: 525 Park Street #250, St. Paul, MN 55103; *Telephone*: 651-222-0022; *Fax*: 651-224-4122; *Email*: info@mngop.com; *Web site*: http://www.mngop.com, http://www.gop-mn.org. *Mississippi*: 415 Yazoo Street, Jackson, MS 39201; *Telephone*: 601-948-5191; *Fax*: 601-354-0972; *Email*: chairman@msogop.org; *Web site*: http://www.msgop.org. *Missouri*: 204 East Dunklin Avenue, Jefferson City, MO 65101; *Telephone*: 573-636-3146; *Email*: contact party through its web site; *Web site*: http://www.mogop.org. *Montana*: P.O. Box 935, 921 Euclid Avenue, Helena, MT 59624; *Telephone*: 406-442-6469; *Fax*: 406-442-3293; *Email*: contact party through its web site; *Web site*: http://www.mtgop.org. *Nebraska*: 1610 N Street, Lincoln, NE 68508; *Telephone*: 402-475-2122; *Fax*: 402-475-3541; *Email*: contact party through its web site; *Web site*: http://www.negop.org. *Nevada*: 8625 West Sahara Avenue, Las Vegas, NV 89117; *Telephone*: 702-258-9182; *Fax*: 702-258-9186; *Email*: contact party through its web site; *Web site*: http://www.nevadagop.org. *New Hampshire*: 134 North Main Street, Concord, NH 03301; *Telephone*: 603-225.9341; *Fax*: 603-225.7498; *Email*: contact party through its web site; *Web site*: http://www.nhgop.org. *New Jersey*: 150 West State Street #230, Trenton, NJ 08608; *Telephone*: 609-989-7300; *Email*: info@njgop.org; *Web site*: http://www.njgop.org. *New Mexico*: 5150A

Northeast San Francisco, Albuquerque, NM 87109; *Telephone*: 505-298-3662; *Fax*: 505-292-0755; *Email*: administrator@gopnm.org; *Web site*: http://www.gopnm.org. *New York*: 315 State Street, Albany, NY 12210; *Telephone*: 518-462-2601; *Email*: info@nygop.org; *Web site*: http://www.nygop.org. *North Carolina*: 1506 Hillsborough Street, Raleigh, NC 27605; *Telephone*: 919-828-6423; *Fax*: 919-899-3815; *Email*: email@ncgop.org; *Web site*: http://www.ncgop.org. *North Dakota*: P.O. Box 1917, Bismarck, ND 58502; 1029 North 5th Street, Bismarck, ND 58501; *Telephone*: 701-255-0030; *Fax*: 701-255-7513; *Email*: info@ndgop.org; *Web site*: http://www.ndgop.com. *Ohio*: 211 South Fifth Street, Columbus, OH 43215; *Telephone*: 614-228-2481; *Fax*: 614-228-1093; *Email*: info@ohiogop.org; *Web site*: http://www.ohiogop.org. *Oklahoma*: 4031 North Lincoln Boulevard, Oklahoma City, OK 73105; *Telephone*: 405-528-3501; *Fax*: 405-521-9531; *Email*: okgop@okgop.com; *Web site*: http://www.okgop.com. *Oregon*: P.O. Box 789, Salem, OR 97308; 2720 Southeast Commercial Street #210, Salem, OR 97302; *Telephone*: 503-587-9233; *Fax*: 503-587-9244; *Email*: info@orgop.org; *Web site*: http://www.orgop. org. *Pennsylvania*: 301 Market Street #900, Harrisburg, PA 17101; *Telephone*: 717-234-4901; *Fax*: 717-231-3828; *Email*: info@pagop.org; *Web site*: http://www.pagop.org. *Rhode Island*: 413 Knight Street, Warwick, RI 02886; *Telephone*: 401-732-8282; *Email*: contact@rigop.org; *Web site*: http://www.rigop.org. *South Carolina*: 1508 Lady Street, Columbia, SC 29201; *Telephone*: 803-988-8440; *Fax*: 803-988-8444; *Email*: chairman@scgop.com; *Web site*: http://www.scgop.com. *South Dakota*: P.O. Box 1099, 415 South Pierre Street, Pierre, SD 57501; *Telephone*: 605-224-7347; *Fax*: 605-224-7349; *Email*: administrator@ southdakotagop.com; *Web site*: http://www.southdakotagop.com. *Tennessee*: 2424 21st Avenue #200, Nashville, TN 37212; *Telephone*: 615-269-4260; *Fax*: 615-269-4261; *Email*: feedback@tngop.org; *Web site*: http://www.tngop.org. *Texas*: 900 Congress #300 Austin, TX 78701; *Telephone*: 512-477-9821; *Fax*: 512-480-0709; *Email*: info@ texasgop.org; *Web site*: http://www.texasgop.org. *Utah*: 117 East South Temple, Salt Lake City, Utah 84111; *Telephone*: 800-230-8824, 801-533-9777; *Fax*: 801-533-0327; *Email*: mail@utgop.org; *Web site*: http://www.utgop.org. *Vermont*: P.O. Box 70, 100 State Street #2, Montpelier, VT 05601; *Telephone*: 802-223-3411; *Fax*: 802-229-1864;

Email: vtgop@vtgop.org; *Web site*: http://www.vermontgop.org. *Virginia*: 115 East Grace Street, Richmond, VA 23219; *Telephone*: 804-780-0111; *Fax*: 804-343-1060; *Email*: info@rpv.org; *Web site*: http://www.rpv.org. *Washington*: 16400 Southcenter Parkway #200, Seattle, WA 98188; *Telephone*: 206-575-2900; *Fax*: 206-575-1730; *Email*: contact party through its web site; *Web site*: http://www.wsrp.org. *West Virginia*: P.O. Box 2711, Charleston, WV 25330; 5019 Southwest Mac-Corkle Avenue, South Charleston, WV 25303; *Telephone*: 304-768-0493; *Fax*: 304-768-6083; *Email*: wvgop@wvgop.org; *Web site*: http://www.wvgop.org. *Wisconsin*, P.O. Box 31, Madison, WI 53701; 148 East Johnson Street, Madison, WI 53703; *Telephone*: 608-257-4765; *Email*: hq@wisgop.org; *Web site*: http://www.wisgop.org. *Wyoming*: 400 East 1st Street #314 Casper, WY 82602; *Telephone*: 307-234-9166; *Fax*: 307-473-8640; *Email*: wygop@coffey.com; *Web site*: http://www.wygop.org.

Revolution (Revolution Party)

Email: revolutionaries@disinfo.net; *Web site*: http://www.revolting.com

The Revolution is a broad-based, non-ideological anti-authoritarian political party/organization that supports converting to clean energy and investigating alternate fuel sources; an end to the war on drugs and freedom for individuals incarcerated solely for illegal drug possession; treating drug use as a health care issue not a law enforcement problem; an end to corporate welfare and stricter control of corporate operations; an end to all income taxes on the first $100,000 of income and a flat tax on all income over $100,000; pardoning all non-violent prisoners who have been incarcerated for victimless crimes; a global minimum wage and worldwide environmental standards; reducing the Pentagon budget by at least 30%; dismantling the Central Intelligence Agency and reforming the federal intelligence gathering apparatus; and opening federally-funded birth control clinics across the country.

Revolutionize Politics in Illinois (Revolutionary Party of Illinois)

P.O. Box 188, South Elgin, IL 60177; *Email*: nomoreil@yahoo.com; *Web site*: http://rpil.org

Revolutionize Politics in Illinois is currently comprised of many third party independents and organizations, including members from the Reform Party, the Independence Party, United Independents, and others. The main purpose of RPIL is to "elect independent candidates to the legislature and put our state government back into the hands of the electorate." The group's plan is to unite numerous, smaller independent groups and other disenfranchised voters in Illinois and to harness their collective power and energy to make changes in government at the state level. The RPIL supports restructuring elementary school curriculum and the ability to recall elected officials.

Right to Life Party of New York

P.O. Box 379, Holtsville, NY 11742; *Email*: contact party through its web site; *Web site*: http://www.nysrtlp.org

The purpose of the Right to Life Party is "to support and work for a constitutional amendment that would reverse the decision of January 22, 1973 by the U.S. Supreme Court" (the *Roe v. Wade* case legalizing abortion). The party works at all levels of government to support legislation restricting and regulating abortion and prohibiting the use of taxpayer funds by the government for abortions. Additionally, the party defends the right of life of all individuals, including those threatened by the "growing pro-euthanasia movement."

The party was founded in 1970 to oppose the legalization of abortion in New York, almost three years before the *Roe v. Wade* decision. The party first made the state ballot in the 1978 gubernatorial election, where its candidate, Mary Jane Tobin, garnered 130,000 votes. In following elections, the party lost support and votes but maintained its ballot status until 2002, when it fell short of the 50,000 votes required to remain on the ballot.

Romantic Transcendentalist Party of the United States

20 Oak Street, North Billerica, MA 01862; *Telephone*: 978-807-1144; *Email*: usrtp@yahoo.com; *Web site*: http://www.geocities.com//usrtp

The Romantic Transcendentalist Party of the United States was started in 2001 and its beliefs are based on the 17th and 18th Century transcendental and romantic beliefs of William Blake, Ralph Waldo

Emerson, and Henry David Thoreau. Its 11 Main Principles include support for a spiritual return to Nature; the goodness of humanity; the value of human spirituality as sacred; the artist as a supremely individual creator; taking pride in America as a nation of liberty and freedom; the use of the senses and emotions over reason and intellect; each human spirit as an individual; the right endowed by creation to be free to do as we please, so long as we do not infringe on the rights of others; the objection and rejection of a cultural norm, and the belief that each person is normal in their individual being; Thoreau's philosophy that "government is best which governs not at all"; and the right to join together in revolution against tyranny.

San Francisco Green Party

1028A Howard Street, San Francisco, CA 94103; *Telephone*: 415-701-7090; *Fax*: 415-701-7092; *Email*: sfgreenparty@yahoo.com; *Web site*: http://www.sfgreenparty.org

Formed in 1991 the San Francisco Green Party, an affiliate of the national Green Party, aims to "encourage all voters to participate in the political process so they can help control the decisions that affect their lives." The party teaches that "human societies must operate with the understanding that we are part of nature and learn to live within the ecological and resource limits of the planet."

The party supports social justice for all; reducing the size and power of the federal government and returning governmental authority back to the state and local level; community-based economics; and honoring cultural, ethnic, racial, sexual, religious and spiritual diversity.

The San Francisco Green Party is part of the Green Party of California, which is in turn part of the Green Party of the United States. The San Francisco Green Party is one of the largest and strongest local Green groups in the U.S. with more than 15,000 registered Greens, more than 3% of the total number of registered voters. The party also has the highest level Green office holder for a major U.S. city, President of the Board of Supervisors.

California is a stronghold for the Green Party as well. With more than 166,000 registered Greens (of the nationwide total of 300,000 in 22 states), the party passed the 1% mark of total registered voters and is growing faster than any other party in the state. The party upholds and supports the 10 key values of the Green Party: grassroots democracy, ecological wisdom, social justice, nonviolence, decentralization, community-based economics, feminism, respect for diversity, global responsibility, and sustainability.

School Choice Party (of New York)

P.O. Box 150013, Brooklyn, NY 11215; *Telephone*: 718-783-0592; *Email*: school_choice_party@aol.com; *Web site*: http://www.geocities. com/SchoolChoiceParty

Believing that the public school system in New York has been steadily deteriorating for more than 20 years, the School Choice Party is dedicated to the idea that parents, not government bureaucrats, should choose a child's school and have a say in the educational curriculum. The party supports giving financial assistance to parents who educate their children at their own expense. Starting locally, the party aims to expand its idea throughout the state of New York.

Social Democrats USA (Social Democratic Party)

P.O. Box 18865, Washington, D.C. 20036; 815 15th Street NW #511, Washington, D.C. 20005; *Telephone*: 202-467-0028; *Fax*: 202-457-0029; *Email*: info@socialdemocrats.org; *Web site*: http://www. socialdemocrats.org

Social Democrats USA (SDUSA) is the successor to the Socialist Party USA, is a member of the Socialist International, and considers itself a close ally of the organized labor movement. The party believes that the world, including America, is ripe for a new Socialist Democratic Movement; is confident in the basic success of democracy; and still feels "burned" by its support of the "failed experiment of communism." While many communist supporters believe that the collapse of Soviet communism meant the end of social democracy, the Social Democratic Party does not share this view and works to introduce and spread the basic ideals of socialism.

The party's history begins at the 1919 Chicago Convention of the Socialist Party of the United States, at which time party loyalists split with the anti-democratic factions that eventually became the Communist Party, USA, while Eugene Debs announced his rejection of "the dictatorship of the proletariat" and protested Lenin's repression of opposition parties in Russia.

Socialist Action Party

298 Valencia Street, San Francisco, CA 94103; *Telephone*: 415-255-1080; *Fax*: 415-255-1082; *Email*: socialistact@igc.org, socialistactionnews@yahoo.com (Party newspaper); *Web site*: http://www.socialistaction.org/sfsa.htm; http://www.socialistaction.org; Youth for Socialist Action's National Office, P.O. Box 16853, Duluth MN 55816; *Telephone*: 715-394-6660; *Email*: mnsocialist@yahoo.com; *Web site: http://*www.socialistaction.org/ysa.htm

The Socialist Action Party is "a group of revolutionary socialists committed to the emancipation of working and oppressed people throughout the world." The party is active in the labor, anti-war, human rights, student, women's, Black and Chicano liberation, gay and all other social movements that challenge the injustices of capitalism and organize people to stand up and fight in their own interests. The party supports a 30-hour work week for 40 hours of pay; strong unions; and fighting capitalism around the world. The party communicates with its members and espouses its message through its newspaper, *Socialist Action*.

The Socialist Action Party was founded in 1983 by a "group of revolutionary socialists who had been long standing activists in the American Trotskyist movement." The party traces its political theory and organizational structure back to the founding of the U.S. Trotskyist movement in 1928, to the Communist League, and eventually through the influences of the Workers Party.

The party supports human needs not profits; an end to racism in all forms; an end to the Democratic and Republican parties as well as all capitalist governments; and a socialist world that is democratically controlled by workers through their own institutions.

Affiliates. *California*: *Email*: trotskyism@aol.com. *Illinois*: P.O. Box 578428, Chicago, IL 60657; *Telephone*: 773-844-1174; *Email*: jpottinger@earthlink.net. *Minnesota*: P.O. Box 16853, Duluth, MN 55816; *Email*: mnsocialist@yahoo.com; *Web site*: http://www.socialistaction.org/lakesuperior.htm; International Falls, MN; *Telephone*: 218-283-3827; *Email*: ifallsysa@hotmail.com; *Web site*: http//www.

socialistaction.org/ifallsysa.htm; *Telephone*: 612-373-8143; *Email*: del-frutas@hotmail.com; *Web site*: http://www.socialistaction.org/twincitiesysa.htm. *Nebraska*: P.O. Box 933, Bellevue, NE 68005; *Email*: ne4socialism@yahoo.com; *Web site*: http://www.geocities.com/ne4socialism. *New York*: New York City, NY; *Email*: spewnyc@aol.com; *Web site*: http://groups.yahoo.com/group/AtlanticSocialists. *North Carolina*: 386 Kenilworth Road, Asheville, NC 28805; *Telephone*: 828-232-4922; Chapel Hill, NC; *Email*: robonica@lycos.com. *Ohio*: Mansfield, OH; *Email*: koryjohnson2004@yahoo.com. *Oregon*: 2725 Southeast 35th Avenue, Portland, OR 97202; *Telephone*: 503-233-1629; *Email*: gary1917@aol.com. *Utah*: Salt Lake City, UT; *Email*: kemuel@killamail.com. *Wisconsin*: P.O. Box 904, Ashland WI 54806; *Telephone*: 715-685-270; *Email*: sackc01@northland.edu; *Web site*: http//www.socialistaction.org/ashlandysa.htm; 1506 North 19th Street, Superior WI 54880; *Telephone*: 715–395–8683; *Email*: lucas-dietsche@hotmail.com; *Web site*: http://www.socialistaction.org/superiorysa.htm.

Socialist Alternative Party

P.O. Box 45343, Seattle, WA 98145; *Telephone*: 206-842-9487; *Email*: info@socialistalternative.org; *Web site*: http://www.socialistalternative.org

Formed in 1986, the Socialist Alternative Party is a national organization "fighting against the exploitation and injustices people face every day. We are union activists fighting for workers' rights and militant, democratic labor unions." The party views the global capitalist system as the root cause of terrorism, war, poverty, discrimination, and environmental destruction. It also believes the dictatorships that existed in the Soviet Union and Eastern Europe were perversions of what socialism is about and the party works for democratic socialism where people will have control over their daily lives. The Socialist Alternative Party is in political solidarity with the Committee for a Workers' International, a worldwide socialist organization in 35 countries on every continent. The party uses its newspaper, *Justice*, to espouse its views.

The party supports no financial cuts in public services; spending increase in health, housing, education, childcare, leisure and community facilities; canceling the national debt with no payments to big investors; free public education for all from preschool to college; free, socialized medicine; abortion rights for women; a minimum wage of $12.50 per hour; a 30-hour work week with 40-hour pay; and revoking all anti-union laws.

Affiliates. *Illinois*: 3329 North Hoyne Avenue, Chicago, IL 60618; *Telephone*: 773-755-3270. *Massachusetts*: Boston, MA; *Telephone*: 617-501-1115. *Minnesota*: 301 West 22nd Street #3, Minneapolis, MN 55404; *Telephone*: 612-760-1980; *Email*: contact party through its web site; *Web site*: http://www.socialistalternative.org/mn. *Nebraska*: 5718 South 98th Plaza #3B, Omaha, NE 68127; *Telephone*: 402-884-6075. *New Hampshire*: Concord, NH; *Telephone*: 603-219-6197. *New York*: P.O. Box 8213, Jackson Heights, NY 11372; *Telephone*: 718-490-9912. *Ohio*: P.O. Box 151281, Columbus, OH 43224; 135 West Lorain Street, Wilder Box 11, Oberlin, OH 44074; *Telephone*: 440-339-9793. *Pennsylvania*: P.O. Box 23013, Philadelphia, PA 19124. *Texas*: 410 Cedar Lane, Channelview, TX 77530; *Telephone*: 281-457-1508. *Utah*: 1411 South Utah Street #9, Salt Lake City, UT 84104; *Telephone*: 801-978-2208.

Socialist Equality Party

P.O. Box 48377, Oak Park, MI 48237; *Email*: contact party through its web site; *Web site*: http://www.socialequality.com

The Socialist Equality Party, the United States part of an international organization, works to "fight big-money politics that has permeated the Democratic and Republican parties and has led to less freedom for Americans" and adheres to the beliefs and platform of the International Committee of the Fourth International. The party maintained a low profile until well-known California politician John Burton ran as the SEP gubernatorial candidate in 2003 and garnered almost 7,000 votes. Since then, the party has revamped its organizational efforts and is expanding into other states.

The SEP began its political life as the Workers League and initially focused its efforts on building a strong labor party in the United States. In 1996, the Workers League changed its name to the Socialist Equality Party, which it felt better reflected its mission to become a "mass socialist party of the working class."

Socialist Labor Party of America

P.O. Box 218, Mountain View, CA 94042; *Telephone*: 408-280-7266; *Fax*: 408-280-6964; *Email*: socialists@slp.org; *Web site*: http://www.slp.org

Initially organized as the Workingmen's Party in 1876, the Socialist Labor Party of America calls itself the original party of socialism in America and adopted its current name in 1877. As the only nationally organized party of socialism in America until 1900, the SLP attracted Socialists of all spectrums; however, the Marxist element became dominant by 1890 and the party adopted its tenor. The SLP ran the first socialist presidential campaign in 1892 and fielded national tickets in every presidential campaign through 1976.

In the early 1890s, the SLP attempted, unsuccessfully, to convert the American Federation of Labor and other unions into militant working-class organizations and in 1896, the party endorsed the Socialist Trade & Labor Alliance, the first attempt in America to build a revolutionary union movement. The ST&LA merged into the Industrial Workers of the World, based in Chicago, in 1905 and in 1908 the SLP helped form a new IWW based in Detroit. The Detroit IWW, later renamed the Workers International Industrial Union, was disbanded in 1924.

The SLP's ultimate political goal is the creation of a classless society based on collective ownership and control of the industries and social services, to be administered in the interests of all society through a Socialist Industrial Union government composed of democratically elected representatives from all the industries and services of the land. Production would be carried on for use instead of profit. The SLP program for achieving this revolutionary change from capitalism to socialism is based on the Marxist tenet that socialism can be achieved only through the class-conscious action "of the working class itself."

The Socialist Industrial Union program, as the SLP program is known, developed by Daniel De Leon (1852–1914), is a continuation of Karl Marx's ideas on a workers' government. In all essentials (political and economic class-wide organization, the breakup of the state, workers' democracy, the seizure of social power by the organized producers, and their socialist reorganization of the economy) the SIU program of the SLP conforms to the democratic premises underlying Marx's concept of socialism. The party uses its publication, *The People*, to provide information to members and the general public.

Affiliates. *California*: P.O. Box 2973, Sacramento, CA 95812; P.O. Box 70034, Sunnyvale, CA 94086; *Email*: slpsfba@netscape.net; P.O. Box 526, Forestville, CA 95436; 851 Van Ness Avenue #211, Fresno,CA 93721. *Connecticut*: 506 Hunting Hill Avenue, Middletown, CT 06457; *Telephone*: 860-347-4003; 3 Jodry Street, Quaker Hill, CT 06375; *Telephone*: 203-447-9897. *Florida*: 5228 South 30th Avenue, Gulfport, FL 33707; *Telephone*: 727-321-0999. *Illinois*: P.O. Box 1432, Skokie, IL 60076. *Massachusetts*: 180 Washington Avenue, Needham, MA 02492; *Telephone*: 781-444-3576. *Michigan*: 49409 Schoenherr Road, Shelby Township, MI 48315; *Telephone*: 586-731-6756. *Minnesota*: 5414 Williams Avenue, White Bear Lake, MN 55110; *Telephone*: 651-429-7279. *New Hampshire*: 4 New Hampshire Street, Seabrook, NH 03874. *New York*: 4 Maple Drive, Great Neck, NY 11021; Buffalo, NY; *Email*: wanblee27@aol.com; New York, NY; *Telephone*: 516-829-5325; 339 Lafayette Street #303, New York, NY 10012; *Telephone & Fax*: 212-982-4586; *Email*: SocialistParty@sp-usa.org; *Web site*: http://www.sp-usa.org; http://www.socialistpartyusa.org. *Ohio*: 9626 York Road, North Royalton, OH 44133; *Telephone*: 440-237-7933; *Email*: slpcleveland@yahoo.com. *Oregon*: P.O. Box 4951, Portland, OR 97208; *Telephone*: 503-226-2881; *Email*: slp.pdx@mindspring.com; *Web site*: http://slp.pdx.home.mindspring.com. *Pennsylvania*: P.O. Box 28732, Philadelphia, PA 19151; Pittsburgh, PA; *Telephone*: 412-751-2613. *Texas*: 12610 Breckenridge Drive, Dallas, TX 75230; *Telephone*: 972-458-2253; 3431 Lantern Lane, Baytown, TX 77521; *Telephone*: 281-424-1040; *Email*: houstonslp@frys.com; *Web site*: http://houstonslp.tripod.com

Socialist Party USA (SPUSA)

339 Lafayette Street #303, New York, NY 10012; *Telephone*: 212-982-4586; *Email*: socialistparty@sp-usa.org; *Web site*: http://www.sp-usa.org

Formally organized in Indianapolis, Indiana in 1901, the Socialist Party has been the voice of democratic socialism in the United States for over 100 years. The party came about with the merger of the Social Democratic Party (led by Eugene Victor Debs) and a splinter group of the older Socialist Labor Party. The Socialist Democratic Party had been organized in 1898 by veterans of the Pullman strike of the American Railway Union and was largely composed of American-born workers. The Socialist Labor Party had its roots in the Marx's First International and the Workingmen's Party of America, and was primarily composed of immigrants in big cities. By the 1880s, under the rule of Daniel De Leon, the SLP had become increasingly intolerant of internal dissent and several splinter groups had been formed in protest, one of which eventually merged with the SDP to form the Socialist Party. Today, the party uses its publication, *The Socialist*, to inform its members and the general public about the party's activities.

From its inception, the Socialist Party drew its support from American radicals and its membership included Marxists of various political stripes, Christian socialists, Zionist and anti–Zionist Jewish socialists, and foreign-language speaking splinter groups. On the divisive issue of "reform vs. revolution," the Socialist Party has always adopted a compromise position, producing platforms calling for revolutionary change but also making demands of a reformist nature. The party has always had to deal with the unresolved issue as to whether revolutionary change could come with or without violence, and its members have always been split on which path to follow. The party has historically stressed cooperatives as much as labor unions, and included the concept of revolution by education and of "building the new society within the shell of the old."

From its beginning, the Socialist Party has always worked to become a major political influence in the United States and in the years prior to World War I it had elected two members of Congress, over 70 mayors, and numerous state legislators and city councilors. Its membership reached 100,000 and its Presidential candidate, Eugene Debs, received close to a million votes in his presidential campaign of 1912 and again in 1920. However, as with any ideologically mixed organization, the party was always dealing with internal disputes and factions who wanted to take the organization in different directions.

During World War I, the Socialist Party in America was one of the very few international socialist movements to maintain its opposition to the war, and many Socialists were imprisoned, including

Debs. In 1919, there was a major split in the party when those who accepted the demand for unconditional allegiance to the Third (Communist) International formed the Communist Party (whose membership composed mostly of the foreign-language federations) and the Communist Labor Party (led by John Reed). Under pressure from the International, the two parties later merged, forming the United Communist Party (later to become the Communist Party USA).

Politically weakened by this split, the Socialist Party did not run its own Presidential candidate in 1924, but decided to join the American Federation of Labor and the railroad unions in support of the independent campaign of Wisconsin Senator Robert La Follette who was hoping to build a permanent Farmer-Labor Party. In 1928, led by Norman Thomas, an opponent of World War I and one of the founders of the American Civil Liberties Union, the Socialist Party regrouped as an independent electoral entity.

The party made great strides leading up to the election of 1932, due mainly to the impact of the Great Depression, and its presidential candidate, Thomas, received 896,000 votes. However, by 1936 the liberal policies of President Roosevelt's New Deal had drained much of the support from the Socialist Party. Later in the year, socialist union leaders in New York switched alliances, called on their membership to vote for Roosevelt, and formed the Social Democratic Federation with the intent of promoting socialism within the ranks of the liberal/labor wing of the Democratic Party. With this additional splintering, the Socialist Party's presidential candidate garnered only 185,000 votes in the 1936 election, a mere 20% of its total vote only four years earlier. The party suffered further weakening within its ranks with the war against fascism (World War II) and the wartime prosperity that ensued.

While it was the Communist Party USA that suffered the brunt of the McCarthy era's wrath, all left-leaning political parties were weakened and by the mid 1950s, little remained of organized radical politics. By this time, membership in the Socialist Party had dwindled to a mere 2,000 and it had basically withdrawn from electoral activities. Under pressure from the Socialist International (a group to which both entities belonged), in 1956 the Socialist Party and the Social Democratic Federation reunited. A dissenting faction within the SDF opposed the merger and went on to form the Democratic Socialist Federation (DSF).

By 1957, with the McCarthy Era over, the SP-SDF was ready to start over and rebuild a major radical party in America. Giving further impetus to this rejuvenation was the fact that the Communist Party had lost a large number of members over its uncritical allegiance to the Soviet government, and these disenfranchised voters were among those the party actively attempted to recruit. Additionally, the party attempted to unite with the Jewish Labor Bund (an international organization of anti–Zionist, non-religious, democratic socialist Jews) and the Independent Socialist League (ISL) (a Trotskyist splinter group founded and led by Max Shachtman, with about 400 members). In 1958 the ISL dissolved and its members joined the SP-SDF. This move ended any hopes of further mergers because it was Shachtman's stated intention to take control of the Socialist Party.

Shachtman and his followers proposed what they called the Realignment, a belief that America did not need another third party but a strong second party, an idea that caused an immediate rift within the Socialist Party. Realignment supporters argued that in its 60 years of existence the Socialist Party had failed not only to bring labor into its fold, but had consistently lost labor support to the Democratic Party. Another argument they used was that, in view of restricted ballot access, the Democratic primaries were a better forum for electoral activity than Socialist candidacies. Both arguments, however, were basically an appeal to a traditional Marxist tenet: labor is the motor for social change. The argument went that if labor would not come to the Socialist Party, it had to go to labor, which meant going to the Democratic Party. Many members accepted the reasoning of this argument but insisted of joining the Democratic Party openly as Socialists.

While the Realignment policy was initially appealing, it quickly lost favor with true socialist believers because the strategy focused solely on gaining power for its own sake while socialist politics was concerned not only with winning power but also with redistributing it to build a new society. Another problem followers had was that the result of Realignment was to diminish any differences between Socialists and liberals, thus reducing their own political power. In addition to growing opposition to the Realignment, socialists began to have other problems in the early 1960s.

The merger with the Jewish Labor Bund had not occurred primarily because of the growing conservatism of the Socialist Party and the issue of Israel. The Bund wanted veto rights over policy issues dealing with Israel and party supporters were against the idea. Another major problem the party faced was the defection of many in its youth section. The Young People's Socialist League (YPSL) had always been to the left of the party and after the ISL merger (which also brought in the ISL's youth section), the YPSL developed the same conflicts with the ISL youth section as had developed between the two main groups as a whole. In the early 1960s, a group within the YPSL obtained control of the Students for a Democratic Society (SDS) (the youth section of the League for Industrial Democracy [LID]), and then disaffiliated it from the LID. At the 1963 YPSL Convention, the left held an overwhelming majority and its views were at odds with the leadership of the Socialist Party. That convention formally dissolved the YPSL and the SDS, now deprived of party support, and disintegrated.

The ISL merger had brought into the fold numerous members who did not agree with the original Realignment theory and their ideas found allies in the older party leadership. Starting in Berkeley, California under the leadership of Hal Draper, a variety of so-called Independent Socialist Clubs were formed, many of which replaced the existing local Socialist Party clubs. Initially these clubs included Socialist Party members but as time passed, more of these members began leaving the party. The final four-pronged problem facing the party was the constant loss of members as left-leaning socialists decided they could not tolerate or support the rightward drift of the party's leadership.

At the 1968 Socialist Party National Convention, the Shachtman-Harrington Caucus held a majority and voted down resolutions demanding American withdrawal from Vietnam and urging independent political action. They also passed a resolution endorsing Hubert Humphrey, elected a majority of the party's National Committee, and installed their own supporters as National Secretary and editor of the party paper. These actions were met with stiff resistance and, in response, the left wing of the party organized itself as a caucus, proceeded to hire a secretary, and started their own newspaper. At their first conference this splinter group called itself the Debs Caucus and continued to function under that name for almost five years. The Debs Caucus had strong support within the party and included a former National Chairman (Darlington Hoopes), the Socialist ex–Mayor of Milwaukee (Frank Zeidler), and many of the state and local Socialist Party organizations, including Wisconsin, Illinois, California, Philadelphia, Washington D.C., and New York City.

Further splintering of the Socialist Party was evident at the raucous and riotous Democratic National Convention in Chicago in 1968. Realignment Socialists were present as delegates supporting Hubert Humphrey while other members of the party, mainly from the Debs Caucus, were in the streets supporting the demonstrators.

By 1970, with Michael Harrington as National Chairman, the Socialist Party became even more divided as the party newspaper was censored to all but official views and the members of the Debs Caucus were being ignored. While Harrington personally opposed the war in Vietnam, he did not support the demand for unconditional withdrawal of U.S. forces, a stand that put him squarely at odds with the entire American left political movement. Because the Socialist Party was isolated from the anti-war movement and other left-leaning thinkers, it was basically the only left-leaning party in America that did not experience an increase in membership in this period.

Harrington and his followers pushed ahead and formed a third caucus, called the Coalition Caucus, with the intent of pursuing the Realignment strategy within the more liberal factions of both the Democratic Party and organized labor. In 1972, a Unity Convention was held to finalize the merger of the Socialist Party with the Democratic Socialist Federation. The Unity Caucus, led by supporters of Shachtman, were opposed to Harrington and his supporters and succeeded in passing a constitutional amendment providing for a "troika" in the Chairmanship, made up of Harrington, Charles Zimmerman of the DSF, and former civil rights leader Bayard Rustin. However, a resolution opposing the Vietnam war failed.

In the 1972 presidential election, the divisions within the party became blatantly clear as each arm of the "troika" supported different candidates. The Shachtman followers supported Henry Jackson during the primaries but took a neutral position during the campaign between McGovern and Nixon. Meanwhile, Harrington and the Coalition Caucus supported McGovern throughout the electoral campaign. And, finally, members of the Debs Caucus supported Benjamin Spock, a candidate of the People's Party.

By the end of 1972, the totally splintered Socialist Party, under the control of the right wing, changed its name to Social Democrats USA, which caused even more unrest as many states and locals within the Debs Caucus were disaffiliated and many others resigned. Early in 1973, the Socialist Parties of Wisconsin, California, and Illinois called for a National Convention in Milwaukee, Wisconsin. Earlier the Debs Caucus had organized the Union for Democratic Socialism (UDS) to act as an umbrella organization for both members and nonmembers of the Socialist Party. The UDS made plans for a major conference discussing the "Future of Democratic Socialism in America" to be held at the same time the three states had called for their National Convention. The result of these meetings was a reconstitution of the Socialist Party USA.

Michael Harrington resigned from SDUSA but played no active role in the reconstituted SPUSA. In 1973, he and his followers founded the Democratic Socialist Organizing Committee, now called the Democratic Socialists of America (after merging with the New American Movement in 1982). The DSA has basically functioned as a socialist faction within the various liberal wings of the Democratic Party and of the American Federation of Labor-Congress of Industrial Organizations.

Since 1973, the Socialist Party USA has focused its efforts on grassroots and local politics. In 1976 the party ran a presidential campaign with former Milwaukee Mayor Zeidler as its candidate. In 1980 the Socialist presidential ticket included David McReynolds, a pacifist on the staff of the War Resisters League, and Sister Diane Drufenbrock of the Order of St. Francis. The 1980 showing gave the party Federal Election Commission recognition as a national political party. The party had no presidential slate in 1984 but returned in 1988 with candidates Willa Kenoyer, a journalist, and Ron Ehrenreich, a credit union officer and university lecturer. In 1992, the party nominated

J. Quinn Brisben for President and union organizer Bill Edwards for Vice President. Edwards died during the campaign and was replaced by author and playwright Barbara Garson. In 1996, the party nominated activist and special education teacher Mary Cal Hollis for president and author and economics professor Eric Chester for Vice-President.

Affiliates. *Alabama*: *Email*: contact party through its web site; *Web site*: http://www.sp-usa.org/states/alabama.html. *Alaska*: *Email*: contact party through its web site; *Web site*: http://www.sp-usa.org/states/alaska.html. *Arizona*: *Email*: contact party through its web site; *Web site*: http://www.sp-usa.org/states/arizona.html. *Arkansas*: *Email*: contact party through its web site; *Web site*: http://www.sp-usa.org/states/arkansas.html. *California*: 2617 South Hauser Boulevard, Los Angeles, CA 90016; *Telephone:* 323-939-8281; *Email*: david@pinko.net; P.O. Box 22822, Oakland, CA 94609; *Telephone*: 510-663-6302; *Email*: bayareasplocal@yahoo.com; *Web site*: http://www.sp-usa.org/states/california.html. *Colorado*: 2625 Pine Street, Boulder, CO 80302; *Email*: sp-co@sp-usa.org; 9624 Grape Court, Thorton, CO 80229; *Email*: fulchi@hotmail.com; *Web site*: http://www.sp-usa.org/states/colorado.html. *Connecticut*: Socialist Party of Central/Eastern Connecticut, P.O. Box 310681, Newington, CT 06131; *Telephone*: 860-423-9776; *Email*: SPCentralCT@gmail.com; *Web site*: http://www.sp-usa.org/states/connecticut.html. *Delaware*: *Email*: contact party through its web site; *Web site*: http://www.sp-usa.org/states/delaware.html. *District of Columbia*: 1822 Lamont Street NW, Washington, D.C. 20010; *Email*: contact party through its web site; *Web site*: http://www.sp-usa.org/states/district-columbia.html. *Florida*: 1706 B Lake Avenue, Panama City, FL 32401; *Email*: flsocialist@socialistpartyflorida.org; *Web site*: http://www.socialistpartyflorida.org; 13938 Manowar Lane, Jacksonville Beach, FL 32250. *Georgia*: *Email*: contact party through its web site; *Web site*: http://www.sp-usa.org/states/georgia.html. *Hawaii*: *Email*: contact party through its web site; *Web site*: http://www.sp-usa.org/states/hawaii.html. *Idaho*: *Email*: contact party through its web site; *Web site*: http://www.sp-usa.org/states/idaho.html. *Illinois*: P.O. Box 578398, Chicago, IL 60657; *Email*: iwch@juno.com; *Web site*: http://www.sp-usa.org/states/illinois.html. *Indiana*: 2440 North

Park Avenue, Indianapolis, IN 46205; *Email*: contact party through its web site; *Web site*: http://www.sp-usa.org/states/indiana.html. *Iowa*: P.O. Box 924, Iowa City, IA 52244; *Email*: contact party through its web site; *Web site*: http://iowasocialistparty.org. *Kansas*: *Email*: contact party through its web site; *Web site*: http://www.sp-usa.org/states/kansas.html. *Kentucky*: *Email*: contact party through its web site; *Web site*: http://www.sp-usa.org/states/kentucky.html. *Louisiana*: *Email*: contact party through its web site; *Web site*: http://www.sp-usa.org/states/louisiana.html. *Maine*: *Email*: contact party through its web site; *Web site*: http://www.sp-usa.org/states/maine.html. *Maryland*: *Email*: contact party through its web site; *Web site*: http://www.sp-usa.org/states/maryland.html. *Massachusetts*: 43 Taylor Hill Road, Montague, MA 01351; *Telephone*: 413-367-9356; *Email*: susandor@crocker.com; P.O. Box 541468, Waltham, MA 02454; *Email*: PeopleUnite@aol.com; *Web site*: http://www.sp-usa.org/states/massachusetts.html. *Michigan*: P.O. Box 3285, Kalamazoo, MI 49003; *Telephone*: 269-599-1248; *Email*: spmi@spmichigan.org; *Web site*: http://www.michigansocialist.net. *Minnesota*: *Email*: contact party through its web site; *Web site*: http://www.sp-usa.org/states/minnesota.html. *Mississippi*: *Email*: contact party through its web site; *Web site*: http://www.sp-usa.org/states/mississippi.html. *Missouri*: *Email*: contact party through its web site; *Web site*: http://www.sp-usa.org/states/missouri.html. *Montana*: *Email*: contact party through its web site; *Web site*: http://www.sp-usa.org/states/montana.html. *Nebraska*: *Email*: contact party through its web site; *Web site*: http://www.sp-usa.org/states/nebraska.html. *Nevada*: *Email*: contact party through its web site; *Web site*: http://www.sp-usa.org/states/nevada.html. *New Hampshire*: *Email*: contact party through its web site; *Web site*: http://www.sp-usa.org/states/new-hampshire.html. *New Jersey*: P.O. Box 8622, Saddle Brook, NJ 07663; *Telephone*: 201-845-5463; *Email*: spnj@sp-usa.org, info@njsocialistparty.org; *Web site*: http://www.sp-usa.org/states/new-jersey.html; P.O. Box 86, Rochelle Park, NJ 07662. *New Mexico*: *Email*: contact party through its web site; *Web site*: http://www.sp-usa.org/states/new-mexico.html. *New York*: 339 Lafayette Street #303, New York, NY 10012; *Telephone*: 212-982-4586; *Email*: spnyc@newyorksocialists.org; *Web site*: http://sp-usa.org/ny/;

P.O. Box 35113, University Station, Syracuse, NY 13235. *North Carolina*: P.O. Box 37553, Raleigh, NC 27627; P.O. Box 217, Richlands, NC 28574; *Telephone*: 919-816-0213; *Email*: ncsocialist@hotmail.com; *Web site*: http://www.ncsocialist.org. *North Dakota*: *Email*: contact party through its web site; *Web site*: http://www.sp-usa.org/states/north-dakota.html. *Ohio*: P.O. Box 204, Yellow Springs, OH 45387; *Email*: contact party through its web site; *Web site*: http://www.sp-usa.org/states/ohio.html. *Oklahoma*: *Email*: contact party through its web site; *Web site*: http://www.sp-usa.org/states/oklahoma.html. *Oregon*: P.O. Box 5633, Portland, OR 97228; *Telephone*: 503-289-3511; *Email*: info@thesocialistparty.org, oregonsocialist@union.org.za; *Web site*: http://www.thesocialistparty.org/spo/, http://www.sp-usa.org/states/oregon.html; 16 Southwest Monticello Drive, Lake Oswego, OR 97035; *Telephone*: 503-636-4150; 3375 Northwest Fifth Avenue, Ontario, OR 97914; *Telephone*: 208-495-2323; 1555 West 18th Avenue #11, Eugene, OR 97402; 6035 North Greeley Avenue, Portland, OR 97217; *Telephone*: 503-740-9947. *Pennsylvania*: 102 Rachel Lane, Coatesville, PA 19320; *Email*: contact party through its web site; *Web site*: http//www.sp-usa.org/sppa/; 273 South Fourth Street, Hamburg, PA 19526; 2211 Bainbridge Street, Philadelphia, PA 19146; 331 Theatre Drive #1–B4, Johnstown, PA 19526; 4618 Carroll Street, Pittsburgh, PA 15224. *Rhode Island*: *Email*: contact party through its web site; *Web site*: http://sp-usa.org/spri/; http://www.sp-usa.org/states/rhode-island.html. *South Carolina*: *Email*: contact party through its web site; *Web site*: http://www.sp-usa.org/states/south-carolina.html. *South Dakota*: *Email*: contact party through its web site; *Web site*: http://sp-usa.org/spsd/; http://www.sp-usa.org/states/south-carolina.html. *Tennessee*: *Email*: contact party through its web site; *Web site*: http://www.sp-usa.org/states/tennessee.html. *Texas*: P.O. Box 2640, Austin, TX 78768; *Email*: sptx@moment.net; *Web site*: http://www.sp-usa.org/lonestar/; Partido Socialista del Valle, PMB 117, East Ruben Torres Sr. #A16, Brownsville, TX 78526; *Telephone*: 956-748-0169, 956-490-4220; *Email*: raucan@msn.com; *Web site*: http://www.geocities.com/sprgv/; http://www.sp-usa.org/states/texas.html. *Utah*: P.O. Box 540571, North Salt Lake, UT 84054; *Email*: contact party through its web site; *Web site*: http://www.sp-usa.org/states/utah.html. *Vermont*: 71 Westminster Road, Putney, VT 05346; *Email*: contact party through its web site; *Web site*: http://www.sp-usa.org/states/vermont.html. *Virginia*: 251 Fitchingfield Court, Sterling, VA 20165; *Email*: sdpva@juno.com; *Web site*: http://www.sp-usa.org/states/virginia.html. *Washington*: P.O. Box 656, Mounlake Terrace, WA 98043; *Email*: contact party through its web site; *Web site*: http://www.sp-usa.org/states/washington.html. *West Virginia*: *Email*: contact party through its web site; *Web site*: http://www.sp-usa.org/states/west-virginia.html. *Wisconsin*: P.O. Box 259824, Madison, WI 53725; 1001 East Keefe Avenue, Milwaukee, WI 53212; *Telephone*: 414-332-0654; *Email*: contact party through its web site; *Web site*: http://www.sp-usa.org/states/wisconsin.html.

Socialist Workers Party (SWP)

152 West 36th Street #401, New York, NY 10018; *Telephone*: 212-594-1014; *Fax*: 212-594-1018; *Email*: themilitant@verizon.net; *Web site*: http://www.themilitant.com

Originally a pro–Trotsky faction within the Communist Party USA, the Socialist Workers Party was formed in 1938 after the Communist Party USA, on orders from Soviet dictator Joseph Stalin, expelled the American Trotskyites. For years the party was the leading voice of Trotskyism in the United States; however, since the 1980s, the party has drifted toward authoritarian politics as espoused by Cuban leader Fidel Castro. The SWP has run candidates for President in every election since 1948, in addition to numerous local candidates for multiple political offices in various states. The party distributes its message and the latest news through its newspaper, *The Militant*.

The Socialist Workers Party traces its origins back to the former Communist League of America, which had been founded in 1928 by members of the Communist Party USA expelled for supporting Russian Communist leader Leon Trotsky against Josef Stalin. In 1934, the Communist League of America merged with the American Workers Party and formed the Workers Party of America (WPA). Members of the WPA, in turn, joined the Socialist Party of America in 1936. The Socialist Party soon expelled the former Workers Party members, along with others recruited to their Trotskyist politics. Those expelled founded the Socialist Workers Party, combining the names of the

Workers Party and the Socialist Party. The new party participated in founding the Fourth International.

In 1940, a split within the SWP, which began as a debate over internal leadership, proved to be the largest feud in the party's history. The majority faction supported Trotsky's position that the U.S.S.R. should remain a workers' state and be supported in any war with capitalist states, despite their opposition to Josef Stalin's regime. The minority faction believed that the U.S.S.R. should not be supported in its war with Finland and some members felt that Russia's leadership had degenerated to such a point that it deserved no support at all on any issue. After much internal dissension, the minority faction split away from the SWP and formed the Workers Party, taking roughly 40% of the party's membership as well as its youth organization, the Young People's Socialist League.

The next major split within the SWP came after World War II when a minority faction called for the party to support the 1948 presidential campaign of Henry Wallace (who ran under the banner of the Progressive Party). This faction also regarded Mao Tse-Tung as a Chinese revolutionary leader. This faction eventually left the SWP in 1958 after supporting the suppression of the Hungarian Rising of 1956, which was a position in contrast to most Trotskyists. This faction left to form the Workers' World Party.

In the 1950s and 1960s the membership of the SWP grew older, maintained a low public profile, and began to lose influence as a party. Things changed for the SWP with the 1959 revolution in Cuba, which prompted the party to support the island nation through the Fair Play for Cuba Committee.

Although the party survived the McCarthy era, it again began to experience a series of revolts and defections as multiple opposition groups formed to protest the direction of the party on numerous fronts, publicly centered on its various internal positions on Cuba and the Cuban Revolution. Its internal dissent led the party closer to the International Secretariat of the Fourth International (ISFI), from which it had split in 1953. In an attempt at reconciliation, the party attempted a reunification of the ISFI and the International Committee of the Fourth International. These efforts led to the 1963 creation of the United Secretariat of the Fourth International (USFI).

Numerous opposition groups rejected the merger and turned against the SWP leadership.

The most important faction opposing the SWP's move toward the USFI was the Revolutionary Tendency, led by James Robertson and Tim Wohlforth, which was critical of the Castro government for running Cuba as a Stalinist-style workers state. A split soon developed between the two men and two new organizations were created by their respective followers, the Spartacist League and the American Committee of the Fourth International.

The SWP survived these defections and later supported both the civil rights movement and the Black nationalist movement, both of which gained strength during the 1960s. The party strongly supported Black nationalist leader Malcolm X, who spoke at several of the party's public forums and had given an interview to *Young Socialist* magazine. After his assassination, the SWP had limited success and hardly any future involvement with his followers and other Black nationalists.

The SWP grew strength and members during the 1960s and into the early 1970s, mainly due to its ardent opposition to the Vietnam War and its activities on college campuses. Additionally, the party was strongly pro–Castro and became more so under the leadership of Jack Barnes, who became National Secretary in 1972. The SWP also published many of Leon Trotsky's works through its publishing house, Pathfinder Press. During this time the party supported Chicano nationalism and helped organize protests demanding legal abortion through the Women's National Abortion Action Coalition. When these movements went into decline and the Vietnam War came to an end, the SWP lost membership and its influence significantly declined.

Reacting to its decline, the party's leadership decided it needed a new focus and turned its attention and organizational skills towards industry and worked to improve the workers' lot in life. The party encouraged its members to take jobs within various industries with the aim of organizing worker factions, performing "communist-political work," and supporting union activity. This change in focus was not well received by all its members and the SWP again had to deal with internal friction, defections, and a seeming loss of purpose.

In the early 1980s the SWP again attempted to re-define itself when its leadership began to move away from its Trotskyist label, specifically rejecting Trotsky's theory of Permanent Revolution, arguing that it failed to make a distinction between the democratic and socialist goals of a workers' revolution. The leadership also argued that adopting a "Trotskyist" label created an unnecessary friction between itself and other like-minded revolutionary groups instead of working towards a collaborative effort to seek common goals. Opposition factions within the SWP rejected this move and continued to support the theory of permanent revolution, while maintaining the Trotskyist label. These factions, while supporting the Cuban and Nicaraguan revolutions, were more openly critical of those movements' leaders, such as Castro. There also continued to be strong resistance toward the SWP's "turn to industry" plan.

The influence of these factions grew within the SWP and eventually led to the formation of an opposition bloc on the party's National Committee. Tension came to a head in 1983 when the opposition was defeated in a vote at the party's National Convention, which led to some members being expelled and others quitting. Those who left the SWP went on to form other socialist organizations, such as the San Francisco, California-based Socialist Action and the Fourth Internationalist Tendency. The SWP has experienced a long period of relative peace ever since.

The Socialist Workers Party has run candidates for President since 1948 and received its greatest number of votes in 1976, when its candidate, Peter Camejo, received over 90,000 votes. In 1986, the party won a lawsuit against the Federal Bureau of Investigation as a result of its spying on the SWP for years.

The SWP's highest profile campaign occurred in the late 1980s and early 1990s when it created the Mark Curtis Defense Committee, when Curtis (an SWP activist and trade union organizer) was convicted on burglary and rape charges in 1988. The party claimed that he had been framed by police for his role in defending immigrant workers. Curtis was eventually paroled.

Although party membership has declined significantly in recent years, it has continued its "turn to industry" policy, while a majority of its members are industrial workers and rank-and-file trade union activists. Additionally, the party continues to support Pathfinder Press, which still publishes a large range of titles by revolutionary leaders, such as Malcolm X and Ernesto "Che" Guevara.

In 2004, the party's presidential campaign achieved ballot access in 13 states and the District of Columbia, even though its candidates were technically unqualified to hold office. Its presidential candidate, Roger Calero, was not an American citizen; and its vice-presidential candidate, Arrin Hawkins, was only 29 years old (not the 35-year-old minimum requirement established in the Constitution).

Southern Independence Party (SIP)

1402 Carol Avenue, Lancaster, TX 75134; *Email*: contact party through its web site; *Web site*: http://www.southernindependenceparty.com

Formed in 2000, the Southern Independence Party, a splinter group founded by dissident members of the Southern Party, is a right-wing political organization based in the southern United States that seeks southern independence and works to reconstitute the Confederate States of America. Even though the Southern Independence Party and the Southern Party espouse basically the same political views, the split was basically caused over infighting between members and a perceived dictatorial leadership.

The SIP insists that it is not a hate group and works to advance the flag of Dixie, Southern Culture, and Southern Tradition; "reveal the true history of the War of Northern Aggression"; promote states' rights and local governmental control; and the restoration of the Confederate States of America as a free and independent nation. The party believes that establishing a separate cultural and political entity within the borders of the United States is supported by history and the number of independent political governments that are currently being established throughout the world within the borders of now-defunct nations.

The SIP supports independence for, not secession by, the Southern States (Alabama, Arkansas, Georgia, Florida, Kentucky, Louisiana, Mississippi, Missouri, North Carolina, South Carolina, Tennessee, Texas, and Virginia) and territories of the Confederacy (Arizona, New Mexico, and Oklahoma). The Southern Independence

Party is working to be officially registered with the Secretary of State's office of each of the Southern States while the Southern Federation Committee oversees the organizing and promoting of the Southern Independence Party.

The Southern Independence Party believes that the "United States in general, and the South in particular, are defined by their historically Western and Biblical-Christian cultural core. This is especially true of the South, whose predominantly Celtic, British and French-derived religious and cultural traditions mixed with the Afro American, Mexican-American and American Indian cultures distinguish it from the rest of the country." Instead of competing with the Democratic and Republican parties for national power, the SIP functions as a broad-based regional political movement operating entirely at the state and local levels.

The party supports the right of citizens to own and bear arms; the abolishment of the Internal Revenue Service; restricting or abolishing the federal Department of Education; a strong military comprised mainly of State National Guard units; withdrawal from the North Atlantic Treaty Organization and all international organizations; voting with paper ballots to allow for accurate hand counts and traceability; and an end to all affirmative action programs.

Affiliates. *Alabama*: *Email*: contact party through its web site; *Web site*: http://www.sipofalabama.org. *Arizona*: Southern Parties of the Southwest, 4610 South Rural Road # 808, Tempe AZ 85282; *Telephone*: 480-831-0309; *Email*: southernpartysw@msn.com; *Web site*: http://www.southernpartysw.org. *Arkansas*: *Email*: contact party through its web site; *Web site*: www.sipofArkansas.org. *Kentucky*: *Email*: contact party through its web site; *Web site*: http://www.kentuckysip.homestead.com. *Louisiana*: *Email*: contact party through its web site; *Web site*: http://www.sipoflouisiana.org. *Maryland*: *Email*: contact party through its web site; *Web site*: http://www.sipofmaryland.org. *Mississippi*: *Email*: contact party through its web site; *Web site*: www.sipofmississippi.org. *Missouri*: *Email*: contact party through its web site; *Web site*: http://www.sipofmissouri.org. *New Mexico*: *Email*: contact party through its web site; *Web site*: http://www.southernpartysw.org. *Oklahoma*: *Email*: contact party through its web site; *Web site*: http://www.sipofoklahoma.org. *Tennessee*: P.O. Box 16,

Granville, TN 38564; *Telephone*: 800-747-8619; *Email*: contact party through its web site; *Web site*: http://www.siptn.org/the_index.htm, http://www.siptn.org.*Texas*: *Email*: contact party through its web site; *Web site*: http://www.sipoftexas.org

Southern Party

Founded in 1999 by League of the South activists, the Southern Party describes itself as a "nationalist party of the South." Touting the "National Flag of Dixie," the party calls for the formation of "a new Southern republic and the re-formation of a Confederate States of America, to include Maryland, Oklahoma and West Virginia."

Basically politically conservative, the Southern Party denounces the "corrupt two-party system; views the Democratic Party as a party of socialism; and the Republican Party as representing the interests of global corporations." The party describes its members as "decent, God-fearing, Southerners" who denounce "racial malice towards people of non-European origin."

For two years after its founding, the party was embroiled in internal conflict for the control of its political message. This dissension led to a number of members leaving and forming the rival Southern Independence Party in 2000. The Southern Party began fielding candidates for local offices in 1999 with some success and formed an alliance in 2001 to endorse future candidates of the Constitution Party for higher-level offices. By the end of 2000, the party claimed a membership of 3,000 including a youth branch called the Southern Party Collegiate Club.

Affiliates. *Arkansas*: *Email*: contact party through its web site; *Web site*: http://www.southernpartyofarkansas.org. *Georgia*: 725 Ridgeview Road, Morganton, GA 30560; *Email*: secretary@spofga.org; *Web site*: http://www.spofga.org. *Kentucky*: *Email*: contact party through its web site; *Web site*: http://www.siptn.org/kentucky. *Louisiana*: *Email*: contact party through its web site; *Web site*: http://www.geocities.com/logos_eros. *North Carolina*: *Email*: contact party through its web site; *Web site*: http://confederatepatriot.tripod.com/ncsp. *South Carolina*: 121 March Road, West Columbia, SC 29172; *Telephone*: 803-926-8960; *Email*: contact party through its web site; *Web site*: http://www.southernpartysc.com

Spirit of America Party

Email: abutom@aol.com; *Web site*: http://www.spiritofameri-caparty.com

The Spirit of America Party supports a strict limit on abortions; significant police and military pay raises; strict limits on immigration; using Indian tribes to patrol America's borders; 100% tax deduction for religious education; one-year draft for all citizens at the age of 19; basic foreign language training for all military personnel; and reciting the Pledge of Allegiance in all work places, schools, and public locations.

Star Party

Email: contact party through its web site; *Web site*: http://www.brantley.net/html/star_party.html

The Star Party supports tax-free savings for education; banning all hand guns for anyone under 18 and a registration of all weapons; a four-day work week with Monday being a community service day; protecting Social Security by progressively raising the retirement age; eliminating the penny as legal tender; limiting all interest rates to 15%; multi-national space exploration; zero tolerance for drug trafficking and hard labor for offenders; and restricting all public smoking.

Statesmanship Party

Route 1, Box 265, Warsaw, MO 65355; *Telephone*: 660-547-2314; *Email*: mostatesmanship@yahoo.com; *Web site*: http://statesmanship.4t.com

The Statesmanship Party has teamed up with the Reform Party of Missouri and the Constitutional Justice Society with the goal of "restoring free and fair elections in Missouri and throughout the United States." The party defines Statesmanship as "preservation of the past, while protecting the future through leadership, wisdom, ethics, integrity, perseverance, accountability, courage, tenacity, skill, activism, rule of law, and common sense."

The party supports equal political access for all candidates and political parties; complete right of privacy with no government interference at any level; term limits for all public offices; and financial support for campaigns being required to originate within the jurisdiction of the election.

Students Rights Party

Email: brianclarkson@lycos.com; *Web site*: http://brianclarkson.tripod.com/studentsrightsparty

The Students Rights Party was formed to give political voice to people under the age of 18. The party supports lowering the voting age to those in the first grade; lowering the age of candidates for all offices to 18, except for judges; and balancing the federal budget within a four year period.

Technotarian Party

Email: contact party through its web site; *Web site*: http://www.technotarian.org

The Technotarian Party focuses its efforts on blue- and white-collar workers through the use of technology and capitalistic opportunities. The party considers itself "liberal, with a strong sense of progressive leanings." The party supports technological solutions to social and political ills; and strong education in Math, Science, and Engineering.

Thermodynamic Law Party

Email: lyle@zapatopi.net; *Web site*: http://zapatopi.net/tlp.html

Founded in 1997 "as an alternative to the stagnant two-party system," the Thermodynamic Law Party is active in over 70 countries worldwide. Its policies are based on the scientific Laws of Thermodynamics and the party seeks to bring society into harmony with those Laws. The party believes that "a full awareness of the nature of Entropy, the Universe's natural movement to disorder and chaos (as stated in the Second Law of Thermodynamics) will give us insight into the course of societal decay and show us how to maximize our political energies to offset its effects."

The party believes governance obeys the laws of thermodynamics (applying scientific and Thermodynamic thinking to problems will provide viable solutions); technology is our friend but not our master (by using technology, the government can become more responsive to the needs of the people); better standards make better living (such as supporting the national switch to the metric system, adopting metric time, and using the exactitude offered with the Kelvin temperature scale); return to traditional values; educational reform (supporting school vouchers, national testing standards, and Head Start); economic growth the thermodynamic way (promoting free trade over protectionist policies; according to the First Law of Thermodynamics, wealth is neither created nor destroyed, it only changes forms); defense through non-entropy (using Thermodynamic principles to safeguard against negative foreign forces; decreasing the nation's Entropy through extensive use of Kelvinian Meditation); energy policies that make sense (applying Thermodynamic techniques learned in industry to increase America's energy efficiency and decrease its dependency on foreign oil); senior citizens are happy citizens (insuring the future existence of Medicare and Social Security); protecting the environment protects our nation (working to conserve and better use of the planet's physical resources); and the hoax of radioactivity (the party believes that radioactivity does not exist and the money that has been spent on so-called nuclear energy and nuclear weapons has actually been embezzled by corrupt government officials).

Third Party of America

P.O. Box 3007, Hollywood, CA 90078; *Telephone*: 323-462-8002; *Fax*: 812-339-0557; *Email*: info@3rdparty.org; *Web site*: http://www. 3rdparty.org/

Active since 1997 and created as an alternative to the current two-party system, the Third Party seeks direct input from the public to mold itself into a politically centrist party that unifies America in the 21st Century. The party encourages a philosophy of "Empathy in Politics" and is dedicated to forming policy positions from a grassroots perspective and supporting local candidates.

Timesizing Party of Massachusetts

P.O. Box 117, Harvard Square Station, Cambridge, MA 02238; *Telephone*: 617-623-8080; *Email*: timesizing@aol.com; *Web site*: http://www.timesizing.com/1polprty.htm, http://www.timesizing.com

Established in 1999, the Timesizing Party of Massachusetts aims to upsize markets by downsizing the work week and the work force. This plan translates into employers adjusting the work week up or down (adding or deducting work hours as needed) instead of hiring or firing workers to meet working demands. The party believes its ideas can be supported by the entire political spectrum: the conservative movement (the "right") can embrace the theory because it focuses on smaller government and bigger markets, while the liberal faction (the "left") can also embrace the theory because it promotes a stronger social safety net. The party states that its theory is "based on working models, American history, economic designs, ecology, work-time economics, linguistics, Limits to Growth theories, and the teachings of Buckminster Fuller."

U.S. Marijuana Party

Telephone: 404-806-5303; *Fax*: 404-806-9704; *Email*: contact party through its web site; *Web site*: http://www.usmjparty.com

The national U.S. Marijuana Party operates extensively through the internet and focuses its activities on working at the grassroots, local, and state-wide level. In addition to marijuana reform, the party supports making prostitution legal, the right of citizens to own and bear arms; and less government intrusion into the lives of its citizens. The party works to address and change local marijuana possession and sales laws on a state-by-state basis (through constitution changes and/or ballot initiatives), with the ultimate goal of creating a national marijuana policy.

Affiliates. *Alabama*: *Email*: contact party through its web site; *Web site*: http://alabama.usmjparty.com. *Arizona*: *Email*: arizonadm@usmjparty.com; *Web site*: http://arizona.usmjparty.com. *Arkansas*: P.O. Box 206, Pottsville, AR 72858; *Telephone*: 866-815-7807; *Email*: arkansasmarijuanaparty@hotmail.com; *Web site*: http://arkansas.usmjparty.com. *California*: *Telephone*: 415-368-7187; *Email*: contact party through its web site; *Web site*: http://california.usmjparty.com. *Colorado*: *Email*: contact party through its web site; *Web site*: http://colorado.usmjparty.com. *Florida*: Tampa; *Telephone*: 813-924-0395; *Email*: contact party through its web site; *Web site*: http://florida.usmjparty.com. *Georgia*: *Telephone*: 770-638-5915; *Email*: contact party through its web site; *Web site*: http://georgia.usmjparty.com. *Hawaii*: *Telephone*: 808-982-7640; *Email*: contact party through its web site; *Web site*: http://hawaii.usmjparty.com. *Illinois*:

1022 Collins Court, Bartonville, IL 61607; *Telephone*: 309-633-1023; *Email*: info@imjp.com; *Web site*: http://illinois.usmjparty.com. *Kansas*: 200 Brookwood Street, Lansing, KS 66043; *Telephone*: 913-727-3316; *Email*: ksmjparty@graffiti.net; *Web site*: http://kansas.usmjparty.com. *Kentucky*: *Telephone*: 859-835-4117; *Email*: contact party through its web site; *Web site*: http://kentucky.usmjparty.com. *Louisiana*: 1526 Pecan, Pine Prairie, LA 70576; *Telephone*: 337-599-3209; *Email*: contact party through its web site; *Web site*: http://louisiana.usmjparty.com. *Maryland*: *Telephone*: 410-486-7965; *Email*: contact party through its web site; *Web site*: http://maryland.usmjparty.com. *Massachusetts*: *Email*: contact party through its web site; *Web site*: http://massachusetts.usmjparty.com. *Michigan*: *Email*: contact party through its web site; *Web site*: http://michigan.usmjparty.com. *Minnesota*: *Email*: contact party through its web site; *Web site*: http://minnesota.usmjparty.com. *Mississippi*: 116 Burgess Drive, Nettelton, MS 38858; *Telephone*: 662-963-0775; *Email*: contact party through its web site; *Web site*: http://mississippi.usmjparty.com. *Missouri*: *Email*: contact party through its web site; *Web site*: http://missouri.usmjparty.com. *Montana*: *Email*: contact_us@mindorgy.net; *Web site*: http://montana.usmjparty.com. *Nebraska*: *Telephone*: 402-435-2047; *Email*: contact party through its web site; *Web site*: http://nebraska.usmjparty.com. *Nevada*: *Email*: contact party through its web site; *Web site*: http://nevada.usmjparty.com. *New Jersey*: P.O. Box 1302, Browns Mills, NJ 08015; *Telephone*: 609-893-3983; *Email*: contact party through its web site; *Web site*: http://newjersey.usmjparty.com. *New Mexico*: *Email*: contact party through its web site; *Web site*: http://newmexico.usmjparty.com. *North Carolina*: *Telephone*: 888-420-2543; *Email*: contact party through its web site; *Web site*: http://northcarolina.usmjparty.com. *North Dakota*: 520 West 5th Avenue, Dickinson, ND 58601; *Telephone*: 701-483-3353; *Email*: contact party through its web site; *Web site*: http://northdakota.usmjparty.com. *Ohio*: *Telephone*: 937-207-7537; *Email*: contact party through its web site; *Web site*: http://ohio.usmjparty.com. *Oklahoma*: 3201 South Parkview Avenue, Oklahoma City, OK 73119; *Telephone*: 405-686-1042; *Email*: spaceytraveler@sbcglobal.net; *Web site*: http://oklahoma.usmjparty.com. *Oregon*: 4259 Northeast Broadway Street, Portland, OR 97213; *Telephone*: 503-235-4606; *Email*:

contact party through its web site; *Web site*: http://oregon.usmjparty. com. *Pennsylvania*: 425 Tearing Run Road, Homer City, PA 15748; *Telephone*: 724-479-8887; *Email*: pennmjparty@graffiti.net; *Web site*: http://pennsylvania.usmjparty.com. *Tennessee*: *Telephone*: 615-310-8709; *Email*: contact party through its web site; *Web site*: http:// tennessee.usmjparty.com. *Texas*: 955 Brandywine, Beaumont, TX 77706; *Telephone*: 409-866-9459; *Email*: contact party through its web site; *Web site*: http://texas.usmjparty.com. *Utah*: *Telephone*: 435-635-3931; *Email*: contact party through its web site; *Web site*: http://utah.usmjparty.com. *Wisconsin*: *Email*: contact party through its web site; *Web site*: http://wisconsin.usmjparty.com.

U.S. Parliamentary Party (Parliament Party, Parliamentary Party)

P.O. Box 970, Paradise, CA 95967; *Email*: vcc@usparliament.org; *Web site*: http://www.parliamentparty.com, http://www.usparliament.org

The Parliament Party was founded in 2003 within the U.S.A. Parliament, which had been founded in 1995. The Parliamentary Party (of California) was founded in 2004 by radio talk-show host Mark Williams in Sacramento, California. The party supports allowing voters to vote for more than one candidate or cross over to more than one party or elective office.

Supporting the "all party system" concept, the party elects 100 Members of Parliament every four years by direct vote of all citizens who wish to participate in the process. Some are active in politics while other "elected" members are not even aware of the party's existence (which includes famous actors and celebrities, sports figures, and anyone else citizens vote to "elect").

The result of this open-ballot system is that the party is made up of members from numerous political groups, social organizations, and others at-large who do not participate at all in its activities. Consequently, most of the party's activities and initiatives are conducted at the local state level.

The result of the party's 7th U.S. Parliament election (whose members will "serve" from 08/05/04 through 08/05/08) is a good indicator of the mix that makes up the U.S. Parliamentary Party organization. Elected members include: Libertarian Party (19 MPs); Green Party (16 MPs); Democratic Party (9MPs); Unaffiliated (7 MPs, including Ozzy Osbourne, Bill Maher, Woody Harrelson, Jim Carrey, Michael Ruppert, Clint Eastwood); Independents (6 MPs, including Ralph Nader, Michael Moore, Arianna Huffington, John Anderson); Pot Party (6 MPs); Republican Party (6 MPs); Parliamentary Party (3 MPs); Conservative Populist Party (2 MPs); Marijuana Party (2 MPs); Natural Law Party (2 MPs); Peace and Freedom Party (2 MPs); Rock Star Party (2 MPs); United Veterans Rights Party (2 MPs); and 16 MPs from a variety of parties that have elected only one seat.

Affiliates. *Alabama*: *Email*: contact party through its web site; *Web site*: http://www.usparliament.org/al-par.htm. *Alaska*: *Email*: contact party through its web site; *Web site*: http://www.usparliament.org/ak-par.htm. *Arizona*: *Email*: contact party through its web site; *Web site*: http://www.usparliament.org/az-par.htm. *Arkansas*: *Email*: contact party through its web site; *Web site*: http://www.usparliament.org/ak-par.htm. *California*: *Email*: contact party through its web site; *Web site*: http://www.usparliament.org/ca-par.htm. *Colorado*: *Email*: contact party through its web site; *Web site*: http://www.usparliament.org/co-par.htm. *Connecticut*: *Email*: Contact Party through its web site; *Web site*: http://www.usparliament.org/ct-par.htm. *Delaware*: *Email*: contact party through its web site; *Web site*: http://www.usparliament.org/de-par.htm. *Washington, D.C.*: *Email*: contact party through its web site; *Web site*: http://www.usparliament.org/dc-par.htm. *Florida*: *Email*: contact party through its web site; *Web site*: http://www.usparliament.org/fl-par.htm. *Georgia*: *Email*: contact party through its web site; *Web site*: http://www.usparliament.org/ga-par.htm. *Hawaii*: *Email*: contact party through its web site; *Web site*: http://www.usparliament.org/hi-par.htm. *Idaho*: *Email*: contact party through its web site; *Web site*: http://www.usparliament.org/id-par.htm. *Illinois*: *Email*: contact party through its web site; *Web site*: http://www.usparliament.org/il-par.htm. *Indiana*: *Email*: contact party through its web site; *Web site*: http://www.usparliament.org/in-par.htm. *Iowa*: *Email*: contact party through its web site; *Web site*: http://www.usparliament.org/ia-par.htm. *Kansas*: *Email*: contact party through its web site; *Web site*: http://www.usparliament.org/ks-par.htm. *Kentucky*: *Email*: contact party through its web site; *Web site*: http://www.usparliament.org/ky-par.htm. *Louisiana*: *Email*: contact party through its web site; *Web site*: http://www.usparliament.org/la-par.htm. *Maine*: *Email*: contact party through its web site; *Web site*: http://www.usparliament. org/me-par.htm. *Maryland*: *Email*: contact party through its web site; *Web site*: http://www.usparliament.org/md-par.htm. *Massachusetts*: *Email*: contact party through its web site; *Web site*: http://www.usparliament.org/ma-par.htm. *Michigan*: *Email*: contact party through its web site; *Web site*: http://www.usparliament.org/mi-par.htm. *Minnesota*: *Email*: contact party through its web site; *Web site*: http://www.usparliament.org/mn-par.htm. *Mississippi*: *Email*: contact party through its web site; *Web site*: http://www. usparliament.org/ms-par.htm. *Missouri*: *Email*: contact party through its web site; *Web site*: http://www.usparliament.org/mo-par.htm. *Montana*: *Email*: contact party through its web site; *Web site*: http://www.usparliament.org/mt-par.htm. *Nebraska*: *Email*: contact party through its web site; *Web site*: http://www.usparliament.org/ne-par.htm. *Nevada*: *Email*: contact party through its web site; *Web site*: http://www.usparliament.org/nv-par.htm. *New Hampshire*: *Email*: contact party through its web site; *Web site*: http://www. usparliament.org/nh-par.htm. *New Jersey*: *Email*: contact party through its web site; *Web site*: http://www.usparliament.org/nj-par.htm. *New Mexico*: *Email*: contact party through its web site; *Web site*: http://www.usparliament.org/nm-par.htm. *New York*: *Email*: contact party through its web site; *Web site*: http://www.usparliament.org/ny-par.htm. *North Carolina*: *Email*: contact party through its web site; *Web site*: http://www.usparliament.org/nc-par.htm. *North Dakota*: *Email*: contact party through its web site; *Web site*: http://www.usparliament.org/nd-par.htm. *Ohio*: *Email*: contact party through its web site; *Web site*: http://www.usparliament.org/oh-par.htm. *Oklahoma*: *Email*: contact party through its web site; *Web site*: http://www.usparliament.org/ok-par.htm. *Oregon*: *Email*: contact party through its web site; *Web site*: http://www.usparliament. org/or-par.htm. *Pennsylvania*: *Email*: contact party through its web site; *Web site*: http://www.usparliament.org/pa-par.htm. *Rhode Island*: *Email*: contact party through its web site; *Web site*: http:// www.usparliament.org/ri-par.htm. *South Carolina*: *Email*: contact party through its web site; *Web site*: http://www.usparliament.org/sc-par.htm. *South Dakota*: *Email*: contact party through its web site; *Web site*: http://www.usparliament.org/sd-par.htm. *Tennessee*: *Email*: contact party through its web site; *Web site*: http://www.us parliament.org/tn-par.htm. *Texas*: *Email*: contact party through its web site; *Web site*: http://www.usparliament.org/tx-par.htm. *Utah*: *Email*: contact party through its web site; *Web site*: http://www.usparliament.org/ut-par.htm. *Vermont*: *Email*: contact party through its web site; *Web site*: http://www.usparliament.org/vt-par.htm. *Virginia*: *Email*: contact party through its web site; *Web site*: http://www.usparliament.org/va-par.htm. *Washington*: *Email*: contact party through its web site; *Web site*: http://www.usparliment.org/wa-par.htm. *West Virginia*: *Email*: contact party through its web site; *Web site*: http://www.usparliament.org/wv-par.htm. *Wisconsin*: *Email*: contact party through its web site; *Web site*: http://www.usparliament.org/wi-par.htm. *Wyoming*: *Email*: contact party through its web site; *Web site*: http://www.usparliament.org/wy-par.htm.

Unification Party

Email: UniParty@aol.com; *Web site*: http://www.geocities.com/capitolhill/lobby/3278/index.html

The Unification Party believes that there are too many political and financial options in the world and if things were simplified, the world would be a better place. The party supports the world unifying under one military and one currency; and the nations of the world yielding power to the United Nations.

United Citizens Party

9834 Highgate Road, Columbia, SC 29223; *Telephone*: 803-419-0801, 803-776-2372; *Fax*: 864-243-0283; *Web site*: http://unitedcitizens party.com

The United Citizens Party (legal name is United Citizens) is a political organization dedicated to opening the political process to all people. The party aims to "work together to elect people who will fight for progressive public policies that promote justice and return power to the people."

First organized in 1969, the party was formed "in response to the Democratic Party's opposition to nominating black candidates and its general hostility to working people and minority interests." The party's primary goal is to elect black candidates to the legislature and local offices in counties with black majority populations. The party ran candidates in 1970 and 1972 and as a result the first three black candidates were elected to the South Carolina House of Representatives since Reconstruction in 1970. The party was reconstituted in South Carolina and in 2002 nominated candidates for Congress and for the South Carolina State legislature. Five party candidates were elected to the South Carolina House of Representatives.

The party supports a livable minimum wage; local actions to provide affordable housing and eliminating homelessness; unionization of all South Carolina companies with over 100 employees; repealing all "right-to-work" legislation; reparations for all Black Americans; repeal of the Patriot Act; repealing mandatory-minimum sentencing guidelines; abolishing the death penalty; abolishing private, for-profit prisons; proportional representation and abolishing the electoral college; free access to reproductive health care; free tuition at public universities for all who qualify; greater community control of schools; and development of renewable energy sources.

United Party USA

Email: contact party through its web site; *Web site*: http://www.freehomepages.com/upnews/unitedparty.html

The United Party USA is a coalition of disenfranchised, excluded and oppressed voters, with Hispanics and Blacks playing a major leadership role and focusing on community actions and union activities. The party focuses its efforts on "representing the oppressed working people in America" and is currently seeking a prominent individual to travel around the country, espouse the party's beliefs, and to act as a spokesman for a nation-wide membership drive.

United States Corporatist Party

1332 Imperial Court, Suite C, Troy, OH 45373; *Email*: usasuperpower@corporatistparty.com; *Web site*: http://www.corporatist-party.org

The United States Corporatist Party is committed to saving

American jobs, farms and industries, and preserving the American standard of living, in contrast to what members see as the goals of the Democratic or Republican parties. The party favors an economic policy known as "Free-Market Corporatism," where prices are permitted to self-adjust according to various markets, while still being subject to indirect or direct government control, as needed.

Since the party is basically a capitalist organization, its primary focus is on tax reform and calling for lower rates and flat taxes, which will be less of a burden on citizens and will encourage business to expand investment, thus stimulating national economic growth. Additionally, the party supports fully-funded state-provided education for all citizens; long-term mandatory jail sentences for drug dealers and producers; laws that ban same-sex marriages; Christianity being the recognized and official religion of the country while allowing for individual religious freedom; laws prohibiting abortion; and international isolationist policies (both political and monetary).

United States National Official Monster Raving Loony Party

Boca Ciega Yacht Club, 4600 South Tifton Drive, Gulfport, FL 33701; P.O. Box 40925, St. Petersburg, FL 33743; *Telephone*: 727-344-5443; *Email*: contact party through its web site; *Web site*: http://www.usloonyparty.tripod.com

First started by rocker Screaming Lord Sutch in England in 1963, the United States National Official Monster Raving Loony Party takes a very light-hearted approach to local and national politics. The party issues daffy manifestos with a laugh and proposes even zanier laws with a serious intent, to make people take action. This party is the Pied Piper of politics that wants to put the PARTY back into political party.

United States Pacifist Party (USPP)

5729 South Dorchester Avenue, Chicago, IL 60637; *Telephone*: 773-324-0654; *Fax*: 773-324-6426; *Email*: blyttle@igc.org; *Web site*: http://www.uspacifistparty.org

Founded in 1983, the United States Pacifist Party was formed to give expression within a democratic, electoral context to the belief that military power profoundly contradicts many religious and philosophic principles, and is a practical mistake in today's world. The party views military traditions and institutions as the key obstacle to the solution of major social evils, such as war, the arms race, poverty, and political oppression.

The small USPP fielded a write-in candidate for President in 1996 and a U.S. Senate candidate in Colorado in 1998. The party opposes military actions in all circumstances and wants to transform the U.S. armed forces into "a non-violent defense and humanitarian service corps." The USPP platform advocates generally left-wing political stances, including slashing the military budget to zero, and is opposed to nuclear weapons. The party ran founder Bradford Lyttle as a write-in Presidential candidate in 2000 but has done little since.

While a graduate student of political science at the University of Chicago, Lyttle developed a mathematical probability model he called the "Apocalypse Equation" that he claimed showed nuclear deterrence, the foundation of U.S. foreign policy for decades, can be expected at any time to produce catastrophic accidents involving nuclear weapons and/or nuclear war. He felt this Equation produced an irrefutable scientific argument that national security could not be founded on military force, and therefore indirectly establishes a scientific basis for pacifism and defense by nonviolent resistance. He realized that the Equation made it possible to argue the realism of pacifism in any political arena and could be made one of the foundations of a pacifist political party. He founded the USPP mainly as an educational vehicle to promote what he called "scientific pacifism." Under the USPP banner, Lyttle ran for President in the 1984 election in the belief that the President determines foreign policy. With little success, he again ran for President as a write-in candidate in 1996 and 2000.

The party supports deactivation of all nuclear, biological, and chemical weapons; elimination of the Strategic Defense Initiative; abolishing the Selective Service System; an end to all overt and covert military aid and intelligence operations; repealing the Patriot Act; establishment of an unarmed service corps trained in strategic nonviolent defense and equipped for mobilization anywhere in the world; termination of all foreign military aid; creation of a Canadian-style single-payer national health care system with universal access; abolishing the death penalty; an open and unfettered immigration policy; normalizing relations with Cuba; a one-person-one-vote democratic world government; and proportional representation in national elections.

United States Peace Government (USPG)

2000 Capital Boulevard, Maharishi Vedic City, IA 52556; *Telephone*: 877-424-3546; *Fax*: 641-472-1165; *Email*: info@USPeaceGovernment.org; *Web site*: http://www.uspeacegovernment.org; http://www.natural-law.org

Founded in 1992 and originally called the Natural Law Party (NLP), the United States Peace Government works through 2000 presidential candidate Dr. John Hagelin's Institute of Science, Technology, and Public Policy to identify and promote scientifically proven solutions to the nation's problems. The USPG is composed of scientists, medical doctors, educators, and interested members from the former Natural Law Party and is dedicated to creating permanent peace in the U.S. and the world.

The two-party dominance of the 2004 election combined with the inability for any third party to gain financial or public support led Hagelin to choose against seeking the party's presidential nomination in 2004 and instead to accept the role of President of the United States Peace Government. Due to the Natural Law Party's inability to marshal national support and the rise of the USPG's profile, the party's Executive Committee decided to suspend national party operations but to keep the state affiliates active.

Shortly after forming, the party obtained ballot access in 32 states, fielded 128 candidates, and was granted "national party" status by the Federal Election Commission, which meant that Hagelin qualified for federal matching funds. In 1993 and 1994, Hagelin worked on Capitol Hill to introduce language into health care legislation that would support funding for proven prevention-oriented health care programs. By 1994 the Natural Law Party's message was gaining support and some of its candidates increased their vote total by 20% over 1992. In 1995 the party gained ballot access in California and Ohio and by 1996 the NLP qualified for the ballot in 48 states and ran 400 candidates for federal, state, and local offices, collecting a total of more than 2.5 million votes nationwide. In 1999 the Natural Law Party began hosting national summits on the hazards of genetically engineered foods and Hagelin announced his candidacy for both the Natural Law Party and Reform Party presidential nominations in a bid to create a powerful coalition of independent voters. The Natural Law Party changed its name in July 2003 to the United States Peace Government.

The party supports prevention-oriented government that will both solve existing problems and prevent future ones from arising; conflict-free politics; an end to negative campaigning; streamlining the federal government and decreasing its intrusion into its citizens lives; vouchers enabling Medicare and Medicaid enrollees to choose any insurance plan or health care provider they desire; the Head Start program; school vouchers to increase school choice; mandating the labeling of genetically engineered foods; development of alternative energy sources; eliminating Political Action Committee and soft-money funding of campaigns; abolishing the Electoral College; decreasing abortions through education but not legislation; creating a "prevention wing" within the military, with a primary purpose of preventing the outbreak of war; existing gun-control legislation as an appropriate balance between public safety and the constitutional right to bear arms; allocating immigration quotas to each nation; and increasing border defense through reassignment of selected military personnel.

Affiliates. *Alabama*: 28 Harbor View Court, Decatur, AL 35601; *Telephone*: 256-350-2823; *Email*: gmcoffey@aol.com; *Web site*: http://www.natural-law.org/states/Alabama.html. *Arizona*: 2727 South Kinney Road, Tucson, AZ 85735; *Telephone*: 520-908-0392; *Fax*: 520-578-8186; *Email*: NLPArizona@aol.com; *Web site*: http://www.natural-law.org/states/Arizona.html. *Arkansas*: P.O. Box 294, Plumerville, AR 72127; *Telephone*: 501-977-0112; *Email*: areasotovote@aol.com; *Web site*: http://www.natural-law.org/states/Arkansas.html. *California*: P.O. Box 50843, Palo Alto, CA 94303; *Telephone*: 831-425-2201, *Fax*: 831-427-9230; *Email*: nlpca@aol.com; P.O. Box 5065, Irvine, CA 92616; *Telephone*: 949-509-7555; P.O. Box 270605, San Diego, CA 92198; *Telephone*: 760-888-9600; *Fax*: 760-233-0299; *Email*: iris4NLP@yahoo.com; *Web site*: http://www.natural-law.org/states/California.html. *Colorado*: 1140 U.S. Highway 287 #400–126,

Broomfield, CO 80020; *Telephone*: 303-885-0705; *Email*: info@coloradonlp.org; *Web site*: http://www.coloradonlp.org. *Connecticut*: P.O. Box 61, Colchester, CT 06415; *Telephone*: 860-961-7546; *Email*: spowens@webmastersct.com; *Web site*: http://www.natural-law.org/states/Connecticut.html. *Delaware*: 1 Russell Road., Landers Park, New Castle, DE 19720; *Telephone*: 302-654-5872; *Fax*: 609-935-1494; *Email*: seatigermattson@aol.com; *Web site*: http://www.natural-law.org/states/Delaware.html. *Georgia*: 5901 Peachtree-Dunwoody Place, Building B #170, Atlanta, GA 30328; *Telephone*: 770-393-4270; *Fax*: 770-396-0067; *Email*: dswerdlin@swerdlin.net; *Web site*: http://www.natural-law.org/states/Georgia.html. *Idaho*: 59 Drake Street, Pocatello, ID 83201; *Telephone*: 208-233-0129; *Fax*: 208-235-1158; *Email*: contact party through its web site; *Web site*: http://www.natural-law.org/states/Idaho.html. *Illinois*: 2357 South 8th Street, Springfield, IL 62703; *Telephone*: 217-553-6075; *Email*: contact party through its web site; *Web site*: http://www.natural-law.org/states/Illinois.html. *Kentucky*: 3820 Nicholasville Road #1009, Lexington, KY 40503; *Telephone*: 859-272-5904; *Email*: sharkiemike@earthlink.net; *Web site*: http://www.natural-law.org/states/Kentucky.html. *Louisiana*: 1828 Fifth Street #1, Slidell, LA 70458; *Telephone*: 985-641-6784; *Email*: mrozenthal@cs.com; *Web site*: http://members.aol.com/lanlp; *Web site*: http://www.natural-law.org/states/Louisiana.html. *Michigan*: 13541 Austin Court, Hartland, MI 48353; *Telephone*: 248-889-0610; *Email*: dddern@aol.com; *Web site*: http://www.natural-law.org/states/Michigan.html; 5950 South Lake Shore Drive, Harbor Springs, MI 49740; *Telephone & Fax*: 231-526-2002. *Minnesota*: 5620 Code Avenue, Edina, MN 55436; *Telephone*: 952-920-9311; *Fax*: 612-560-3844; *Email*: robjoful@aol.com; *Web site*: http://www.natural-law.org/states/Minnesota.html. *Nevada*: 2900 Fantasy Lane, Sparks, NV 89436; *Telephone*: 775-425-8000; *Fax*: 775-425-3000; *Email*: lois@telemetry.com; *Web site*: http://www.natural-law.org/states/Nevada.html. *New Hampshire*: 65 Dorchester Way, Nashua, NH 03064; *Telephone*: 603-889-0170; *Email*: cori_dollette_peele@yahoo.com; *Web site*: http://www.natural-law.org/states/New_Hampshire.html. *New Jersey*: 189 Swimming River Road, Tinton Falls, NJ 07724; *Telephone*: 732-389-5453; *Fax*: 732-389-1299; *Email*: mjexcels@myexcel.com; *Web site*: http://www.natural-law.org/states/

New_Jersey.html. *New Mexico*: 25B Paseo Galisteo, Santa Fe, NM 87708; *Telephone*: 505-660-5288; *Email*: baruch88@yahoo.com; *Web site*: http://www.natural-law.org/states/New_Mexico.html.*New York*: 58 West 58th Street #9A, New York, NY 10019; *Telephone*: 917-710-2093; *Fax*: 212-725-1020; *Email*: AYLC@msn.com; *Web site*: http://www.natural-law.org/states/New_York.html. *North Carolina*: 236–2 RC Cook Road, Blowing Rock, NC 28605; *Telephone*: 828-268-0012; *Email*: catherine@boone.net; *Web site*: http://www.natural-law.org/states/North_Carolina.html. *Ohio*: 915 Washington Street, Genoa, Ohio 43430; *Telephone & Fax*: 419-855-1346; *Email*: slotnicks4@aol.com; *Web site*: http://www.natural-law.org/states/Ohio.html. *Pennsylvania*: 100 West Avenue, Jenkintown, PA 19046; *Telephone*: 215-681-4370; *Fax*: 215-886-2978; *Email*: billsmithnlp@hotmail.com; *Web site*: http://www.geocities.com/natural-law-pa/; *Web site*: http://www.natural-law.org/states/Pennsylvania.html. *Rhode Island*: 136 Riverside Drive #2, Tiverton, RI 02878; *Email*: plautus1@msn.com; *Web site*: http://www.natural-law.org/states/Rhode_Island.html. *Tennessee*: P.O. Box 3214, Chattanooga, TN 37404; *Telephone*: 423-698-1141; *Email*: dicksims@earthlink.net; *Web site*: http://www.natural-law.org/states/Tennessee.html. *Vermont*: 1075 Butternut Hill Road #2, Waitsville, VT 05673; *Telephone*: 802-496-8026; *Fax*: 802-496-6215; *Email*: anne@pixelridge.com; *Web site*: http://www.natural-law.org/states/Vermont.html. *Virginia*: 4830 Valley Pike, Stephens City, VA 22655; *Email*: patrickd@visuallink.com; *Web site*: http://www.va-natural-law.org, http://www.natural-law.org/states/Virginia.html. *Washington*: 5228 North Winnifred Street, Ruston, WA 98407; *Telephone*: 253-732-8626; *Fax*: 253-759-6714; *Email*: nlp@iopener.net, macampbell@yahoo.com; *Web site*: http://www.natural-law.org/states/Washington.html. *West Virginia*: P.O. Box 668, Shepherdstown, WV 25443; *Telephone*: 304-876-5431; *Email*: kwilliam@shepherd.wvnet.edu; *Web site*: http://www.natural-law.org/states/West_Virginia.html. *Wisconsin*: P.O. Box 314, Mukwonago, WI 53149; *Telephone*: 262-363-4410; *Email*: sukham@ix.netcom.com; *Web site*: http://www.natural-law.org/states/Wisconsin.html. *Wyoming*: P.O. Box 595, Wilson, WY 83014; *Telephone*: 307-733-0734; *Fax*: 307-739-1995; *Email*: contact party through its web site; *Web site*: http://www.natural-law.org/states/Wyoming.html.

United States Taxpayers Party (see Constitution Party)

United States World Political Party (USWPP)
P.O. Box 163114, Columbus, OH 43215; *Email*: contact party through its web site; *Web site*: http://worldpoliticalparty.com

The United States World Political Party accepts the idea that individuals have different temperaments, talents, and convictions; yet have a common interest in the preservation of the earth and the world and the advancement of politics on all levels. The party recognizes the importance of individual human will and effort and seeks to provide opportunities for development and prosperity of all individuals.

The party ardently opposes terrorism and believes the offensive use of advanced killing technologies against civilians or to disrupt popularly elected constitutional governments is criminal and warrants appropriate defensive military reaction, followed by educational action to attempt to assist in the implementation and development of constitutional popularly elected governments.

In general the USWPP adheres to the views of the World Political Party as long-term goals, but recognizes that a period of transition will be necessary. During the transition toward a popular world political reality, the party believes that "every effort must be made to preserve within the United States the Constitutional freedoms of its citizens." In the near future, the party expects to create a World Political Institute for the purpose of advancing the educational priorities of the party and for training the public servants of the future.

The party supports voluntary human population control; encouraging individual participation in government at all levels; the training of a public service force that would better understand both international and local perspectives; strong environmental laws; complete nuclear disarmament; and the destruction of all weapons of mass destruction.

Unity Party of America
Email: mail@unityparty.us; *Web site*: http://www.unityparty.us

The Unity Party of America is a political organization dedicated to "advancing national unity on commonsense solutions." The party supports a balanced budget constitutional amendment; elimination of all income tax on annual income below $30,000 and a flat tax of thirty percent on annual income over $30,000; full tax deductions for health care costs; affirmative action programs based on economic circumstances and not on the color of one's skin; an amendment to the Constitution lowering the voting age to 16; and allowing naturalized citizens to become President of the United States.

In 2003 the party began its life as Runners for Clark (RFC), one of the numerous nationwide organizations that routinely crops up across America in support for various political presidential candidates. RFC was created to support the 2004 presidential campaign of General Wesley K. Clark and by the time he quit the campaign, Runners for Clark had formed 19 chapters in 16 states.

No longer having a specific candidate to support, in 2004 RFC adjusted its focus toward a national view and changed its name to Unity Runners and began supporting candidates who agreed with their political beliefs, regardless of their party affiliation. Realizing the need for a middle-of-the-road political party in reaction to the animus created between the political left and right in America, the party refocused its efforts toward moderate politics and changed its name to the Unity Party.

Affiliates. *Alabama*: unitypartyalabama@yahoo.com. *Alaska*: unitypartyalaska@yahoo.com. *Arizona*: unitypartyarizona@yahoo.com. *Arkansas*: unitypartyarkansas@yahoo.com. *California*: unitypartycalifornia@yahoo.com. *Colorado*: unitypartycolorado@yahoo.com. *Connecticut*: unitypartyconnecticut@yahoo.com. *Delaware*: unitypartydelaware@yahoo.com. *Florida*: unitypartyflorida@yahoo.com. *Georgia*: unitypartygeorgia@yahoo.com. *Hawaii*: unitypartyhawaii@yahoo.com. *Idaho*: unitypartyidaho@yahoo.com. *Illinois*: unitypartyillinois@yahoo.com. *Indiana*: unitypartyindiana@yahoo.com. *Iowa*: unitypartyiowa@yahoo.com. *Kansas*: unitypartykansas@yahoo.com. *Kentucky*: unitypartykentucky@yahoo.com. *Louisiana*: unitypartylouisiana@yahoo.com. *Maine*: unitypartymaine@yahoo.com. *Maryland*: unitypartymaryland@yahoo.com. *Massachusetts*: unitypartymassachusetts@yahoo.com. *Michigan*: unitypartymichigan@yahoo.com. *Minnesota*: unitypartyminnesota@yahoo.com. *Mississippi*: unitypartymississippi@yahoo.com. *Missouri*: unitypartymissouri@yahoo.com. *Montana*: unitypartymontana@yahoo.com. *Nebraska*: unitypartynebraska@yahoo.com. *Nevada*: unitypartynevada@yahoo.

com. *New Hampshire*: unitypartynewhampshire@yahoo.com. *New Jersey*: unitypartynewjersey@yahoo.com. *New Mexico*: unitypartynewmexico@yahoo.com. *New York*: unitypartynewyork@yahoo.com. *North Carolina*: unitypartynorthcarolina@yahoo.com. *North Dakota*: unitypartynorthdakota@yahoo.com. *Ohio*: unitypartyohio@yahoo.com. *Oklahoma*: unitypartyoklahoma@yahoo.com. *Oregon*: unitypartyoregon@yahoo.com. *Pennsylvania*: unityparty pennsylvania@yahoo.com. *Rhode Island*: unitypartyrhodeisland@yahoo.com. *South Carolina*: unitypartysouthcarolina@yahoo.com. *South Dakota*: unitypartysouthdakota@yahoo.com. *Tennessee*: unity partytennessee@yahoo.com. *Texas*: unitypartytexas@yahoo.com. *Utah*: unitypartyutah@yahoo.com. *Vermont*: unitypartyvermont@yahoo.com. *Virginia*: unitypartyvirginia@yahoo.com. *Washington*: unitypartywashingtonstate@yahoo.com. *West Virginia*: unitypartywestvirginia@yahoo.com. *Wisconsin*: unitypartywisconsin@yahoo.com. *Wyoming*: unitypartywyoming@yahoo.com.

Vermont Grassroots Party

1614 Gilbert Road, Williamstown, VT 05679; *Telephone*: 802-433-5441; *Email*: vgp@vtgrassrootsparty.org; *Web site*: http://www.vtgrassrootsparty.org

The Vermont Grassroots Party aims to end the cannabis prohibition and all that follows from this concept. The cannabis prohibition represents to the party "the worst of lawmaking and a real assault on our environmental ethics, economic freedoms, access to medicines, individual liberties and personal responsibility." The party is not a single-issue entity and has a platform addressing numerous issues, including improving national education systems, transportation, economic development, a strong environment, civil liberties, personal responsibility, governmental restraint, medical care, and social protections.

Vermont Progressive Party

P.O. Box 281, Montpelier, VT 05601; 73 Main Street #29, Montpelier, VT 05602; *Telephone*: 877-798-2795, 802-229-0800; *Email*: info@progressiveparty.org; *Web site*: http://www.progressiveparty.org

The Vermont Progressive Party focuses its efforts on helping working men, women, and families. Members of the party believe that everyone who works full-time should be able to meet his or her basic needs, have access to health care, and be able to send their children to college. The party also works to protect the state's landscape and environment.

The party supports campaign finance reform; promoting economic, social and environmental justice; the tax burden being shared by those able to pay; elimination of all nuclear weapons; and redirecting military spending to human/social needs.

In 1981, Independent candidate Bernie Sanders upset a longtime incumbent mayor of Burlington, the state's largest city, and the coalition that had helped put him in office came to be known as the Progressive Coalition. The Coalition went on to help elect members to the city council, another mayor, and were an important part of Sanders becoming the only Independent Congressman in 1990.

The Coalition enjoyed continued electoral success and helped get other local and state candidates voted into office. In 1999, the Coalition was organized in enough local cities to qualify as an official statewide party and adopted its current name.

Veterans Party of America

1441 South Dr. Martin Luther King Jr Street, Saint Petersburg, FL 33705, *Telephone*: 727-822-8387; *Email*: veteransparty@aol.com; *Web site*: http://www.veteransparty.us

Founded in 2003, the Veterans Party of America exists to support and honor those men and women who have served in the nation's military forces since America's inception in 1776 and to ensure they receive all the rights and benefits they have earned. The party represents the rights and needs of veterans across the political spectrum and its top priority is improving the lives of those who served. In 2004, the party fielded a few candidates, including one running for U.S. Senate from Florida.

Affiliates. *Alabama*: *Email*: contact party through its web site; *Web site*: http://www.veteransparty.us/AL01.htm. *Alaska*: *Email*: contact party through its web site; *Web site*: http://www.veteransparty.us/ AK01.htm. *Arizona*: *Email*: contact party through its web site; *Web site*: http://www.veteransparty.us/AZ01.htm. *Arkansas*: *Email*: contact party through its web site; *Web site*: http://www.veteransparty.us/

AR01.htm. *California*: *Email*: contact party through its web site; *Web site*: http://www.veteransparty.us/CA01.htm. *Colorado*: *Email*: contact party through its web site; *Web site*: http://www.veteransparty.us/ C001.htm. *Connecticut*: *Email*: contact party through its web site; *Web site*: http://www.veteransparty.us/CT01.htm. *Delaware*: *Email*: contact party through its web site; *Web site*: http://www.veteransparty. us/DE01.htm. *Florida*: *Email*: contact party through its web site; *Web site*: http://www.veteransparty.us/FL01.htm. *Georgia*: *Email*: contact party through its web site; *Web site*: http://www.veteransparty. us/GA01.htm. *Hawaii*: *Email*: contact party through its web site; *Web site*: http://www.veteransparty.us/HI01.htm. *Idaho*: *Email*: contact party through its web site; *Web site*: http://www.veteransparty.us/ ID01.htm. *Illinois*: *Email*: contact party through its web site; *Website*: http://www.veteransparty.us/IL01.htm. *Indiana*: *Email*: contact party through its web site; *Web site*: http://www.veteransparty.us/IN01. htm. *Iowa*: *Email*: contact party through its web site; *Web site*: http://www.veteransparty.us/IA01.htm. *Kansas*: *Email*: contact party through its web site; *Web site*: http://www.veteransparty.us/KS01. htm. *Kentucky*: *Email*: contact party through its web site; *Web site*: http://www.veteransparty.us/KY01.htm. *Louisiana*: *Email*: contact party through its web site; *Web site*: http://www.veteransparty.us/ LA01.htm. *Maine*: *Email*: contact party through its web site; *Web site*: http://www.veteransparty.us/ME01.htm. *Maryland*: *Email*: contact party through its web site; *Web site*: http://www.veteransparty.us/ MD01.htm. *Massachusetts*: *Email*: contact party through its web site; *Web site*: http://www.veteransparty.us/MA01.htm. *Michigan*: *Email*: contact party through its web site; *Web site*: http://www.veteansparty. us/MI01.htm. *Minnesota*: *Email*: contact party through its web site; *Web site*: http://www.veteransparty.us/MN01.htm. *Mississippi*: *Email*: contact party through its web site; *Web site*: http://www.veterans party.us/MS01.htm. *Missouri*: *Email*: contact party through its web site; *Web site*: http://www.veteransparty.us/M001.htm. *Montana*: *Email*: contact party through its web site; *Web site*: http://www.vet-eransparty.us/ MT01.htm. *Nebraska*: *Email*: contact party through its web site; *Web site*: http://www.veteransparty.us/NE01.htm. *Nevada*: *Email*: contact party through its web site; *Web site*: http://www.vet-eransparty.us/NV01.htm. *New Hampshire*: *Email*: contact party through its web site; *Web site*: http://www.veteansparty.us/NH01.htm. *New Jersey*: *Email*: contact party through its web site; *Web site*: http://www.veteransparty.us/NJ01.htm. *New Mexico*: *Email*: contact party through its web site; *Web site*: http://www.veteransparty.us/NM01.htm. *New York*: *Email*: contact party through its web site; *Web site*: http://www.veteransparty.us/NY01.htm. *North Carolina*: *Email*: contact party through its web site; *Web site*: http://www.veteransparty.us/NC01.htm. *North Dakota*: *Email*: contact party through its web site; *Web site*: http://www.veteransparty.us/ND01.htm. *Ohio*: *Email*: contact party through its web site; *Web site*: http://www.veteransparty.us/OH01.htm. *Oklahoma*: *Email*: contact party through its web site; *Web site*: http://www.veteransparty.us/OK01.htm. *Oregon*: *Email*: contact party through its web site; *Web site*: http://www.veteransparty.us/OR01.htm. *Pennsylvania*: *Email*: contact party through its web site; *Web site*: http://www.veteransparty.us/PA01.htm. *Rhode Island*: *Email*: contact party through its web site; *Web site*: http://www.veteransparty.us/RI01.htm. *South Carolina*: *Email*: contact party through its web site; *Web site*: http://www.veteransparty.us/SC01.htm. *South Dakota*: *Email*: contact party through its web site; *Web site*: http://www.veteransparty.us/SD01.htm. *Tennessee*: *Email*: contact party through its web site; *Web site*: http://www.veteransparty.us/TN01.htm. *Texas*: *Email*: contact party through its web site; *Web site*: http://www.veteransparty.us/TX01.htm. *Utah*: *Email*: contact party through its web site; *Web site*: http://www.veteransparty.us/UT01.htm. *Vermont*: *Email*: contact party through its web site; *Web site*: http://www.veteransparty.us/VT01.htm. *Virginia*: *Email*: contact party through its web site; *Web site*: http://www.veteransparty.us/VA01.htm. *Washington*: *Email*: contact party through its web site; *Web site*: http://www.veteransparty.us/WA01.htm. *West Virginia*: *Email*: contact party through its web site; *Web site*: http://www.veteransparty.us/WV01.htm. *Wisconsin*: *Email*: contact party through its web site; *Web site*: http://www.veteransparty.us/WI01.htm. *Wyoming*: *Email*: contact party through its web site; *Web site*: http://www.veteransparty.us/WY01.htm.

We the People, the People's Party
P.O. Box 253, Jackson, NH 03846; *Telephone*: 603-383-4285; *Fax*:

603-383-6793; *Email*: petersWTP@aol.com; *Web site*: http://www. WeThePeople-WTP.org

Formed in 1995, We The People, The People's Party (which bills itself as the "American People's Party") works to take big money out of politics and to return governmental control back to the people. The party's co-founder, Jeffrey Peters, ran for President as a write-in candidate in 2000. He formed the "Boston TV Party" in 2000 to protest the exclusion of third party and independent candidates (such as himself) from the televised Bush-Gore Presidential Debate. Under various forms of its name (such as "The American People's Party," "We the People," and "The People's Committee"), the party is registered in all 50 states.

The party believes the country needs (and wants) a more centrist-based political party that is not available from either the Democrats ("who are being controlled by the left-wing liberals") or the Republicans ("who are being controlled by right-wing reactionaries").

Workers Party, USA (WP-USA) (Workers World Party [WWP])

55 West 17th Street, New York, NY 10011; *Telephone*: 212-627-2994; *Fax*: 212-675-7869; *Email*: ww@workers.org; *Web site*: http:// www.workers.org; P.O. Box 25716, Chicago, IL 60625; *Telephone*: 312-409-1127; *Email*: wp@workersparty.org; *Web site*: http://www. workersparty.org

The Workers Party, USA is a Marxist-Leninist political party founded by Michael Thorburn in 1992 and was established to "bring the working class out as an independent class force." The WP-USA shares much of the Communist Party USA's ideology and publishes a bi-weekly newspaper, *The Worker*, and a quarterly journal called *The Worker Magazine*.

As with all Communist-style political organizations, the party believes that capitalism in the United States has reached its final stage of monopoly and can no longer provide jobs for a growing number of workers; immediate withdrawal of all U.S. troops abroad, the withdrawal of the U.S. from all aggressive military pacts and alliances, such as the North Atlantic Treaty Organization, an end to the militarization of U.S. society; free, comprehensive health care; and free education at all levels, from infant care through the university.

The (international) Workers World Party (American headquarters: 55 West 17th Street, 5th Floor, New York NY 10011; *Telephone*: 212-627-2994; *Fax*: 212-675-7869; *Email*: ww@workers.org; *Web site*: http://www.workers.org) was formed in 1959 by a pro–Chinese communist faction that split from the Socialist Workers Party. The WWP believes in direct action and not democratic elections. Although the WWP's stated mission is to support worker revolutions, the party was criticized for endorsing the Soviet Union's actions when it suppressed worker uprisings in Hungary in the 1950s, Czechoslovakia in the 1960s and Poland in the early 1980s.

The party mainly operates through its newspaper, *Workers World*, and supports worldwide socialism, specifically the idea that ownership of the productive wealth built up by workers can't remain in the hands of a privileged few. Members of the party describe themselves as "independent Marxists who respect the struggles for self-determination and progress of oppressed nations ... Our goal is solidarity of all the workers and oppressed against the dominant imperialist system."

In 1980, the WWP fielded its first candidate for president. In 1996 its candidate (Monica Moorehead) was on the ballot in 12 states, and she ran again in 2000, garnering almost 5,000 votes while being listed on the ballot in four states. The international party sponsors or directs numerous popular front groups including International ANSWER (an anti-war organization), the All People's Congress, the International Action Center, the Nicaragua Network, the Alliance for Global Justice, Pastors for Peace, the Korean Truth Commission, the Movement for a People's Assembly, the National People's Campaign, the Independent Commission of Inquiry on the U.S. Invasion of Panama, and the Campaign to Stop Settlements in Occupied Palestine.

Affiliates. *California*: 5274 West Pico Boulevard #203, Los Angeles CA 90019; *Telephone*: 323-936-1416; *Email*: la@workers.org; 3930 Oregon Street #230, San Diego CA 92104; *Telephone*: 619-692-4496; 2940 16th Street #207, San Francisco CA 94103; *Telephone*: 415-561-9752; *Email*: sf@workers.org. *Colorado*: *Email*: denver@workers.org. *District of Columbia*: P.O. Box 57300, Washington D.C. 20037; *Email*: dc@workers.org. *Georgia*: P.O. Box 424, Atlanta, GA 30301; *Telephone*: 404-627-0815. *Illinois*: 27 North Wacker Drive #138, Chicago IL 60606; *Telephone*: 773-381-5839; *Fax*: 773-761-9330; *Email*: chicago@

workers.org. *Maryland*: 426 East 31 Street, Baltimore, MD 21218; *Telephone*: 410-235-7040; *Email*: baltimore@workers.org. *Massachusetts*: 284 Armory Street, Boston MA 02130; *Telephone*: 617-983-3835; *Fax*: 617-983-3836; *Email*: boston@workers.org. *Michigan*: 5920 Second Avenue, Detroit MI 48202; *Telephone*: 313-831-0750; *Email*: detroit@workers.org. *New York*: P.O. Box 1204, Buffalo NY 14213; *Telephone*: 716-566-1115; *Email*: buffalo@workers.org; 55 West 17 Street, New York NY 10011; *Telephone*: 212-627-2994; *Fax*: 212-675-7869; *Email*: ww@workers.org; 71 Inglewood Drive, Rochester, NY 14619; *Telephone*: 585-436-6458; *Email*: rochester@workers.org. *Ohio*: P.O. Box 5963, Cleveland OH 44101; *Telephone*: 216-531-4004; *Email*: cleveland@workers.org. *Pennsylvania*: P.O. Box 9202, Philadelphia PA 19139; *Telephone*: 610-352-3625; *Email*: phila@workers.org; 100 Grandview Road, State College PA 16801; *Email*: 814-237-8695. *Texas*: P.O. Box 130322, Houston TX 77219; *Telephone*: 713-861-5965; *Email*: houston@workers.org. *Virginia*: P.O. Box 14602, Richmond VA 23221; *Email*: richmond@workers.org. *Washington*: 1218 East Cherry #201, Seattle WA 98122; *Telephone*: 206-325-0085

Workers Socialist Party of the United States (WSP-US)

1205 Thomas Palmer Court, Lawrenceville, GA 30043; *Email*: contact party through its web site; *Web site*: http://www.socialism.org.i8.com

The Workers Socialist Party of the United States describes itself as a "revolutionary political organization whose sole aim is the establishment of a new society, based on Socialism, that would be a world of social ownership, democratic control and free access." The party advocates the abolition of social classes through production based solely on meeting people's needs and believes, like almost all socialist organizations, that the capitalistic system has gone as far as it can in solving problems of the working class.

Founded in 1916 after splitting from the Socialist Party of America, the WSP-US believes that all economic wealth is the result of the application of human energy to the materials provided by nature and that no special elite group of people should be allowed to control the source of wealth; the wealth of the world is produced by workers who obtain a living by selling their bodily and mental energies to the capitalists and anyone whose principal means of living is secured by selling his energies to an employer is a member of the working class; the result of the social labor of the working class is the production of a quantity of wealth far greater than that which is represented by their wages and salaries and it is this surplus on which the capitalist class lives; the goals of these two groups are in conflict since the working class tries to sell their labor power for as high a price as they can get while the capitalist class tries to buy the workers' labor power for as low a price as possible; the wealth produced is not distributed according to the needs of the worker but is sold for the purpose of making a profit for the capitalists; capitalist competition in the world market often results in war; the unemployed are used by the capitalists to keep wages as low as possible and are needed to ensure a steady stream of available workers—which means that unemployment is a natural byproduct of a capitalist system; the unemployed make conditions worse for the working class by causing greater competition for jobs which usually results in lower wages and a lower standard of living; and the way to break this cycle is not through reformist movements but by converting the means of production from private ownership to common ownership by the whole community.

Working Families Party

88 3rd Avenue, Brooklyn NY 11217; *Telephone*: 718-222-3796; *Fax*: 718-246-3718; *Email*: wfp@workingfamiliesparty.org; *Web site*: http://www.workingfamiliesparty.org

Formed in 1998 by a variety of groups (including members from the United Auto Workers, the Communication Workers, the Association of Community Organizations for Reform Now, Citizen Action, and the New Party), the Working Families Party is a grassroots, community and labor based organization that operates in New York State. The goal of the party is to ensure that elected officials are aware of, and held responsible for, issues that are important to working class families, including jobs, health care, education, housing, school investment, and fair taxes. While currently a statewide organization, the party's future plans are to expand nationally.

The party's first task was to collect 50,000 votes in the gubernatorial race to qualify for official state ballot status. In a very short period of time and working only from a grassroots level, the party met its goal in the 1998 race by receiving just over 51,000 votes. Since its inception, the party has joined forces with more than 70 organizations, established local chapters throughout the state, and garnered a growing share of the vote in each subsequent election.

World Socialist Party of the USA

Box 440247, Boston MA 02144; *Email*: wspus@mindspring.com; *Web site*: http://www.worldsocialism.org/usa

Founded in 1916, the World Socialist Party of the USA (an integral part of the international socialist movement) is a Marxist organization whose members believe "that true socialism can only work when it is established worldwide." The party renounces violence, Soviet-style totalitarianism, formal financial instruments, and all forms of leadership; instead advocating a "classless, wageless, moneyless, free access society without any national borders."

Founded in 1904, the World Socialist Movement works to maintain the original socialist principles of Marxism: the emancipation of the working class is made by workers themselves; Socialism means the end of the market system not the nationalization of capitalism; and capitalism cannot be reformed in the workers' interests. In Great Britain members committed to Marxism left the Social Democratic Federation in 1904 and formed the Socialist Party of Great Britain (SPGB). Later that same year, the Socialist Party of Canada (SPC) was established by a group of Marxist believers.

The SPGB and SPC refused to support their respective governments during World War I and many members of these two groups scattered throughout the world to avoid conscription, spreading the ideas of Marxism wherever they went. In the United States, the Socialist Party of America (SPA) was formed by believers of Marxism and those who opposed the war. The SPA–Michigan came under the influence of the already established branch in Detroit, the center of the auto-industry and auto workers.

In 1916 political activities in Detroit were very active due to the mix of various Marxist groups, including the SPA, the SPC, and unaffiliated labor workers, but activities were splintered and unorganized. Out of this chaos the Socialist Party of the United States (SPUS) was formed, even though the SPA (and the Michigan SPA) continued to operate as separate entities. In 1918 the Michigan SPA began publishing *The Proletarian*, which adopted the Declaration of Principles of the SPGB. Its accepting SPGB principles caused the group to be expelled by the SPA in 1919, which led the Michigan SPA to unite with like-minded supporters and other expelled SPA entities to form the Communist Party. However, soon after, the Michigan SPA left the Communist Party and formed the Proletarian Party.

At about the same time, the SPUS discovered that the name "Socialist Party" had been copyrighted by the SPA, causing the organization to change its name to the Workers Socialist Party (WSP). In 1917 the United States entered World War I and began a crackdown on anti-war groups, which forced the WSP to curtail its activities for a period of time.

Meanwhile, from 1918 to 1920, the SPA was very active in New York City where the idea of socialism had been well received. Many political adherents from various socialist movements (including some from the SPA in Detroit) formed the Socialist Educational Society (SES) in 1921. While the New York SES gained membership and influence during the 1920s, the earlier-established SES in Detroit lost membership and eventually became inactive by 1924. Socialism was also active in Boston, Massachusetts in the early 1920s aided by several SPA members arriving from Detroit.

In 1929 the WSP began publishing *The Socialist* in New York as its official newspaper. It was discontinued a year later, revived for a brief period in 1937, and in 1939 merged with the current *The Western Socialist*, which had started in Winnipeg, Canada and was a joint publication of the WSP and the SPC.

Also in 1929, the SES was reorganized as the Workers Socialist Party, with locals in New York and Boston. During the Depression years, membership in the WSP increased steadily, along with its influence. Outside of the Communist Party, the Boston WSP was the most active and widely-known of the Marxist organizations in the New England area. During the 1930s, WSP activities spread to the west coast, mainly in Los Angeles and San Francisco, from which many local groups are still active today.

Through membership attrition, the failure of socialism to attract enough adherents to challenge capitalism, and a lack of national focus, the 1940s and 1950s saw a decline in WSP membership and influence. Social and cultural confrontations and ideological conflicts between the numerous socialist organizations were kept in check by the common goal of winning World War II during the 1940s. Immediately after the war years, the nation enjoyed a period of prosperity and growth, and a brief respite from confrontational politics.

Unprecedented prosperity in the United States convinced workers to more willingly accept values and institutions that originated from the capitalist class. The prospect of a better life seemed attainable for all citizens and the future looked bright for subsequent generations. In the light of this social and political climate, the WSP was not able to marshal its forces against a perceived national complacency and lost relevance and members.

In an attempt to clarify its role and appeal to an international following, in 1947 the WSP changed its name to the World Socialist Party, emphasizing socialism as a worldwide system of society and trying to avoid being confused with the Trotskyist Socialist Workers Party. Another change was the party moving its national headquarters to Detroit in 1949 before returning to Boston in the mid 1950s.

The World Socialist Party, along with other non–American political entities, came under extreme pressure during the McCarthy Era of the late 1950s but were able to survive and spread their beliefs to a receptive international audience. The social and political turmoil of the 1960s gave impetus to party growth as many young people around the world were searching for direction in their attempt to make the world a better place.

Since the 1970s, the WSP has continued to grow slowly and to attract new adherents. The party's membership roles, growth of local chapters, and international political influence historically have been tied to how the working class perceives its current economic and political well-being. The WSP is convinced that as capitalism loses its luster and ability to solve problems faced by workers, the party's core beliefs will be embraced by an electorate eager for change.

Affiliates. *California*: 233 North Mar Vista Avenue, Pasadena, CA 91106; *Telephone*: 626-584-9390; Riverside, *Email*: wspriverside@

post.com; Santa Cruz, *Email*: cruzcab@cruzio.com; San Diego: *Email*: wspsandiego@hotmail.com. *Colorado*: Colorado Springs, *Email*: wspcs@softhome.com. *Georgia*: Athens, *Email*: chelives@punts1.cc.uda.edu. *Illinois*: Chicago, *Email*: worldsocialismchicago@hotmail.com. *Michigan*: Detroit, *Email*: aburdua@avci.net. *New York*: *Email*: itzar@aol.com. *Ohio*: Toledo, *Email*: argentum@accesstoledo.com. *Oregon*: Portland, *Email*: wsppdx@yahoo.com. *Pennsylvania*: Philadelphia, *Email*: thoshs@verizon.net. *Vermont*: Brattleboro, *Email*: wspvt@yahoo.com.

Young Communist League — USA (YCL)

235 West 23rd Street, New York, NY 10011; *Telephone*: 212-741-2016; *Fax*: 212-229-1713; *Email*: yclwebmaster@yclusa.org; *Web site*: http://www.yclusa.org

The Young Communist League — USA is the youth affiliated movement of the Communist Party — USA and operates as an independent organization. The YCL is "devoted to the interests of all young people, is dedicated to the revolutionary cause of the working class of our country, and the transformation of the United States through mass democratic struggle into a socialist society ... the primary goal of the YCL is to help our members become Communists ... through studying Marxism-Leninism and active participation in day to day struggles of the working people and youth for a better life."

Affiliates. *California*: 1251 South St. Andrews Place, Los Angeles, CA 90019; *Telephone*: 213-733-3415; 3940 High Street, Suite B, Oakland, CA 94619; *Telephone*: 510 336-0617; *Email*: ncalview@igc.org. *Connecticut*: P.O. Box 1437, New Haven, CT 06506; *Telphone*: 203-624-4254. *Illinois*: 3116 South Halsted, Chicago, IL 60608; *Telephone*: 312-842-5770; *Email*: CPI@rednet.org. *Maryland*: P.O. Box 39187, Baltimore, MD 21212. *Massachusetts*: 550 Massachusetts Avenue, 2nd Floor, Cambridge, MA 02139; *Telephone*: 617-287-9672; *Email*: jacruz@argo.net. *Michigan*: 16145 Woodward Highland Park, MI 48203; *Telephone*: 313-883-3244. *Missouri*: P.O. Box 11523, St. Louis, MO 63105; *Email*: tonpec2000@yahoo.com. *New Mexico*: P.O. Box 613, Albuquerque, NM 87103; *Email*: Eshaw72789@aol.com. *New York*: 235 West 23rd Street, 6th Floor, New York, NY 10011; *Telephone*:

212-924-0550; *Email*: ycl@yclusa.org. *Ohio*: 4307 Lorain Avenue, Cleveland, OH 44113; *Telephone*: 216-281-7141; *Email*: 103650.2622@ CompuServe.com. *Pennsylvania*: 4515 Baltimore, Philadelphia, PA 19143; *Telephone*: 215-222-8895; *Email*: epa@cpusa.org; 5024 Penn Avenue, Pittsburgh, PA 15224; *Telephone*: 412-661-6115; *Email*: Dwinebr696@aol.com. *Rhode Island*: Center for Workers Education, P.O. Box 25015, Providence, RI 02905. *Texas*: P.O. Box 226147, Dallas, TX 75222; *Telephone*: 214-757-0391. *Washington*: P.O. Box 24806, Seattle, WA 98124; *Telephone*: 206-725-1555; *Email*: wacpusa@home. com.

Young Democratic Socialists (YDS)

198 Broadway #700, New York, NY 10038; *Telephone*: 212-727 8610; *Fax*: 212-608-6955; *Email*: lucas@dsausa.org; *Web site*: http://www.dsausa.org/yds

Young Democratic Socialists (the nation's largest socialist student and youth organization) is the youth section of the Democratic Socialists of America and is the only American member of the International Union of Socialist Youth, the largest political youth coalition in the world. With members and local organizations across the United States, YDS is a diverse network of young activists who "share a vision of a more humane future."

Local YDS chapters are autonomous and set their own agendas on their campuses and in their communities. Members are encouraged to join the Committee for New Directions, an exploratory group working to develop new and dynamic models for organizing. YDS works with the National Youth and Student Peace Coalition to support the Books-Not-Bombs Agenda.

The YDS believes that the Republican Party is anti-youth and basically supports Democratic candidates without actually joining the party. The YDS encourages activists to work with the College Democrats and other progressive groups on campus to form coalitions; register young voters in local communities and participate in election day get-out-the-vote activities; host fund raising activities for grassroots progressive and democratic organizations; assist with election protection activities organized by the National Association for the Advancement of Colored People and the American Civil Liberties Union; and creating voter guides that educate citizens on national and local issues and candidates.

The Young Democratic Socialists support "workers on and off campus in their struggles for dignity, respect, and a decent standard of living, by increasing corporate accountability and promoting a democratic socialist vision and path to social justice." The YDS encourages campus officials not to use union-busting tactics if school workers want to form a union; pressures elected officials to support the Employee Free Choice Act; and works against anti-union and anti-worker government laws and corporate policies.

The YDS main office works to connect chapters and organizes campus speakers to discuss the future of the low-wage, multi-service economy in the United States; develops educational materials on specific worker struggles; and provides background materials on the labor movement and the importance of strong, democratic, militant unions. To be most effective, the YDS believes that, in general, it needs to work closely with unions and the Democratic Party, thus giving the organization as large a platform as possible from which to deliver its message. The unions and the Democratic Party are the entities the YDS believes are the most like-minded and are working towards the goals the YDS supports.

The YDS supports increasing federal funding for education and for programs aimed at low-income and undocumented students; no military recruitment on high school or college campuses; repealing provisions of the Patriot Act that violate youth and students rights; campus administrators publicly disclosing all military-related research and all financial relationships with weapons manufacturers and severing all such contracts; and college administrations establishing recruitment and retention programs for communities adversely affected by incarceration, specifically low-income youth and youth of color.

Bibliography

Aldrich, John H. *Why Parties? The Origin and Transformation of Political Parties in America.* ISBN 0-2260-1272-7. Chicago: University of Chicago Press, 1995.

Cohen, Jeffrey E., Richard Fleisher, and Paul Kantor, editors. *American Political Parties: Decline or Resurgence?* ISBN 1-5680-2585-8. Washington, D.C.: Congressional Quarterly Books, 2001.

Diamond, Robert A. *Congressional Quarterly's Guide to U.S. Elections.* ISBN 0-87187-072-X. Washington, D.C.: Congressional Quarterly Books, 1976.

Green, John C., and Paul S. Herrnson. *Responsible Partisanship?: The Evolution of American Political Parties Since 1950* (Studies in Government and Public Policy). ISBN 0-7006-1217-3. Lawrence: University Press of Kansas, 2003.

Kruschke, Earl R. *Encyclopedia of Third Parties in the United States.* ISBN 0-87436-236-9. Santa Barbara, CA: ABC-Clio, 1991.

Schapsmeier, Edward L., and Frederick H. Schapsmeier. *The Greenwood Encyclopedia of American Institutions: Political Parties and Civic Action Groups.* ISBN 0-313-21442-5. Westport, CT: Greenwood Press, 1981.

Schramm, Peter W., and Bradford P. Wilson, editors. *American Political Parties and Constitutional Politics.* ISBN 0-8476-7819-9. Lanham, MD: Rowman & Littlefield, 1993.

White, John Kenneth, and John C. Green, editors. *The Politics of Ideas: Intellectual Challenges Facing the American Political Parties.* ISBN 0-7914-5044-9. Albany: State University of New York Press, 2001.

In addition to each entry's web site, the following on-line locations also provide comprehensive and in-depth information focused on political parties in the United States:

The History Guy, ampolparties@historyguy.com; http://www. historyguy.com (detailed listing of American political parties and all things related to U.S. political operations).

International Political Resources, http://www.politicalresources. net/usa1.htm (includes American and international political parties).

Politics 1, 409 Northeast 17th Avenue, Fort Lauderdale, FL 33301; 954-557-4911; publisher@politics1.com; http://www.politics. com (comprehensive web site of political groups in the United States).

Project Vote Smart, One Common Ground, Philipsburg, MT 59858; 888-868-3762, 406-859-8683; http://www.vote-smart.org (in-depth information about American politics, government operations, and political parties in the United States).

Index